In this important book David Gushee gives the lie to the sorry myth that evangelicals are all right-wing extremists. Not only does he show that many are politically progressive, but also that most of them are actually or potentially political moderates with a strong biblical conscience.

 —**George Hunsinger**, *McCord Professor of Theology, Princeton Theological Seminary*

The Future of Faith in American Politics challenges Jim Hightower's famous maxim that the only things in the middle of the road are yellow stripes and dead armadillos. Gushee offers here a cogent and balanced agenda for evangelical activism, a most welcome addition to this important conversation.

 —**Randall Balmer**, *Professor of American Religious History at Barnard College, Columbia University*

Gushee offers a valuable survey of evangelical subgroups and their varied responses to some of the most significant and divisive ethical issues of our time. It is a timely response to questions that demand informed and immediate attention in the academy and the pulpit.

 —**Bill J. Leonard**, *Dean and Professor of Church History, Wake Forest University Divinity School*

Will there be a kinder, gentler, wiser evangelical ethos in the future—less strident, rigid, politically entrenched, and reactive, and more thoughtful, robust, politically independent, and constructive? If so, I believe it will develop in large part because of David Gushee and the new/renewing identity articulated in this important book.

 —**Brian D. McLaren**, *Author (brianmclaren.net)*

Gushee makes a strong case for an emerging evangelical "middle" in American politics. For that middle to become more than an occasional, aggregate voice, however, its constituents will have to take more seriously than they do now the responsibilities of citizenship and government. Today, that middle lacks leaders in government and the political process with the comprehensive agenda Gushee advocates.

 —**Jim Skillen**, *President, The Center for Public Justice*

THE FUTURE OF FAITH IN AMERICAN POLITICS

THE FUTURE OF FAITH
IN AMERICAN POLITICS

The Public Witness of the Evangelical Center

David P. Gushee

[signature]

October 5, 2010

BAYLOR UNIVERSITY PRESS

Cover Design by Donna Habersaat
Book Design by Ellen Condict

Excerpts from "Moral Formation and the Evangelical Voter."
Originally authored by David Gushee and Justin Phillips in Journal of
the Society of Christian Ethics 26.2 (2006). Reprinted by permission.

Further permissions found on p. 320.

Gushee, David P., 1962-
  The future of faith in American politics : the public witness of the
evangelical center / David P. Gushee.
     p. cm.
  Includes bibliographical references and index.
  ISBN 978-1-60258-071-8 (pbk. : alk. paper)
  1. Christianity and politics--United States. 2. Evangelicalism--
United States. 3. United States--Church history. I. Title.

  BR516.G87 2008
  261.70973--dc22

                        2007040739

Printed in the United States of America on acid-free paper with a
minimum of 30% pcw recycled content.

To Ron Sider—
Pioneering voice of evangelical conscience, mentor, model, friend

CONTENTS

APPENDICES

FOREWORD

You must read this book. Why? It not only explains who the players are in an evolving religious and political "awakening" occurring within the evangelical world but explains the ideas, conflicts, and controversies that are making news.

Evangelicals, of course, believe every person needs an awakening, or a born-again experience. That conversion, along with a commitment to the Word of God and a desire to share that faith with others, includes up to one-quarter of all adults in the United States, according to surveys. So what's going on with us?

David Gushee has done a significant body of work to help us understand this easily misunderstood religious community. He has been able to capture the spirit of what is happening—the ideas, conflicts, and controversies—because he is both a scholar and an activist helping to inspire and guide it.

Essentially, this is a battle for the soul of the evangelical believer in America. On one side are those who want to keep the agenda focused on three things—abortion, judges, and gay marriage. On the other side are those of us who want to move forward on a broader agenda that includes international religious freedom, poverty and hunger, creation care, human rights, and peacemaking. We want this broader agenda without sacrificing our traditional commitments to protecting human life and the traditional family. Why should that be controversial?

Essentially because the argument over the broadness of a political agenda is a proxy battle over this question: "Who speaks for evangelicals?" Many of us, particularly the younger generation, are tired of lockstep loyalty to the Republican Party. As one blogger put it, "We wake up each morning and see an elephant on the pillow next to us."*

In the debates in our nation over the war in Iraq, torture, and the faith-based initiative, for example, the evangelicals have divided but not contentiously so. But on the most charged issue of all—climate change— the evangelicals have been divided and the methodology and tactics of the religious right have come into dispute.

Not only did the late Reverend Jerry Falwell charge that action to protect creation was "Satan's attempt to redirect the church's primary focus," but two dozen other conservative Christian leaders also warned that global warming "is dividing and demoralizing" evangelicals. In a letter to the National Association of Evangelicals (NAE), they denounced leaders such as myself and Dave Gushee for urging outspoken action against global warming. In my case, they demanded that I essentially shut up or resign.

I did neither, and David Gushee has been a friend and collaborator during this time of trial. Like me, he has seen his share of criticism from his fellow believers for speaking out for biblical truth. Their admonitions were clear: Go along with the status quo or we will see you removed from your career and employment. Now, if this isn't unredemptive, what is? Dave has always responded with charity toward his critics by turning the other cheek. But he has not capitulated to intimidation.

This is courage, the kind demonstrated by such biblical figures as Daniel in the Court of King Darius (Daniel 6). Daniel had risen to a place of influence in Babylonian politics and culture. The satraps of the king's court were jealous and sought to have him expurgated. But Daniel was a man of principle and courage. He neither yielded to pres-

---

*   That is a reference to the Godfather movie in which an opponent of the Corleone family finds himself in bed with the head of a horse; *Wall Street Journal*, September 28, 2007, A1.

sure to compromise, nor wavered in his commitment to God. He pronounced truth and was faithful.

Today, we need a new generation of evangelicals who will rise to the challenge of biblical truthtelling, and do so in a winsome manner within the church, government, and all the institutions of society. Will there be opposition? Count on it. Truth always invites opposition. But God will bring good out of bad circumstances.

A new generation of leaders who are both activists and scholars are seeing God work in this way. He is using them to build his Kingdom. Dave Gushee is one of these individuals who exemplify this new generation. I commend this extraordinary book—and also the man and the personality behind it—to the entire evangelical world. It will encourage and sustain you. There is hope in the next generation.

May all those who read this book be inspired. May you be motivated to go into the world to make a difference, just as Daniel did in his day. If you do, the world will never be the same.

Richard Cizik
Vice President for Govenmental Affairs
National Association of Evangelicals

PREFACE

This is a book about the relationship between evangelicals and American politics. Therefore, every sentence will be subject to dispute. Except perhaps those sentences that get the ball rolling by telling my own personal story.

In 1979 I was a seventeen-year-old brand-new Christian, a fresh convert to evangelical Christianity in its Southern Baptist form. I lived in northern Virginia, land of the federal government and myriad lobbying groups.

A woman in my church approached me that spring with a lucrative offer: Would I be willing to appear briefly in a film that her organization was making? I would receive $200 for just a few hours work. With prom approaching, the money sounded awfully nice.

So it was that I found myself with dyed brown hair, dressed in a Soviet army uniform, on the set of *Can Soviet Imperialism Be Stopped?* My job was to pour a bucket of red paint over a standing globe, beginning ominously in the vicinity of West Germany. I need to report (in all humility) that I was excellent that day. I poured the paint just right, was handed the money after one take, and went on to the prom the very next night with dyed hair but flush with cash.

I did not understand at the time that I was making a propaganda film for one of the most hard-line right-wing organizations in the United States, Howard Phillips's Conservative Caucus. Sadly, though, there is no mention of this great film on their Web site.

By 1986 I had graduated from college and come under the influence of the progressive wing of Protestant Christianity. I worked for a peace organization in Louisville while attending Southern Baptist Theological Seminary. I supported the nuclear freeze campaign, which led to a particularly memorable moment one wintry evening in Chicago, circa 1987. Jesse Jackson was running for president. He was scheduled to speak to the freeze group on that frozen night. He came in late and sat down right next to me on the front row. He tapped my shoe and said, "How ya doin'?" *Yes, Jesse Jackson sat next to me and tapped my left shoe.* It was a highlight of my young life. The crowd shouted, "Run, Jesse, run."

From 1987 to 1989 I lived in New York City, where I pursued a doctorate in Christian ethics at Union Theological Seminary. I had gone there in part to broaden my horizons after lengthy immersion in Southern Baptist culture. I loved my ethics program at Union but often felt like a stranger in a strange land. I discovered how conservative (relatively speaking) I really was.

One day the National Association of Evangelicals (NAE) sent conservative *Catholic* intellectual George Weigel to Union Seminary to talk to the school's few evangelicals. We gathered in the Bonhoeffer Room (where the great German theologian had stayed during his famous Union days). There, Weigel tried to disabuse us of any peacenik inclinations in relation to the Soviet Union or nuclear weapons. A few years later the Soviet Union was dead, ending that particular argument. Later in life I would again encounter both Weigel and the NAE.

In 1990, I needed a job. Halfway through a doctoral program, with a child and another on the way, I interviewed for an editorial position with *The Other Side*, a radical evangelical magazine (now defunct) located across from an abandoned house in the depressed Germantown section of Philadelphia. Based on biblical principles, they were offering poverty-level wages of $14,000 a year. During the interview one staff member helpfully told me that she trash picked to supplement her income and that I would come to enjoy trash picking as well. I fled, vowing never to return. (Not exactly, but that is how I remember it.) A few months later I took a position with Ron Sider and Evangelicals for Social Action (ESA), living just around the corner from that abandoned house. I never did take up trash picking. I did, however, find with ESA the kernel of a sociopolitical vision that has never left me.

In 1992–1993 I was working at ESA, finishing my doctorate, and looking without much success for my first teaching post. Finally I got the chance to interview at Southern Baptist Theological Seminary, my alma mater. I got the job. I was on campus in April 1993 on the same day that Dr. R. Albert Mohler Jr. was named president of Southern. The school swung sharply to the right.

As an evangelical in an influential ethics post formerly held by a pro-choice professor, I had, for a time, numerous opportunities to enter the inner sanctum of the conservative Southern Baptist Convention (SBC). I drafted a 1994 SBC statement condemning the killing of abortion doctors. I remember the drafting meeting, in a high-up executive suite in Nashville, where most of the powers in the SBC gathered to comb through the text I had written. The next year I had a similar experience while working with a top-level group on the SBC's repudiation of its historic racism. It was thrilling. But such involvement soon ended. I wasn't quite "right" enough. I see that now.

Right, left; left, right . . . today I identify with what I call an emerging evangelical center, neither left nor right. This book is about that evangelical center and makes a case for its great importance for the future not just of evangelicalism but of the United States. This evangelical center can be found in the editorial pages of some of our magazines, in the classrooms of most seriously Christian colleges, in the current vision of some of our think tanks and parachurch organizations, and in the vision of some of our most important churches and their pastors. I believe it offers the best way forward for us in the notoriously controversial engagement of our faith with American public life.

And yet it is not quite good enough to say we should move to the center from the right and the left. Any right-center-left language is political, borrowed from the world. We need a biblically grounded rethinking of Christianity's entire engagement with American culture. I offer here at least a rethinking of our engagement with American public policy.

INCONTESTABLE FACTS

Little can be said about this issue without evoking controversy, but I would suggest that there are four incontestable facts related to evangelicals and politics today.

1. *Conservative evangelical (I will use the term* evangelical right) *political activism is evoking a heated backlash.* This backlash comes from dissident evangelicals, from the nonevangelical Christian left, and from many other voices from the secular left and sometimes the political right. This backlash is in turn evoking a counterbacklash, with various defenses of the evangelical right now on offer. And, of course, the evangelical right already understands itself as a defensive movement—in other words, a reaction to prior challenges to traditional Christian values.

2. *Battles over evangelical right involvement with politics are merging into the broader "culture wars" environment that is tearing our country apart.* It is increasingly difficult to distinguish a particularly Christian voice in the red state/blue state, right/left polarization of American public discourse. Conservatives like Ann Coulter, Rush Limbaugh, and Ramesh Ponnuru do not speak as Christian thinkers, but their arguments hit religious themes. The left is only now finding its religious voice and is (increasingly) trying to fire back with religious themes in this deeply religious nation. The screeching tone of the argument (it is not a conversation) is contributing to the depressing, even dangerous, polarization of American society and the loss of a sensible center—despite what ought to be soothing evidence that most average Americans are not culture warriors at all.

3. *Many sense that our culture is in crisis but see the churches as part of the problem rather than part of the solution.* Political divisions, hatred of the cultural "enemy," fiscal irresponsibility, growing income inequality, eroding international standing, government gridlock, business and political corruption, religious/ethnic balkanization, special interest politics, endless political gamesmanship, the disappearance of statesmanship: these and many other problems threaten our nation. Yet the church seems unable to rise

above these problems; instead it is enmeshed in the culture wars, in backlash upon backlash, conflict upon conflict.

4. *A growing number of visible evangelicals, including the "evangelical pope," Billy Graham, are disillusioned with politics, especially with conservative evangelical engagement in politics.* They sense that something has gone dramatically wrong, and they are attempting to call the church back to its core mission. I think they need to be heard. It is time for a complete rethinking of evangelical public engagement.

That is what I intend to offer in this book. I invite you along for the ride, wherever you find yourself religiously or politically. If you are interested in what is happening at the intersection of evangelicalism and politics in the United States, this book is for you. If you think all evangelicals are right-wing theocrats, join me here and let me introduce you to other branches of the evangelical community. In this book I offer something of an insider's account of what is happening in the evangelical center that is emerging with growing confidence and impact in these days—and perhaps inevitably, evoking a heated reaction from the evangelical right. I want to introduce you to this evangelical center, urge my own evangelical community to converge on this center and join our cause and urge nonevangelical and non-Christian readers to learn more about us. If nothing else, I want this book to help end the public misperception of evangelical public witness as either unipolar (Christian right) or bipolar (right vs. left). We are in fact multipolar (right, left, and center). I hope that this will be indisputably clear by the end of this volume.

Here is how we will proceed. Part I, Evangelicals and Public Life: Across the Spectrum, begins with a chapter that seeks to clear away practical and theoretical obstacles to Christian, especially evangelical, engagement with public life. Having made the case that evangelicals can and must enter the public square, the next two chapters profile what I will describe as the evangelical right and the evangelical left. Major groups, personalities, and beliefs of these branches of the evangelical world are considered here. Chapter 4 turns to the evangelical center. Here I will follow the pattern established in previous chapters to describe broadly the groups, personalities, and beliefs of this emerging evangelical center. Part II, Finding the Center: Key Issues for Evangelical

Public Engagement, offers analysis of four key moral/policy issues that reside at the borderlines between the evangelical left, right, and center: torture, marriage, climate, and war. These chapters are intended to offer a centrist take on these issues and to commend that stance for broader evangelical adoption. After a concluding chapter, several primary documents of the evangelical center are printed as appendixes, along with my own analysis of two of them. The book concludes with an extensive bibliography of major books now available related to evangelical public engagement.

One last note before we dive in: Though I write against the backdrop of a massive flow of books and articles on the issues discussed here, you do not have to be a scholar to read this book. I write for a broad public readership. Some of the many books and articles that inform my study here are mentioned in the source notes related to each chapter, which are included at the end of the book. You could read these books and articles on faith and politics for the rest of your life and never be done. But you do not have to be committed to doing that to want to read this book. You do have to care about the bitterly contested interaction between evangelicals and American culture. You do have to be looking for an alternative to the main voices that are being heard right now. If that is what you are looking for, read on.

ACKNOWLEDGMENTS

The completion of this book leaves me greatly indebted to many friends and to my precious family. I am forever grateful to them, even while absolving them of any responsibility for any flaws and limits of this work.

As with every one of my book projects, I am most grateful to my wife, Jeanie, and my children, Holly, David, and Marie, for supporting me amidst the burdens and distractions of book writing.

This book began as a jointly authored paper presented at the Society of Christian Ethics with my Union University graduate and current Fuller Seminary doctoral student, Justin Phillips. Chapter 3, on the evangelical left, especially still bears his fingerprints.

In preparing that original essay, I had the help of many of the figures discussed in the document. I am grateful to Rich Cizik, Ron Sider, David Neff, and Bob Andringa for reviewing the manuscript and adding helpful comments that strengthened it. More broadly, I am grateful for their confirmation that I might just be onto something with my thesis about an evangelical center.

The actual preparation of the book involved the considerable help of a group of Union University students, undergraduates all: Josh Hays,

Matt Elia, Brent Parrish, Bess Perrier, and Amanda Norris. Josh compiled the Further Reading list, Matt researched the evangelical relief and development organizations, and together they double-checked my Web research; Brent and Bess served as guides to the music world; Amanda researched the gay marriage issue. Thank you, my friends.

As always, I am grateful to my mother-in-law, Earlynn Grant, for her review and copyediting of the manuscript.

I thank my friend Jim Patterson, professor of church history at Union, for his careful review of the book at the historical and sociological levels.

I am grateful to my editor, Carey C. Newman, for cracking the whip on his weary author and pushing me forward when I was tempted to settle for second best.

As for my administrative assistant, Mary Head, all I can say is that without her this book would have been inconceivable. Her research, editing, and compiling of the notes made her contribution invaluable. Thank you, Mary.

This book represents the culmination of many years of experiences in the evangelical world. I am grateful to the patrons or sponsors who in various ways at various stages helped push open these doors: Glen Stassen, David Dockery, Richard Land, David Neff, Jim Skillen, Larry Rasmussen, and Rich Cizik are among the most significant of these.

But as I think about my own journey as a Christian, as an evangelical, as a writer and editor, and as an activist, I continue to come back to the pivotal role played in my life by Ron Sider, my employer at Evangelicals for Social Action (ESA) from 1990 to 1993 and friend for life.

Therefore it is to Ron Sider that I dedicate this book.

PART I

Evangelicals and Public Life
Across the Spectrum

Chapter 1

CLEARING THE GROUND

The purpose of this book is to stake a claim to an emerging evangelical center in American public life and to describe the public moral witness of that evangelical center by contrasting it with its right-leaning and left-leaning alternatives.

At one level, this work claims to be descriptive. I am arguing that among the 60 to 80 million evangelicals in the United States one can identify a political center that is increasingly vibrant and promises to play an increasingly significant role within evangelical Christianity and in the United States. I am going to describe people, institutions, and perspectives on public policy that I suggest characterize this emerging evangelical center. I will also describe some of the people, institutions, documents, and perspectives that can be characterized as belonging to the evangelical right and evangelical left to help clarify what makes the center different. This detailed description of the evangelical center is a new contribution to the seething debate about the role of religion, and especially evangelicalism, in American politics and public life. A few of the more astute observers—both journalistic and scholarly—have noticed at least some elements of this emerging evangelical center, but it has never been described as a whole or in any detail.

At a second level, I am quite frankly moving beyond description to prescription. I am not just describing an evangelical center in this book. My intent is to make a case for the center and its perspectives when contrasted with alternatives to the right and left. I argue that the emerging evangelical center offers a more faithful and more fruitful rendering of Christian convictions in the public arena than that which can be found elsewhere. I will also defend the kind of public engagement that the evangelical center offers by contrast with its evangelical alternatives and against those who cast aspersion on any evangelical public engagement whatsoever. I will argue that secularists and others who are skeptical of evangelical involvement in politics would be both wise and right not just to tolerate this kind of evangelical public engagement but also to look for ways to dialogue with us and to partner with us, as some are now doing. There are too many of us simply to ignore us or scorn us. It is indeed, as one writer has put it, "The Evangelical Moment."[1] We are, in fact, as another observer has said, the "new American mainstream."[2] We help settle elections, as so many noted after 2004. Engaging with us rather than heaping contempt on us simply makes sense. It will prove healthier both for us and for American culture. I will say more about this theme later in the book.

I opened with the metaphor of staking a claim to some "ground" in the faith and politics debate. Before one can build on land to which one has staked a claim, that ground must be cleared of its various obstacles and obstructions. In the rest of this chapter, I want to clear the ground of three particular obstacles to my project.

THE SECULARIST OBSTACLE
Christians Are Theocrats Who Should Stay Out of Politics

My shelf is bulging with books written in the last few years by people who argue that Christians, especially evangelicals, are dangerous "theocrats" who must be kept out of politics and public life altogether—unless, perhaps, they can be trained to bury their religious convictions before they enter the public square. The most fearsome of these critics are perhaps Kevin Phillips and Chris Hedges, but "their name is Legion."[3] And this is a matter not just of popular debate but also considerable scholarly attention. I will not engage the debate in great depth here. But the issue does need to be addressed at least in a preliminary way. Not to put too fine a point on it, are politically engaged Christians properly to be viewed as fascist theocrats?

First foray: Citizens who care about politics and public life are an asset to a democracy, certainly by contrast with the many free riders (at least 40 percent of the population, if one looks just at presidential voting statistics) who enjoy the benefits of democratic life without making any contribution to it whatsoever. Seriously Christian people who attempt to exercise their citizenship responsibilities with care should be celebrated, not scorned, as should any other American citizen who does the same. Let us at least begin there.

The secularist concern about Christians who engage politics is that they/we are attempting to impose a theocracy in what is instead a secular, pluralistic democracy. If this means that Christians bring our religious faith to bear on our moral values, and that these values in turn have an impact on our political thinking and voting behavior, we plead guilty as charged. But I would hasten to add that human beings cannot avoid bringing their deepest worldviews and moral convictions to bear on political life. Politics is value laden because it concerns core issues related to human well-being and the just governance of human communities. There is no value-neutral perspective with which any American engages in political reflection or behavior. All of us (for a million different reasons) believe certain things about what is right and wrong, just and unjust, important and unimportant, and we bring those beliefs with us into public life. Tens of millions of Americans root their most important moral convictions in their religious faith. Certainly that is the hope of those of us who lead religious communities: that we will be successful in training our congregants to draw precisely such connections. To ask religious Americans to bracket off their core beliefs before entering the voting booth is unfair, unrealistic, and unnecessary.

Sometimes we Christians are accused of being theocrats simply because of the content of our moral or policy convictions. By definition, anyone who is opposed to, say, the current status of abortion laws, is a theocrat. I would submit that this belief is little more than a reflexive and unthinking prejudice rooted in a strong difference of convictions.

To be accused contemptuously of theocracy because of one's belief about a major moral issue is both hurtful and unfair. It also tends to evoke similarly heated responses, which sadly worsen the spiral of mistrust and misunderstanding and thus exacerbate the overall "culture wars" atmospherics.

I would, however, acknowledge that at least some of the hue and cry about theocracy stems from real problems in the way many of the most visible evangelicals have engaged public life. In particular, right-wing Christian politics has been characterized by certain tendencies that do raise questions about whether some of these people and groups genuinely understand or accept the constitutional limits on the establishment of religion in the United States. There is indeed a fringe of right-leaning Christians that wants the United States to embrace the harshest features of biblical law (the so-called Reconstructionists), some who explicitly reject the First Amendment, some who seem to want religious tests for public office, and many who claim that the United States is a "Christian country." More subtly, as I will suggest later, much of the rhetoric of the evangelical right reflects a nostalgia for a less religiously and morally pluralistic age, when specifically Christian practices dominated American public life in a way that is now impossible and *should be* impossible under our constitutional system (Christian prayers in school, and so forth). The evangelical right also tends to offer a rendering of the founders and the early period of American life that downplays religious diversity and constitutional protections for religious liberty and treats even skeptical deists as if they were frontier evangelists. All of these are factors contributing to the theocracy charge, and they are real issues.

The way for evangelicals to clear the ground of this "theocratic" objection is therefore twofold. At one level, we must gently but firmly push back against anyone who would deny us the right to participate in public life on the basis of our values, as long as we are just as willing to grant all citizens of every worldview and moral conviction the legitimacy of their own faith-based participation in American public life. Secondly, we must frankly acknowledge the ways in which our own behavior and rhetoric has evoked a legitimate fear among our fellow citizens, explore the reasons for this fear, and reform our public rhetoric and political practice accordingly.

We also can serve the nation by clarifying for concerned onlookers the depth and breadth of particularly worrisome convictions among our nation's conservative Christians—whether they are rare, common, fading, growing, or such. One contribution that can be made by the emerging evangelical center can be found right here. The center tends to be more sensitive to and supportive of the constitutional structure bounding religion in American law than does the evangelical right. We are also less inclined to romanticize the supposed religiosity of the American founders or to pine nostalgically for an earlier age in American history. And we tend to have a pretty good feel for the ebb and flow of particular convictions within the bounds of our community.

THE SECTARIAN OBSTACLE
The Church Is All the Politics Christians Need

The second obstacle needing clearing before we can begin might be called the sectarian objection, though perhaps that is to paint with too broad a brush. I want to consider here several different kinds of concerns, all of which emerge from within the faith community or among some of its leading scholars. Together they add up to a formidable set of objections to evangelical Christian political engagement. I will address them under what might be called their key slogans.

1. "THE CHURCH'S MISSION IS TO PREACH THE GOSPEL, SO WE SHOULD STAY OUT OF POLITICS."

Some object to Christian public witness on the grounds of Christian *missional* concerns. The mission of the church is to "go and make disciples of all nations" (Matt 28:19), which includes some combination of worship, evangelism, missionary activity, service to neighbor, theological reflection, and instruction. Many Christians claim that neither Jesus nor the New Testament churches participated in worldly politics, and thus we are not authorized to do so today. These are just a few of the arguments for the abandonment of worldly politics for a purified religious mission.

There is much to commend in this focus on the church's mission and its core elements of preaching, teaching, theology, service, discipleship, and worship. There is indeed an appealing purity about many of these elements of the church's work that simply cannot be found in the hurly-burly of politics. And I agree with Karl Barth when he wrote in 1932 that the church "should keep precisely to the rhythm of its own relevant concerns, and thus consider well what are the *real* needs of the day by which its own programme should be directed."[4] I would claim that a proper understanding of the content of these relevant churchly concerns actually draws the church into the political arena, at least for a *certain kind* of public engagement focusing on the declaration and embodiment of core moral values of Christian faith—rather than, say, partisan electioneering or personal attacks on candidates.

There are various ways to describe or situate the work of public moral witness in terms of the broader Christian mission. One might say that it is an extension of the church's *preaching and teaching* ministry; because the church studies and proclaims the Bible and is governed by the Bible's authority, it will not be able to avoid addressing publicly significant moral issues that are addressed in the pages of scripture. Or one could place public witness in the context of the church's *evangelistic* ministry, as we bear witness to God's justice or to God's love in Christ for the world and for each person by advocating government policies that reflect love, justice, and the sacredness of life.[5] We could suggest, as does a major centrist-evangelical declaration called "For the Health of the Nation," which will be considered extensively in this book, that Christian public witness is an aspect of Christian *neighbor love*, for as we advocate just public policies related to taxation or international relations or marriage, we seek to serve the neighbor's needs—and thus to love our neighbors as ourselves.[6] One classic formulation of the relationship of the various aspects of the church's work came from Dietrich Bonhoeffer, when he proclaimed in his *Ethics* that the gospel is to ethics or social engagement as the "ultimate" is to the "penultimate."[7] The ultimate is the message of salvation by grace through faith in Jesus Christ. The penultimate is care for human bodily and social existence. The ultimate is more important than the penultimate but also intimately related to it and in fact dependent on it because the human person is a body-soul unity and exists only in community.

To confine the church's mission to a message and a ministry that entirely excludes political engagement is to risk truncating the Christian proclamation quite profoundly. And yet, of course, we are also at risk of putting so much emphasis on the political dimension of the Christian mission as to neglect or truncate the gospel in an entirely different way. So the objections of those who are concerned about the integrity of the church's mission must be taken seriously indeed. I am among those who have written of a concern for a distortion of Christian mission in these politically charged days. We must navigate between the extremes of withdrawal from politics and obsession with politics.

2. "GOD'S KINGDOM IS NOT OF THIS WORLD."

Greg Boyd, an influential Minneapolis evangelical pastor and theologian, is among those claiming these days that Christian political engagement is misguided because it misunderstands the nature of God's kingdom.[8] Grounding his argument especially on his translation of John 18:36 ("my kingdom is not from this world"), Boyd argues that the kingdom of God is fundamentally distinct from the kingdoms of this world. Jesus taught a kingdom in which greatness is defined by sacrifice and service. The kingdoms of this world all operate on the basis of models of power and domination.

Boyd's position is rooted not just in scripture, but also in his reading of history, and in his disdain for the evangelical right and embarrassment about what Christian political activists have been doing. But I think that his core claim about the nature of Christ's kingdom is most at stake in his work.

Any kind of serious study of this core biblical concept, "the kingdom of God," reveals that it has proven itself frustratingly amenable to a variety of interpretations, while sometimes it seems to drop off the theological and rhetorical landscape altogether. For a concept that was clearly so central to the message of Jesus Christ himself, this astonishing variability is more than a little worrisome.

In our own book, *Kingdom Ethics*, Glen Stassen and I seek to show from the Old Testament, from intertestamental literature and Jewish practice, and from Jesus' teachings in the New Testament, that the kingdom of God did have specifiable, this-worldly content.[9] When Jesus came preaching the kingdom, he was specifically intending to convey that God acts to bring justice, peace, healing, inclusion of the excluded, and rescue from oppression and suffering. God is "saving" the world in Christ, understood as a holistic salvation that meets the full range of human needs as we experience them in this sinful world. So the kingdom of God really means that state of affairs in which God's will is done, and therefore his reign is acknowledged and rightly honored. This kingdom stands in continuity with the entire witness of the Old Testament and reflects the core theological claim that God is sovereign over this world as its creator and king. The kingdom of God is therefore both spiritual and political, both this worldly and other worldly. Christians work for the kingdom through all that we do, including sacrificial acts of service and public witness on behalf of the victimized, the oppressed, the tortured, the wrongly imprisoned, the sex slaves, those suffering in war, and so on. For this reason, the message of the kingdom is not a message that must pull us out of engagement in public life and politics. It does, however, prescribe much about the way we engage public life and what we seek to accomplish when we do so.

3. "THE CHURCH DOESN'T DO POLITICS; IT IS ITSELF A POLITICS."

Nonacademic readers may be unaware of the enormous and growing influence of a trend in Christian thought that eschews political engagement for an emphasis on the internal practices of the Christian church. Most associated with the work of Duke Divinity School professor Stanley Hauerwas and the influential late Anabaptist theologian John Howard Yoder, this position has both a descriptive and prescriptive dimension.[10] Descriptively, the claim of Hauerwas has been that American Christians, and especially American Christian ethicists, have focused almost entirely on the *polis* (political community) called the United States of America. The *nation* has almost entirely displaced the *church* as a focus of moral reflection and action. It is as if the nation-state has come to stand in for the church as both our primary identity and the primary object of our reflections. In technical terms, one might say that secular politics has entirely eclipsed ecclesiology. More starkly, one might say that we have succumbed to political idolatry. We bow before flag rather than God.

This shift to a focus on the nation is problematic in many ways, not the least of which is that this tendency is completely out of keeping with the New Testament witness. The moral instruction that is offered in the New Testament is offered by Jesus and the apostles to those who would seek to be followers of Christ in the context of the believing church. It is *parenesis*, or internal community instruction, offered by the apostles to other disciples for the purpose of encouraging faithful Christian living. There is no question of displacing loyalty to Christ with loyalty to Caesar.

Moreover, as Hauerwas and Yoder have noted, this parenesis is linked to the prescribed practices of Christian community. These practices, or commanded activities, include a rich range of behaviors, such as forgiveness, hospitality, prayer for enemies, service to the poor, almsgiving, confession of sin to one another, observance of the Sabbath, nonparticipation in war, peacemaking, mutual help in time of need, and so on. And it includes a prescribed body of worship practices including preaching, prayer, giving, and the Eucharist. Many fine works in recent Christian ethics have been developing reflections both on this intracommunal moral instruction and on the range of practices that were and sometimes still are understood to be expected of the church. This literature has brought together Christians from an astonishing range of traditions toward a shared vision and a kind of post-Enlightenment, postliberal, postmodern renewal of confidence in the church's ancient practices, often accompanied by a complete rejection of the practices of any other community, especially the seductive nation-state.

The prescriptive or normative claim that follows from this view goes something like this: The church is called precisely to embody an alternative politics that is constituted by its core practices. The most important thing we do for the world is to be the church. As we live out these practices, teach one another the way of Jesus, and become a community of character, we serve the world precisely as we were instructed to do in the New Testament. This is itself a political act: Worship is political; serving the poor is political; neighbor love is political; and it is all the politics we are called to be involved in. Remembering this helps us avoid the confusion of loyalties that comes when we offer our attention, and soon enough our primary allegiance, to the nation-state.

This "ecclesial politics" position is deeply attractive in many ways. It is especially appealing to those of us who see all too clearly the failures, the pretensions, the violence, and often the evil that goes on in the name of the state. Some who articulate this view root it quite deeply in a resistant posture in relation to the modern state and its tendency toward totalitarian claims on the life of its citizens. Anyone who has made even a cursory study of the evils done in the name of the state and by the state over the past century cannot help but be attracted to this critique.

My response to this powerful perspective is a "yes, but." Yes, what you say about the internal life of the church and the great significance of its practices is true. But you should also pay attention to the more politically explicit teachings of the Old Testament and the political content of the teaching of Jesus. Yes, what you say about the vanity, folly, and downright evil of the world's kingdoms and governments is true, at least much of the time. But you obfuscate some important distinctions when you seem to tar all governments with the same brush, as if Nazi Germany and modern Denmark are indistinguishable. Yes, the church local and universal is our primary community of allegiance. But even the most committed Christian does still live both in the *ekklesia* and in one or another modern nation-state. And what happens in those nation-states matters to the well-being of everyone who lives there and everyone who is affected by their actions. For those who live in the United States, still the world's most powerful and influential nation despite the bad decisions and tragic events of recent years, even the most basic sense of neighbor love ought to motivate Christians to attempt to have a voice in the domestic and international policies of our troubled but beloved land. The United States is not the church, it is not the kingdom, it cannot bring in the kingdom. But its dollars and policies bring life or death, justice or injustice, participation or exclusion, to billions of people. Our nation will help stop sex trafficking, or it will not. It will provide considerable funding to AIDS treatment, or it will not. It will torture prisoners, or it will not. It will help heal our damaged global ecosystems, or it will not. It will bomb Iran, or it will not. It will harvest embryonic stem cells, or it will not.

I think it is quite possible, and indeed quite necessary, to incorporate the concerns of ecclesial politics without acceding to its stark either/or. Christians are reminded that our core community is the church and that all politics is indeed ecclesial and local in this sense. It is true that our basic proclamation and practices are redolent with moral significance often missed entirely by our theologically shallow church leaders. It is certainly true that nothing we say in public debate will be taken seriously if our own internal life does not reflect the practiced allegiance to the same values we proclaim publicly. For every moral teaching of the Bible, we must always ask, and probably in this order: What does this mean for me as an individual Christian, for us a family, for our congregation as a community of faith, and for our nation and the global human community? It is not either/or, either the church or the state; it is both/and, both the church and the state, and beyond.

4. "WE NEED TO ABANDON THE CHRISTENDOM MENTALITY."

Closely connected to the issues we have been considering is the charge that the engagement of faith with American public life reflects a vestige of the Christendom mentality, which must be rejected at all costs.[11] The claim here is historical, theological, and moral. Essentially, the argument is that ever since the official christianization of the Roman Empire in the fourth century, western Christians have become intoxicated by political power. We have grown accustomed to being in charge, to determining the outcome of political life, and to making history come out right. No one gives up this kind of power easily, and one can argue that it has brought good to the world at points.

But it has corrupted us. We have paid for it by, among other things, compromising Jesus' clear teachings about violence in order to align ourselves with the state's use of power. More broadly, we have been willing to do almost anything to maintain our access to political power. And now that we are losing our grip on that power in much of the Western world, we are frustrated and aggrieved. Much of what drives evangelical right political engagement, these voices argue, is this sense of aggrievement and lost entitlement.

Again, there is much to commend in this perspective. I am among those who agree that there is no going back to any form of Christendom, nor should there be. But I do not agree that the effort to affect the direction of public policy on the basis of Christian moral values is invariably an expression of the Christendom mentality. Trying to prevent Muslim detainees from being tortured in CIA "black sites," for example, cannot fairly be viewed as an effort intended to aggrandize Christian power or restore a lost Christendom. It is instead an effort on the part of Christians as Christians to bear faithful witness to biblical values. It is an effort to call our government to act in keeping with American law and values. And it is an act of solidarity with mistreated and suffering people. Sensitivity to the Christendom worry can definitely help us avoid major mistakes in our public-policy activism, but it should not cause us to abandon that activism altogether.

5. "LET'S TAKE A TIME-OUT FROM POLITICS."

Evangelical involvement with politics is confronted by another kind of plea for withdrawal. Let's call it the "time-out" option. It has surfaced most recently in the book by David Kuo, ex–Bush White House staffer on the faith-based initiative.[12] Kuo has clearly been scarred by his perception that the Bush team, including the president, has manipulated and used evangelicals, including Kuo himself, for their own crass electoral purposes. He calls evangelicals to renounce their "political seduction" and to take a two-year time-out from politics. He seems ashamed of his involvement with the Bush White House and appalled by his discovery of his own political seduction and betrayal.

Similar themes surfaced in the 1999 book by veteran conservatives Cal Thomas and Ed Dobson.[13] They describe an evangelical movement "blinded by might" and at risk of sliding into shameful heresy through their single-minded focus on politics as the heart of Christian faith. They argue that conservative Christian involvement in politics has "failed." They call for a reorientation of perspective and priorities away from secular politics and toward cultural change rooted in classic church missional priorities. Thus, in the end, the Thomas/Dobson argument dovetails with the objection rooted in the church's mission with which we began this section.

These laments from disillusioned, politically engaged Christian conservatives resonate deeply with many of us. I have sounded such notes myself at times. But, on balance, they reflect a weakness in evangelical life as it relates to politics, and one that it is past time we overcame.

Many observers have noted that our reentry into the political arena since the 1970s and 1980s, after decades of disengagement, has been accompanied by certain signs of immaturity and inexperience and by some holes in our theological foundation for political engagement.

Among those problems has been our tendency toward a reactive, episodic, boom-and-bust cycle of political engagement. Evangelicals rallied in the 1980s to try to stop abortion. Many hitched their wagons pretty tightly to Ronald Reagan, newly christened as an antiabortion crusader. When *Roe v. Wade* was not overturned, quite a few evangelicals grew disillusioned with politics and at least *threatened* to go back to their churches and homes and forgo further involvements. The same pattern has been repeated in relation to particular hot causes, favorite politicians, and parachurch organizations. We invest our hope and effort heavily in cause/politician/organization X, but when disappointed, we turn bitterly away from X and threaten to take our marbles and go home, as James Dobson threatened to do in 2004 in relation to the Bush White House.

At a theological level, it is likely that this boom-and-bust cycle is rooted in an inadequate biblical understanding of human nature, culture, and politics. There is really nothing in the Bible that should lead us to expect that a brief, focused, even frenzied effort to transform a culture or to "win" on a moral issue will result in decisive victory for the gospel. The stubborn presence of sin both in human hearts and in human cultures, the pull of self-interest, money, power, and pride, and the immense difficulty of even approximating justice in any dimension of human experience, all mean that political involvement will inevitably be a long, hard slog with at least as many defeats as victories. If the expectation is victory on an issue—or more, transformation of a culture—as the price of continued involvement, we will find ourselves abandoning politics every few years like spoiled children abandoning their vexatious playmates. We need much more patience than this.

Perhaps our eschatology (theology of the last things/end of time) plays a hidden role here. Many skeptics have noted with alarm the role that the eschatology of some of us plays in relation to Israel. Many evangelicals have a particular end-times scenario in mind which involves some rather decisive activity in and around the plains of Megiddo.[14] But that is not what I have in mind. I am thinking about our general tendency toward what might be called an eschatology of urgency. It comes naturally to us because we take the Bible seriously, and the New

Testament is most insistent that we be ready for Christ's return at any moment. It is not easy to reconcile that with a vision that involves bearing public moral witness over decades or even centuries. But that is precisely what we must be able to do. Indeed, we must hold the tension, keep it taut and firm at all times; we are a people ready for Christ's return at a moment's notice or a thousand years from now. And so we work for the peace of the city in which we find ourselves now as if we and our children's grandchildren are just the beginning of the story. We dig in deep, even while at some level we keep our bags packed.

As evangelicals, these theological obstacles to our political engagement may best be dealt with overall through a transition to a concept of "bearing witness" rather than culture wars or even basic short-term win-lose politics. It is always possible—indeed obligatory—for Christians to bear witness to their publicly relevant moral convictions. We bear witness with our lives (thus, we do indeed "let the church be the church") and with our public articulation of our beliefs in sermons, books, letters to the White House, press conferences, declarations, conversations with our senators, and so on. Bearing witness is not something one can ever say has "failed" because it was never predicated upon achieving something other than truthful, faithful speech. Bearing witness does not compromise the mission of the church, instead, rightly practiced, it is part of the mission of the church. Bearing witness does not involve hitching our wagon to politicians, parties, votes, or particular parachurch organizations. Therefore it does not rise and fall as these rise and fall. Just as we do not abandon teaching our children the Bible even when they fail to understand it or live it out, and just as we do not abandon sermons even though they often fall on deaf ears, so we do not abandon public moral witness even when it seems to land on stony ground. So let us move past the time-out idea and dig in—more realistically and patiently than ever before—for the long hard slog of faithful Christian witness until Christ himself returns.

THE TECHNICAL OBSTACLE
Definitional Problems

Thus far I have been attempting to clear the ground of obstacles to the project of staking a claim to the emerging evangelical center in

American public life. I have suggested ways to respond to both the secu-larist objection and various versions of a sectarian objection. One final task lies before us at this stage: dealing with technical obstacles created by tangled definitional issues related to our key terms.

First there is the not insignificant matter of defining the "evangeli-cals" who are the subject of our inquiry. This is a matter of lively debate in American historiography and sociology of religion. For our purposes, I would suggest three possible approaches to defining the evangelicals who are the subject of our study.

One approach is to define evangelicals denominationally. John C. Green, a leading researcher on evangelical engagement in politics, defines evangelicals as "individuals affiliated with historically white denomina-tions and congregations in the Evangelical Protestant tradition."[15] Green finds that 26 percent of the adult population fell within this definition of evangelicalism as of 2004. One concrete way of getting at that defini-tion is to consider the sixty denominations affiliated with the National Association of Evangelicals (NAE), along with a host of schools, para-church organizations, ministries, missions organizations, commissions, individuals, and so on. Evangelicals know who they are because they affiliate with evangelical denominations and organizations.

Green's definition has the serious problem of excluding the majority of black, Latino/a, and other nonwhite evangelicals. This leads to the vexing problem, relevant not only to Green's work, that it is not clear whether nonwhite evangelicals are meant when researchers or media people talk about the voting behavior of "evangelicals." Green himself deals with this in his research by often breaking out separate catego-ries for nonwhite evangelicals, partly because their voting patterns tend to be significantly different from white evangelicals. Peter Heltzel sug-gests in his forthcoming book on evangelical political behavior that black evangelicals need to be treated as a distinctive category when dis-cussing evangelicals.[16] Similar conclusions have recently been offered related to Latino/a evangelicals.[17] Given my own particular experiences and context, I will speak primarily of white evangelicals, though I will attempt to offer treatment of key black and Hispanic evangelicals as well. The spectrum just looks different once one moves beyond the white evangelical world.

A second way to define evangelicals is by specifying the particular content of their religious beliefs or practices. Sociologists Christian Smith and Michael Emerson take this route in their important book on evangelicals and race, *Divided by Faith*.[18] For these authors, evangelicals are part of the broader set called "conservative Protestants." They are distinguishable from other Christian believers because they "hold that the final, ultimate authority is the Bible," they "believe that Christ died for the salvation of all," they press for people to accept Christ and therefore be "born again," they believe in the importance of sharing their faith with others, and they believe in "engaged orthodoxy," or bringing their faith to bear on the culture in which they live. (Notice that this cluster of beliefs is equally applicable across racial lines. White and nonwhite evangelicals do not differ *theologically* in any significant way.)

Reflecting a third way of defining our movement, Smith and Emerson also count as evangelicals anyone who self-identifies as an evangelical (rather than a Catholic, mainline Protestant, etc.) when asked to name their primary religious affiliation. They claim that when these two ways of defining evangelicals are employed, some 25 percent of the U.S. population meets this definition (with 90 percent of these being white).

Another complexity in defining evangelicals is that at a theological level evangelicalism does not offer anything particularly *new* to Christian theology or practice. Indeed, part of the self-understanding of many evangelicals is that they are simply holding on to traditional or orthodox Christian beliefs and behaviors in a secular and religious context in which such beliefs are under pressure and constantly eroding. Most church historians trace evangelicalism to the early church, then to the Protestant Reformation, then to the Puritans, then European Pietism, the Methodist revivals, frontier evangelism and revival efforts in the United States, and in the twentieth century as an heir to the fundamentalist side of the historic fundamentalist-modernist controversy. In each case, evangelicals are reformist conservatives in the sense that they are conserving some version of classic Christian orthodoxy while reforming churches that (they believe) have drifted from such orthodoxy. Understood in a kind of theologically purist way, there should not exist a self-defined evangelicalism anywhere; if our "movement" succeeded, precisely as a call back to classic Christianity, we would make ourselves obsolete by renewing the life of existing denominations. Every Christian would be an evangelical, and so no one would have to be. But of course this has not happened, and so evangelicals as an identifiable religious community can (more or less) be isolated and identified and not just as a reformist strain within existing denominations. Everything clear now?

If we assume that the American population has now reached 300 million, it is a safe estimate to say that as many as 75 million Americans could be defined as evangelical Christians using the three parameters we have identified here. Some know they are evangelicals; others do not. Some make it their primary identity; others do not. But whatever these differences, they represent an identifiable and massive portion of the American population. That much, at least, is sure.

Another definitional problem we must consider briefly is the whole question of whether we ought to even use a taxonomy of left, center, and right either to describe the spectrum of evangelical opinion or the contribution of evangelicals to the broader American political discussion. (I intend to say both that there is an identifiable right-center-left breakdown within evangelical life itself and that this internal evangelical spectrum of opinion tracks pretty closely with the broader American political spectrum.) Criticisms of any such approach could come from a variety of directions.[19]

One criticism is that it gives away too much to contemporary politics. It could be seen as contributing to the whole problem of evangelicals' orienting themselves not according to scripture, which does not use directional political taxonomies at all, but instead in terms of worldly politics. Our goal as Christians is not to be liberal, moderate, or conservative, right, center, or left, but instead to be obedient to God's commands and to live out the meaning of the gospel.

My response is first to agree absolutely with this basic claim. But then I want to suggest the possibility that being obedient to God's commands, being faithfully biblical in the current American context, ends up leading to policy positions that *most of the time* land in the political center of the American landscape. This is a highly provisional claim, based on the always changeable lay of the land in the public life of one particular nation. It is also deeply affected by the left versus right

polarization that has so marked our political life in recent decades and
has opened up a vast space in the center of the political landscape. In
principle it is always possible that the landscape itself could shift in
such a way that faithful adherence to biblical principles would lead
evangelicals to policy positions that would look either consistently liberal (left), consistently conservative (right), or even consistently radical. If we lived in Franco's Spain in 1940, we might look like leftists;
if we lived in Sweden today, we might look like rightists; in Imperial
Rome, Christians were derided as radicals. But in the United States of
America as of 2008, I am arguing that the best and most faithful rendering of our core moral principles would place us most of the time in
the center. I hope to illustrate this throughout the book.

Another possible objection to this political taxonomy is that it is too
comfortable with the current political establishment, and therefore it
risks sacrificing Jesus' radicalism to fit in on Capitol Hill. In response I
would say that it is true that some of the positions (and certainly some of
the *practices*) that reflect the best reading of the biblical evidence actually
are much more radical than the left-center-right landscape really allows.
For example, few American politicians of any stripe are willing to call
for the abolition of the death penalty, but I have come to believe that this
view best reflects the overall biblical witness. This one would put me to
the left of the left, in some cases. In the same way, the radical economic
thinking and practices of the "new monastics," as symbolized by the
life and work of such individuals as Shane Claiborne in Philadelphia,
go far beyond what anybody in Washington is talking about in terms
of action on behalf of, and alongside of, the poor. Over on the other
side of the spectrum, the kinds of steps that many of us think need to
be taken to strengthen marriage, such as making divorces much more
difficult to obtain (especially when there are children involved) go further than even most conservative politicians or evangelical right leaders
(leading flocks full of divorced people) are willing to go (see chapter 6).
Likewise, the growing doubts that some of us are entertaining about the
moral wisdom of in vitro fertilization and other reproductive technologies can be viewed as to the right of the right, or as perhaps busting the
spectrum altogether, because the origins of these concerns can be traced
to sources that emerge from both left and right.

Probably the most compelling critique that I have seen of the whole left-center-right taxonomy is in the work of George Lakoff, the linguist/cognitive scientist. In his book, *Thinking Points*, Lakoff suggests that so-called centrists or moderates—who simultaneously hold some progressive and some conservative convictions—should actually be considered "biconceptuals." They are able to integrate convictions that flow from strongly opposed ideologies.[20] Thus a biconceptual" can be *both* fiscally conservative *and* progressive on social issues like abortion.

As I take you into the world of evangelical politics and map the evangelical right, left, and center for you, you may conclude that the center is actually "biconceptual," and that this is exactly its appeal; the evangelical center is able to be passionate about human problems that concern *both* the right *and* the left. This global, holistic moral vision is precisely what our culture needs, and precisely what represents the best rendering of Christian morality.

Let us wrap up this discussion simply by saying that any political taxonomy is a time-bound, culture-bound, explanatory device rather than truth from beyond. Insofar as it is helpful in making sense of the public witness of evangelicals, we can use it with profit. If it should ever cease to be useful, we can abandon it. It is not the native language of Christian scripture or the church. It is derivative and secondary. But it is helpful language especially in communicating to those who are outside of our community of faith where we stand on issues. I find that it immediately helps the media, students, and non-Christians to make sense of what my own work is about and what the kinds of people we will be talking about in this book are trying to accomplish.

I have sought in this chapter to clear the ground of secularist, sectarian, and technical objections to the project of this book, staking a claim to an emerging evangelical center. It is time to move into the substance of our work, beginning with an analysis of the evangelical right.

Chapter 2

THE EVANGELICAL RIGHT

"The Church won the 2004 election," Jerry Falwell said at the Southern Baptist Convention Pastors' Conference in June 2005.[1] "And don't let anyone tell you any differently." Reverend Falwell was obviously not speaking of the universal church—that part of it to be found in the United States more or less mirrored the nation in its fractured voting patterns. He was, however, referring to white evangelical Protestants, an overwhelming majority of whom voted to reelect George W. Bush as president of the United States.[2]

Following the 2004 presidential election an explanation for the outcome emerged and was widely accepted: Evangelical Christians decided the election, voting en masse for George W. Bush, spurred on by religious convictions and a particular vision of "moral values," thus propelling him to a second term, a majority victory, and a so-called mandate. This interpretation of the 2004 election, widely accepted as conventional wisdom, was not quite so compelling when the best polling data and postelection analysis were examined.[3]

Yet there was some truth to the claim. And certainly the perception of its truth had its own enormous cultural and political impact. For a time it profoundly strengthened the hand of conservative evangelical political activists in the culture and in their electoral home in the Republican

Party. It also evoked an enormous backlash both in religious and secular circles, a backlash that continues to this day. For those most appalled by Bush's policies, evangelicals emerged as the most visible object of blame, scorn, and derision. Evangelicals unhappy to be associated with this depiction moved quickly to distinguish themselves from their coreligionists. It looked like the United States was fracturing politically along religious lines, like Northern Ireland or the former Yugoslavia.

One purpose of this book is to offer an accurate depiction of an evangelical landscape with more diversity than is commonly acknowledged. I will try to show throughout this book that evangelicals are certainly more than that group commonly called the "Religious Right." And yet the right pole of the evangelical spectrum (to be called "evangelical right" here) is a formidable force that deserves careful analysis. I will attempt to offer my own take on this group, rooted in my own experiences, available data, and research.

Meeting the Evangelical Right

It is hard not to encounter the evangelical right in everyday life, especially in the southern United States. One point of contact for me has been Christian radio. For a time I had a regular role as a co-host of a show on a local affiliate of American Family Association (AFA) radio. Christian radio stations like this one compete with public radio stations on the lower end of the FM dial. My station manager delighted in the news that as his signal had grown more powerful; he was sometimes successful in overriding National Public Radio (NPR) and knocking it into the realm of static. It makes an apt symbol—NPR versus AFA, slugging it out on the western end of your radio dial. They signify two very different visions of the world, of news and of the good life. Few people, I think, listen to both.

AFA radio featured a mix of news, talk shows, and Christian music. The news came via a feed from AFA's headquarters in Tupelo, Mississippi. It invariably reflected a hard-edged, sometimes snide conservatism in its reporting, something like a less-polite, more explicitly Christian version of Fox News: "Liberal politicians moved to weaken the family again today; Billy Christian has the story from Washington." AFA's news stories focused heavily on the major issues on the organization's agenda, notably abortion and homosexuality. After the news updates, local AFA talk-show hosts offered their almost invariably hard-line conservative perspectives on the issues of the day. Some focused more on matters of personal finance or spiritual growth. Public service announcements noted major revivals, Christian concerts, and other church events. Musical interludes offered inspiring music in various Christian genres, generally upbeat songs intended to cheer their audiences to "press on" in the Christian life.

A regular listener would learn that the Christian faith as proclaimed on AFA radio means a mix of conservative politics, opposition to abortion and homosexuality, inspiring music to give strength for daily living, and appeals for support of various Christian events and causes. After awhile, I found the reflexive narrowness of this political agenda just too much to bear, and so I gave it up. Yet Christian radio rolls on, a major force in the evangelical right subculture that nurtures the worldviews of millions of Americans. Now I usually encounter Christian radio in the form of hostile questions from hosts who strongly reject evangelical involvement of folks like me on such issues as climate change. There is little question that Christian radio is dominated by the right wing of the evangelical subculture, though there are some signs of change in recent days.

❉ ❉ ❉

Who are these people, the "conservative evangelicals" or "evangelical right"? Let's start at the organizational level. The conservative evangelical activist community can be described as a network of independent but interconnected churches and parachurch organizations. They share a range of perspectives and values while each pursuing its own particular agenda and niche in the evangelical nonprofit marketplace, to some extent competing with one another for market share. Their organizations are customarily built around charismatic founder-leaders who become inextricably identified with the structures that they create (often leading to major succession problems when it is time for these leaders to retire from active service). These leaders rise to the top in conservative evangelical life as a result of some combination of charisma, organizational ability, perceived expertise, fundraising prowess, and media ability/ exposure. It is not uncommon within evangelicalism for these church-related but mainly parachurch-leading personalities to be (somewhat ironically) described as evangelical bishops and cardinals. They play a hugely influential role in evangelical life and are often looked to as both convictional gatekeepers (they set the boundaries of acceptable belief) and authoritative emissaries of the community to the outside world.

Without attempting to be exhaustive or to pretend to have ascertained market share or exact level of influence, I suggest that as of the time of this writing the following ten organizations are among the lead-

Table 1
Conservative Evangelical Activist Groups and Current Leaders

Activist Group	Leader
AFA	Donald Wildmon
Christian Coalition	Roberta Combs
Concerned Women for America (CWA)	Beverly LaHaye
Eagle Forum (EF)	Phyllis Schlafly
Family Research Council (FRC)	Tony Perkins
Focus on the Family	James Dobson
High Impact Leadership Coalition	Harry Jackson
Moral Majority Coalition	Jerry Falwell (successor undetermined as of this writing)
Southern Baptist Convention Ethics and Religious Liberty Commission (ERLC)	Richard Land
Traditional Values Coalition (TVC)	Lou Sheldon

ing voices in the evangelical right, at least in terms of their political activism. Several of those named here are important because of who their leaders are, with their organizations trailing behind them essentially as their organizational embodiment. In other cases, the organization is more visible than the new or relatively unknown person who currently serves as its leader.

The scope of the evangelical right is not adequately represented by this identification of these ten major groups. Its size may perhaps be better understood by consideration of the loose coalition of dozens of organizational leaders who coalesced in 2002 under the leadership of veteran conservative activist Paul Weyrich. This secretive and influential coalition, under the name The Arlington Group, has been chaired by James Dobson (probably the single most visible evangelical right activist today) and is served by its own full-time staff. It provides a forum for member groups to discuss shared goals, debate strategy and tactics, and strengthen the overall educational and lobbying efforts of the member bodies.[4] This coalitional effort marks a significant departure from what Weyrich himself describes as the traditionally individualistic and often competitive approach of conservative activist organizations.

Turning to those organizations themselves, let us briefly describe those just named, looking at their structures, leadership, and goals.

Focus on the Family

The organization popularly known as Focus was founded in 1977 by psychologist James Dobson, who still serves as chairman of its board and its mouthpiece to the outside world.[5] Originally founded with the primary aim of helping Christians strengthen their families, over the years Dobson has turned his attention sharply in the direction of political activism and by now is more or less ubiquitous in the public culture wars debates. Today the mission statement of Dobson's organization covers both its original family support function and the newer political agenda. Notice the classic evangelistic language here: "To cooperate with the Holy Spirit in sharing the Gospel of Jesus Christ with as many people as possible by nurturing and defending the God-ordained institution of the family and promoting biblical truths worldwide."

To set itself up for more explicit public-policy activism, Focus on the Family Action, Inc. (FOFA) was founded in 2004 as a 501(c)(4) organization distinct from the original Focus on the Family. Its self-description: "Since its inception, Focus Action has been instrumental in the battle against judicial tyranny and the fight to protect traditional marriage."

Together, these related organizations are now a massive Colorado Springs-based enterprise with annual revenues totaling nearly $145 million, primarily through contributions. Focus employs hundreds of people, and its headquarters building is a major tourist attraction in Colorado.

The public-policy agenda of Focus (specifically, FOFA) is clearly articulated throughout all Focus materials: "FOFA will focus on policy matters such as: Federal and state constitutional amendments to protect marriage as an institution between one man and one woman, the protection of human life in all its various forms, and the appropriate role of state and [f]ederal judicial systems as designed by the founding fathers of the United States of America." Focus and Dobson have been prominent in opposing gay marriage, abortion, assisted suicide, and embryonic stem-cell research. They have also joined the chorus of conservatives opposed to the direction of the state and federal judiciary, and they weighed in heavily in support of John Roberts and Samuel Alito for the Supreme Court. Although defending "traditional values" related to sex, family, and marriage is the central public policy agenda for the organization, the Focus CitizenLink web page includes access to materials related to a broader range of issues. These other concerns include education, gambling, religious persecution, political Islam, pornography, and worldview/culture. Still, preserving the two-parent heterosexual family from its perceived enemies remains the "focus" of Focus and of Dobson.

Family Research Council

Family Research Council (FRC) was founded in 1983 under the leadership of the ubiquitous Dobson, who at the time apparently wanted an organization distinct from his own Focus on the Family to work on public-policy research and advocacy related to family issues.[6] The most visible leader in FRC history was Gary Bauer, appointed as head in 1988; he served until an unsuccessful run for president in 2000 and today leads his own relatively small organization called American Values. These days FRC's profile is rising again under Tony Perkins, a former Louisiana state legislator who is perhaps best known for his role in writing the nation's first "covenant marriage" law (see chapter 6). FRC was the lead sponsor of the controversial Justice Sunday events in spring/summer 2005, in which various conservative activists attacked the direction of the judiciary and called for an end to "judicial activism" and for full Senate votes for President Bush's judicial nominees.[7] Perkins is a fixture in the media firmament.

FRC describes its mission as follows: "The Family Research Council champions marriage and family as the foundation of civilization, the seedbed of virtue, and the wellspring of society. FRC shapes public debate and formulates public policy that values human life and upholds the institutions of marriage and the family. Believing that God is the author of life, liberty, and the family, FRC promotes the Judeo-Christian worldview as the basis for a just, free, and stable society." The organization roots this mission in a statement of core principles, which includes belief in a sovereign God who has made human beings in his image, a consequent belief in the sacredness of human life, and a conviction that the family is a natural institution that structures the relationship between a man and a woman. Government, says FRC, "has a duty to promote and protect marriage and family in law"; that is, the heterosexual marriage and consequent family. FRC goes on to argue that the American system of law and justice was founded on Judeo-Christian values, which ought to be preserved. They also argue for the importance of a vibrant civil society sector for the health of American democracy.

Although this fairly sophisticated statement of core principles is essentially indistinguishable from that of Focus, FRC has been especially committed to its founding emphasis on research. It is clear that FRC wants to serve as something of a traditional-values Washington think tank; its issue repertoire is wide ranging, though the focus on sex, marriage, life, and judiciary issues is clear. It publishes not just tracts but also rather extensive essays and lectures related to its major issues. Like most of the groups we will consider here, it also offers careful monitoring of state and federal public policy developments and urges its supporters to pay attention to its numerous action alerts and to become politically involved on various measures and issues. Its Web site includes a section that tracks the votes of all federal legislators on the issues of greatest concern to FRC. Similar action alerts are common in the conservative evangelical activist community, just as in other activist communities.

Southern Baptist Convention Ethics and Religious Liberty Commission

Unlike any of the other organizations to be considered in this section, the Ethics and Religious Liberty Commission (ERLC) is an official denominational office, an expression of the convictions and priorities of the 16-million-member, 163-year-old SBC.[8] Formerly known as the Christian Life Commission, the name of the organization was changed in the 1990s to ERLC after a "conservative resurgence" led to a change in leadership in the denomination as a whole. (Disclaimer: As a Southern Baptist ethicist, I worked with ERLC on several projects from 1993 to 1996.)

The strong move to the right in the SBC is clearly reflected in the public stance of ERLC and the role that is played by its leader, Richard Land. ERLC, officially "the public policy arm of the Southern Baptist Convention," essentially functions as a large and powerful evangelical right advocacy organization. It is a member of The Arlington Group, participates in coalition efforts sponsored by other groups mentioned in this section, and embraces the "faith and family" language that is used so consistently by Focus, FRC, and other right-leaning organizations.

Under Land's leadership, ERLC has organized itself in ways similar to those we have already seen. Its polished Web site mentions the weekly radio broadcasts that Land hosts and refers to his consistent presence as a source in the mass media. ERLC offers a wide range of print materials and sponsors a group of research fellows whose thinking supports the development of the organization's policy positions. The ERLC Web site reflects classic SBC piety in offering biblical quotations on a wide range of moral and policy issues. One feature that does set ERLC somewhat apart from other conservative activist groups is the range of its policy repertoire, which includes traditionally "left" concerns, such as ecology, race, human rights, and world hunger. Although these are not the issues that receive most of ERLC's public attention (which instead reflects a by-now familiar focus on abortion, gay marriage, stem cells, morality in the media, and the need for conservative judges), their presence does indicate a breadth of moral interest that is different from many conservative evangelical organizations. This relative breadth of vision is also refleted in Land's recent book, *The Divided States of America?*. Here Land focuses especially on church/state issues, and treats classic "right" concerns like abortion and gay marriage in tandem with progressive stances on less familiar themes such as racism and immigration. The book is packaged as a centrist "between left and right" approach and in this way moves toward the centrist evangelicalism I advocate.

American Family Association

The American Family Association (AFA), discussed previously, was founded by Rev. Donald Wildmon in 1977.[9] The first line of its striking self-description aptly reflects its spirit: "AFA is for people who are tired of cursing the darkness and are ready to light a bonfire." This fiery mission is aimed in the following way: "The American Family Association represents and stands for traditional family values, focusing primarily on the influence of television and other media—including pornography—on our society." AFA's primary focus on the morality of the media sets it somewhat apart from other evangelical right groups, which currently tend to feature the media issue as a minor rather than a major theme. This also explains why AFA has focused so many resources on maintaining an extensive media presence.

AFA's electronic and print materials do address other issues. These include the state of the church in the United States, focusing especially on the theological and moral drift of the churches where this is apparent; education issues, including the evolution/intelligent-design debate and liberalism in higher education; marriage and family, focusing especially but not exclusively on homosexuality-related issues; gambling (opposed); financial planning for Christian families (in favor); and pro-life issues, including opposition to abortion and the harvesting of embryonic stem cells.

AFA stands out from other groups profiled here in the aggressiveness of its tone and tactics. Unlike many of the other evangelical right groups, AFA frequently attempts to initiate boycotts of offensive television shows, movies, and music, and their sponsors. Their published materials express constant outrage at various offenses against the moral vision that they believe is not unique to their own Christian perspective but foundational to historic American values and to the well-being of American culture. Along with their public advocacy and activism, AFA attempts to serve families seeking to steer clear of unwholesome media.

An angry sorrow is apparent in everything AFA does. It is a grief over the direction of our nation that sometimes borders on the apocalyptic. Consider this statement from their Web site: "America desperately needs a moral rebirth. We should be ashamed of the kind of immoral society we are leaving our children and grandchildren. We need to implore God's blessings on our country. We need to ask God to forgive our sinfulness and restore our moral perspective." Although AFA may be particularly strident in its language and aggressive in its approach, its perspective and concerns are shared quite widely among adherents of the evangelical right.

Traditional Values Coalition

Traditional Values Coalition (TVC), founded in 1980 by Rev. Louis Sheldon and now led by executive director Andrea Lafferty, describes itself as "an interdenominational public policy organization speaking on behalf of over 43,000 churches."[10] In its self-presentation TVC emphasizes its interracial and interethnic membership and support base and claims that its membership now includes most U.S. denominations and people in Puerto Rico. Unlike many other conservative evangelical groups, TVC focuses on a church-based strategy, hoping to reach pastors and other church leaders who, in turn, can be the engine driving public-policy activism of various sorts.

TVC's issue agenda focuses on "the restoration of the values needed to maintain strong, unified families," and includes specific concern for such issues as education, "homosexual advocacy," family tax relief, pornography, the right to life, and religious freedom. Divided into a lobbying organization and an educational enterprise, TVC seeks to "educat[e] and support churches in their efforts to restore America's cultural heritage." TVC clearly identifies biblical teachings with American values, thus making them "Traditional Values": "Traditional Values are based upon biblical foundations and upon the principles outlined in the Declaration of Independence, our Constitution, the writings of the Founding Fathers, and upon the writings of great political and religious figures throughout the ages." These values include traditional sexual morality (heterosexuality, practiced in a lifetime marriage alone), opposition to abortion and euthanasia, opposition to pornography and other addictive behaviors, and support for patriotism, the armed forces, and citizen/Christian political engagement. TVC supports limited government, low taxes, free enterprise, and religious liberty, understood as "the right to freely exercise our religious faith" in a context supportive of the idea that "religious faith is the cornerstone of freedom in our nation." TVC's sharply worded press releases and recent advocacy mirror that of other conservative evangelical activist groups in opposing gains for gay marriage or the recognition of homosexual relationships, opposing "judicial activism" and some recent Supreme Court decisions, including the decisions restricting the display of the Ten Commandments, supporting Bush appointees for the Supreme Court, "unmasking the homosexual agenda," supporting parental-notification measures in abortion bills, and defending conservative Bush appointees to judicial and executive posts.

Concerned Women for America and the Eagle Forum

Two of the ten conservative evangelical activist organizations are led by women and primarily geared toward (conservative) women's values: Concerned Women for America (CWA) and the Eagle Forem (EF).[11] We will consider them together for brevity and see if they strike any notes that are different from the traditionally male-led groups.

CWA, a twenty-eight-year-old organization based in Washington, was founded by Beverly LaHaye, an ardent evangelical right activist and writer who is now CWA's board chair. LaHaye is well known in her own right as an evangelical leader-activist, and her name recognition is enhanced by her connection with her husband, Tim, now most famous for his coauthorship of the fabulously successful *Left Behind* series. Describing itself as "the nation's largest public policy women's organization," CWA's mission statement reads as follows: "The mission of CWA is to protect and promote Biblical values among all citizens—first through prayer, then education, and finally by influencing our society—thereby reversing the decline in moral values in our nation." The vision statement of CWA emphasizes the goal of "restor[ing] the family to its traditional purpose." CWA attempts to achieve this vision through a mix of Washington-based research and lobbying efforts together with state-based offices to encourage grass-roots activism, along with CWA's Web presence and print materials. CWA especially emphasizes its e-mail network of over 32,500 subscribers; this group functions as an activist network for whatever projects or issues the CWA leadership seeks to promote at a given time.

CWA organizes its work into six issue areas, which they label as follows: definition of the family, sanctity of human life, education, pornography, religious liberty, and national sovereignty. CWA's stances on the family, sanctity of life, and pornography issues are familiar to us by now as the overall approach of the conservative evangelical camp. On education the core value is to "reform public education by returning authority to parents," a theme that is also picked up by EF. On religious liberty the commitment of CWA is to "support the God-given rights of individuals in the United States and other nations to pray and worship without fear of discrimination or persecution." CWA's statement about "national sovereignty" is striking in its tone and unique among the groups we have surveyed thus far: "CWA believes that neither the United Nations nor any other international organization should have authority over the United States in any area, including economics, social policy, military, and land ownership." This is not an unusual perspective on the political right in the United States, though it is hard to locate any evidence of how CWA finds biblical support for this view as a core value along with its other commitments. Further exploration of that particular issue area on the CWA Web site reveals a number of articles offering support for Bush Supreme Court appointees, opposition to the judicial filibuster, and general criticisms of the United Nations (UN) and various UN treaties.

EF, founded in 1972, is the institutional platform for Phyllis Schlafly, its president, who first came to national prominence in the 1970s as the most strident female opponent of the Equal Rights Amendment—the defeat of which Schlafly claims considerable credit for on her Web page. Though Schlafly does not publicly position her organization as evangelical, her Web site describes the group as "leading the pro-family movement since 1972" and quotes scripture; it has had a considerable evangelical following. The current EF mission statement reads as follows: "to enable conservative and pro-family men and women to participate in the process of self-government and public policy making so that America will continue to be a land of individual liberty, respect for family integrity, public and private virtue, and private enterprise."

The public policy agenda EF presents on its Web page is sharply conservative and libertarian, with a tinge of isolationism and a hint of nativism. Thus EF, like CWA, is opposed to the UN and international conferences and treaties and other supposed encroachments on U.S. sovereignty. Interestingly, it opposes U.S. war-making unless our national security is clearly threatened, and the Congress is properly consulted. It supports a missile defense system, free enterprise, low taxes, election reform, English as the official national language, and the right to keep and bear arms. It opposes government gathering of personal information, judicial activism and the "Imperial Judiciary," abortion, same-sex marriage, embryonic stem-cell research, government-funded day care, the "dumbing down" of educational standards, anything supported by the NEA, any rights or privileges for illegal immigrants, the "feminization of the military," and women in combat roles. Perhaps most strikingly, EF does not just oppose, it says that it "exposes" the "radical feminists," and "honor[s] the institution of marriage and the role of the fulltime homemaker." This strong attack on the feminist movement and mention of the gender-roles issue, especially the focus on upholding the value of the full-time homemaker, sets EF apart from all other conservative evangelical groups profiled here. This is important to note—the evangelical right, in general, has definitely lowered its emphasis on the gender issue in light of overwhelming social changes in recent years.

The Christian Coalition and the Moral Majority

The first significant evangelical right organization was the Moral Majority (MM), founded in 1979 by the late Rev. Jerry Falwell. Most observers would agree that the second major evangelical right group was the Christian Coalition (CC), founded in 1990, most associated with its leaders Pat Robertson and eventually Ralph Reed. Both organizations disappeared from public view; the MM closed up shop in 1989, and CC simply lost momentum as its voice was outshouted by other organizations after 2000. But now both groups are back—sort of.

The Moral Majority Coalition (TMMC) is the new name that Falwell gave to his organization.[12] Described on Falwell's Web site in 2005 as a "21st century resurrection of the Moral Majority," TMMC was founded just after the 2004 election "to utilize the momentum of the November 2 [2004] election to maintain an evangelical revolution of voters who will continue to go to the polls to 'vote values.'" Falwell initially served as national chairman of this new iteration of the Moral Majority, with his son Jonathan as executive director, and Tim LaHaye as chairman of the board. This structure makes for an interesting example of the dynastic quality of many conservative evangelical Christian organizations and the interlocking network of leading figures. (Interestingly, neither the younger Falwell nor LaHaye is now mentioned on the TMMC site. The organization's future is uncertain.)

After describing its founding and purpose, TMMC said in 2005 that "one of our primary commitments is to help make President Bush's second term the most successful in American history. He will certainly need the consistent prayer and support of the evangelical community as he continues to spearhead the international war on terror and the effort to safeguard America." Besides supporting President Bush, TMMC laid out a four-pronged agenda:

1. to conduct a voter registration drive in conservative churches and parachurch organizations over the next four years,
2. to conduct get-out-the-vote campaigns,
3. to engage in the massive recruitment and mobilization of social conservatives through various mass media venues,
4. to encourage prayer for America's "moral renaissance."

The CC, led since 2003 by Roberta Combs, describes itself as "America's leading grassroots organization defending our godly heritage."[13] The most visible feature of the CC Web site throughout much of the summer of 2005 was a photo of Judge John Roberts with the following statement beside it: "Be it resolved, that we the under-signed strongly support President Bush's conservative nominees to the Supreme Court, and that we will support efforts to end Senate obstruction and will fight for 'up or down' votes by the full Senate on ALL of the President's judicial nominees." CC describes its mission as "representing the pro-family agenda and educating America on the critical issues facing our society. Whether it is the fight to end Partial Birth Abortion or efforts to improve education or lower the family's tax burden, the Christian Coalition stands ready and able to work for you." The hallmark of CC activity is its voter guide; the organization claims to have distributed 70 million of these "nonpartisan" documents prior to the 2004 elections. The organization also undertakes commu-nity organizing, Washington lobbying, and media efforts to marshal the influence of conservative, "pro-family" citizens. CC describes itself as a "political organization" encouraging Christian citizens to rise up and shape public policy in accordance with a "pro-family" vision. "We continuously work to identify, educate, and mobilize Christians for effective political action! Such action will preserve, protect and defend the Judeo-Christian values that made this the greatest country in his-tory." Its vision statement, written in 2003 after the ascension of Combs to leadership, emphasizes the spiritual (rather than merely political) focus and purpose of the organization. Combs is described here as "the woman who put the 'Christian' back in Christian Coalition," presum-ably in contrast to her highly political (and now deeply tainted) prede-cessor, Ralph Reed.

Still, the activities of CC remain much as they have been through-out its history—working hard to advance a politically conservative agenda. Its 2005 congressional agenda, fourteen items strong, included passing Social Security reform, making the president's 2001 tax cuts permanent, passing two bills limiting the jurisdiction of the courts and a bill limiting the impact of any international treaties or instruments on the United States, fighting gay marriage, cloning, abortion, and embry-onic stem-cell research, and a bill to protect the Pledge of Allegiance and encourage abstinence-only sex education in schools. Its 2007 con-gressional agenda added such items as protecting religious television programming, passing "net neutrality," confirming conservative judges, opposing religious discrimination in the military, and getting a vote on the Federal Marriage Amendment.

CC briefly returned to the headlines in 2006, when Florida mega-church pastor Joel Hunter was offered the organization's presidency and then withdrew from the post before taking it up. Hunter is a significant figure who helps to clarify the difference between the evangelical right and the evangelical center. His commitment to broadening CC's agenda to include such issues as global warming met with sufficient CC board opposition to prevent him from assuming the organization's presidency. We will say more about Hunter and his agenda later in this book.

The Black Evangelical Right
Bishop Harry Jackson and Kay Coles James

The black evangelical community has produced its own activist leaders and networks. It is possible to identity, at least tentatively, a black evan-gelical right, left, and center. The spectrum is skewed by the continu-ing impact of the tragic realities of racial injustice in the United States. While white evangelical right groups rarely mention racism and its con-crete legacy, black evangelicals cannot avoid such issues. (This is one really good reason why white evangelicals of all stripes need to hang out more with black evangelicals and listen seriously to their agendas.) So the black evangelical right shows a more holistic moral concern—one that engages issues such as race and poverty—than does the white evan-gelical right. Still, I think that there are black evangelical leaders and groups who are properly classified as evangelical right. Let us consider two of them here.

Bishop Harry R. Jackson Jr. is founder of the High Impact Leadership Coalition (HILC) and pastor of Hope Christian Church, a charismatic congregation of 3,500 in Lanham, Maryland. As a con-servative black evangelical, he actively speaks out on political matters and has declared that the church must be the guardian of "America's moral compass." His HILC put forth the "Black Contract with America on Moral Values," in which six key issues are targeted: family recon-struction, wealth creation, education reform, prison reform, health care, and African relief. This agenda is significantly more inclusive than other conservative (white) evangelical declarations.

HILC asks those who sign the Black Contract to "pray for spiritual renewal in America, promote the values of the contract, vote for future legislation to encompass these points, and vote for politicians, regardless of party, who champion these values."[14] To Jackson, however, the Republican Party is clearly the way to go. In 2004, Jackson issued a formal statement that urged Americans to support President Bush as the candidate who stood for righteousness and justice. "In my view," he said, "God has been preparing the heart of President Bush to take a radical stand for social justice in his next term." His support of the Republican Party is primarily based on the "moral agenda" it promotes. The left, he claims, has done nothing to protect the two million black babies that were aborted over the past four years. The right places a stronger emphasis on sexual and marriage issues, which Jackson sees as addressing the fact that over 70 percent of black babies are born to unwed mothers.

Although Jackson is vehemently outspoken against gay marriage and abortion (which he calls black genocide) and makes these two issues the most dominant in his writing and activism, he also begs Christians to expand their definition of "God's moral issues" to include "practical guidelines for living. Churches and Christian leaders are needed to discuss the morality of war, how to deal with poverty, and world hunger." World poverty, clean water, the Darfur crisis, and the AIDS epidemic are moral issues that Jackson sees as "new frontiers for social action." These issues, while not the core of the right's agenda, do not belong to the left because, says Jackson, the left is seriously lacking moral integrity. "My greatest prayer," he said in a 2006 interview, "would be that the Democratic Party would come back from the precipice of moral madness."

In April 2007 Jackson wrote, "I believe that evangelical church[es] must take the lead in defining the key moral issues of our day in clear measurable terms. We must be willing to discuss the hot topics that capture popular attention, while maintaining our core commitment to preaching the gospel, the sanctity of life, the defense of marriage, and the protection of religious liberty in the public square."

Kay Coles James is a black evangelical woman with a strong background in conservative politics. She served in the George H. W. Bush administration as assistant secretary for public affairs at the Health and Human Services Department and as associate director at the Office of National Drug Control Policy. She worked for a time as senior fellow and director of the Citizenship Project at the Heritage Foundation where she promoted conservative policies on Social Security, health care, and education. She has also served as dean of the school of government at Regent University, where Pat Robertson is president and chancellor, and as senior vice president of the FRC. In 2001 President George W. Bush named her as director of the U.S. Office of Personnel Management (OPM).

Personal responsibility and a pro-life ethic are integral pieces of James's outlook. She has placed a major emphasis on small government, believing that most programs run by the government should, in fact, be in the hands of the church. James contends that real culture change happens outside of the government sector. Although it happens less quickly, nongovernmental organizations advance that change with a deeper and more meaningful impact.

In her book *Transforming America from the Inside Out*, James asserts that the term "Cultural AIDS" is more appropriate than culture wars when discussing the battle for morality in America. In a 1996 interview, she explained why she uses this term.

> Those institutions in our culture that historically provided a shield for us against the pathologies of our communities are breaking down. These pathologies—violence, pornography, child abuse, chemical addiction—have existed in world culture since the very beginning of time. But what has allowed us as a nation to fight off those particular pathologies is that we had a very strong immune system—things like strong families, strong faith, strong institutions, a moral base, a strong sense of virtue. As a result of our immune system now being broken down, we are susceptible to these viruses.

In light of that susceptibility, James has become an ardent spokesperson and activist for the pro-life ethic. A "pro-life culture" is one in which abortion, poverty, homelessness, and euthanasia are dealt with as affronts to human dignity, and she has dedicated herself to this with passion.

James spent her childhood supported by welfare and living in public housing, and she sees the welfare system (offering what she calls "misguided compassion") as impairing instead of empowering the poorest members of society. She emphasizes those who have "accepted personal responsibility for their lives," taken charge of their destinies, and become successes. "People rise or sink to their level of expectation, and I think that many who have this misguided compassion have really lowered the bar to the point that many poor people in America really don't believe that they can accomplish anything."

James acknowledges that to be black in the United States is to be forced to deal with the reality of racism, and she is greatly affected by that reality on a daily basis. However she breaks with the "liberal black community" in how to address it. Instead of seeking institutional changes, she thinks racism should be dealt with swiftly on an individual basis. Poverty, racism, poor schools and lack of economic activity are real obstacles in James's eyes, but not a reason why a person should not go on to achieve. "I accept no excuses," she says, "including racism. So I think that while I acknowledge that racism exists, I may have a very different strategy of how to deal with it."

THE NARRATIVE OF DECLINE, DEFENSE, AND COMBAT

Conservative evangelical political activists have a story to tell, and its outlines appear in the materials of just about every one of their organizations. I want to tell it here in a way that they themselves would recognize and affirm. Critique will come later. The story goes something like this:

> The United States of America was once the greatest nation on earth, because it was founded on Judeo-Christian principles, and these governed both the private and public lives of its citizenry. Americans were people of strong faith, who believed in God and the Bible, attended church, got married (to the opposite sex), raised children in the fear and admonition of the Lord, and contributed lives of service and virtue to their communities.
>
> However, America went into decline when its commitment to this faith and way of life was shaken by the introduction of an alien faith and vision of life. This alien ideology is secularist, morally relativist, and profoundly corrosive to the well-being of families and the society as a whole. It shook the norms of heterosexual-only sexuality,

the sacredness of life, and other key components of Judeo-Christian morality. This ideology is now firmly entrenched, especially in the institutions of education and in the judiciary, both of which must be wrestled back to their founding values and vision, in part as an act of self-defense for Christians and churches and in part to serve the well-being of society as a whole.

Evangelical right organizations exist to educate American Christians about what has happened to their beloved country, to train and mobilize them for social and political action, and to fight hard for a return to traditional values at every opportunity. Because it is impossible to find common ground with cultural liberals and secular-ists, the only alternative is to beat them in the court of public opinion and in politics. Thoughtful Christians must join together, mobilize for action, and take back their society.

There are interesting nuances and variations on the themes of this powerful shared narrative that is now so central to U.S. public life, as well as in the strategies the groups pursue. For example, some conserva-tive evangelical activist groups still offer concrete help to Christians in actually navigating these morally treacherous cultural waters (Focus, AFA); others focus almost entirely on public social change efforts. Some organizations are careful in delineating the biblical/theological basis for their beliefs and for their social agendas (Focus, FRC); others merely proclaim their allegiance to the "traditional values" they hold as more or less self-evident truths, values often involving a conflation of American and Christian themes and texts.

Some of these groups are self-consciously intellectual and seek to win the battle of ideas; these, along with a number of other nonpolitical organizations and initiatives not profiled here usually offer a broader cultural-engagement strategy. Others are more populist and emphasize winning the battle of the ballot box for values that are self-evidently right. Some organizations are more overtly partisan or political than oth-ers; for example, most never mention President Bush or the Republican Party on their Web sites, whereas others have been quite direct about their support for the president (such as TMMC, though less today than when Bush was at the height of his popularity among evangelicals). Even in the former case, however, the alignment of the agendas of these organizations with that of the Bush White House and the Republican

Party has been more than apparent and is especially obvious when matters not clearly related to biblical values are discussed.

While all evangelical right groups express support for "traditional family values," of these nine groups only Schlafly's EF addresses an issue once viewed as central to such values—the "God-given" role of the woman as wife, mother, and full-time homemaker. And none of the groups say much about potential public policy measures that might slow down the epidemic of divorce, certainly a major family values issue of our time. Perhaps this means that even the evangelical right knows when certain fights are lost, or it does not want to offend its potential supporters, such as the millions of divorced, working, Christian women who are a significant part of its base.

Most evangelical right groups mention foreign-policy issues rarely or never, but of those that do, an anti-internationalist, isolationist strand is far stronger than any prointerventionism (e.g., the Iraq War). Evangelical right organizations are self-consciously patriotic, they "support the troops," they want schoolchildren to say the Pledge, but they do not generally emphasize or focus on foreign-policy issues as part of their moral agendas for American life.

The rhetoric of evangelical right groups tends to display a level of self-confidence closely tied to the latest political developments. When President Bush and his agenda were riding high, these groups brimmed with self-confidence. After the reversals of the 2006 election, they reverted to a more defensive and angry tone, which seems to be the "native language" of most activist groups and is probably helpful in rallying the troops and raising money.

Whatever the latest political developments, evangelical right groups continue to grow more and more sophisticated in the hurly-burly business of grass-roots organizing, public opinion shaping, lobbying, and get-out-the-vote efforts. These organizations have the support of millions of Americans. There are many more organizations that we have not profiled here. Surely they played a role in affecting conservative evangelical voting behavior in the 2004 election and occupy a strategic position in American public life. One measure of their influence is how rare it has been for President Bush to undertake a policy opposed by this interconnected coalition of activist groups. He has needed them and listened to them; they have supported him almost unquestioningly. Now a new cadre of potential presidential successors is emerging for 2008 and seeking their support. At least serious two candidates (Mike Huckabee and Mitt Romney) are running explicitly as social conservatives and therefore as representatives of the evangelical right bloc in the Republican Party.

WHAT'S TO LIKE AND NOT TO LIKE IN THE EVANGELICAL RIGHT

I refuse to demonize the evangelical right. The groups profiled do not deserve such treatment. They are neither fascists nor theocrats. They are not enemies of American constitutionalism or democracy. However, I do think that my religious brethren exhibit certain tendencies that require critical engagement and correction. I will here offer an evangelical centrist take on what's to like and not to like in the right. I hope these comments can be received in the spirit in which they are offered.

The evangelical right political activist community is to be commended for its passionate and active concern about the direction of the nation. These men and women are attempting to exercise their citizenship responsibilities by making use of the tools available in a free society—free speech, grass-roots organizing, lobbying, voting, and so on. They do what they do because they care about the United States, and they use the tried-and-true methods that have been employed in this country for more than two centuries. The fact that they are often effective in using such tools is commendable in itself, whether or not one agrees with the substance of their positions. It means the participatory democratic system is working.

Evangelical right activism represents an effort to bring faith to bear on the world. It is rooted in a commitment to Christ and one particular understanding of what that commitment means for culture, law, and politics. It is to be preferred to disengagement, or to quietist withdrawal from the world, or to a soul-winning-alone strategy of Christian mission—as we discussed previously.

This branch of the evangelical world is patriotic. It still finds great meaning in traditional symbols of national identity, such as the flag, the Pledge of Allegiance, displays of the Constitution, and the traditions associated with the armed forces. In a nation in which (at least arguably) such patriotism is oh-so-passé and is giving way to a self-absorbed individualism, this tendency is in its way commendable. It just needs to be disciplined by a broader and deeper Christian moral vision and by a democratic constitutionalism that can set proper boundaries for its expression.

That leads us to the following claim: Contrary to the fears of many critics, most in the evangelical right do respect the structures of American constitutional democracy. The appeal to traditional values, whatever its flaws, includes respectful elevation of the founding documents, such as the Declaration of Independence, the Constitution, and, yes, the Bill of Rights, including the First Amendment. It is true that most evangelical right groups want to see the First Amendment interpreted in such a way as to offer maximum room for the free exercise of faith in the public square. To use the language of centrist evangelical thinker Steve Monsma, they embrace the "benevolent neutrality" rather than "strict separationism" line on church-state issues.[15] This is certainly a debatable position, but it is not restricted to some kind of out-there fringe in American public life. It is one perspective in a lively current debate across multiple venues. It has engaged the Supreme Court in a number of close decisions in recent years and is broadly shared in the evangelical community.

It is certainly true that less careful evangelical leaders sometimes make statements that suggest their obliviousness to the boundary lines that broadly characterize our constitutional order. These need to be named and rejected when they occur. Let us rule out of hand, for example, the Reconstructionists who argue for the imposition of Old Testament law on the United States, which they treat as a kind of new Israel under direct divine rule. This fringe group represents only a tiny fraction of the most conservative regions of evangelicalism and would not come close to winning a majority vote in any evangelical context that I have ever experienced.

One might follow Noah Feldman's helpful distinction in arguing that the real boundary line in the church-state arena is whether the individual or group accepts the legitimacy of the constitutional structure that requires religious and moral views on public policy to be mediated through the restrictions established by the First Amendment. So if the question is whether the evangelical right accepts that religion is legally disestablished in the United States, and that all religions have the right to the free exercise of their faith in this country, the answer is clearly yes in almost every case—even if it is sometimes a grudging yes. What the evangelical right seeks in this area includes the freedom for full-throated exercise of their faith, the freedom to articulate their moral values in the public arena like everyone else, and at least some kind of respectful nod in the direction of public acknowledgment of the role of (Judeo-)Christian faith and morality in the history of our nation. Where conservative Christians (like Katharine Harris of Florida in the 2006 Senate race) go beyond that and seem to argue for the full establishment of Christian faith or for religious tests for public office, they are generally repudiated by their coreligionists on the evangelical right and at the ballot box. (The same thing happened to Judge Roy Moore, "The Ten Commandments Judge," in Alabama.) Grass-roots evangelical right folk are often less careful about these boundary lines than are the kinds of organizations that I am considering in this chapter, and the organizations themselves sometimes slip over the line, some more than others. Though this is problematic when it occurs, the evangelical world in general has matured to the point that no one need fear a theocratic takeover by the Christian right.

As an evangelical centrist, I find numerous elements within the moral values and policy agendas of the evangelical right that I can embrace. I think that my views here would be broadly representative of other centrist evangelicals. For example, we are generally in full agreement with the right's concern about the deterioration and deinstitutionalization of marriage. We share the belief, drawn from the Bible but also from experience, that the best context for the raising of children is a loving two-parent family. We grieve for the millions of children being raised in contexts of suffering, instability, divorce, cohabitation, and serial monogamy. (I could wish the evangelical right actually said *more* about these issues!) Where evangelical right organizations provide concrete help to marriages and families, centrists are fully supportive.

Centrist evangelicals are also deeply concerned about abortion. We oppose abortion-on-demand and the structure of U.S. abortion law that was established by *Roe v. Wade*. Besides the direct loss to the world of millions of human beings made in the image of God, mass abortion has cheapened the meaning and value of human life and has helped open the way to other forms of such cheapening, such as the manipulation, use, and destruction of human embryos. Centrists oppose the creation-for-destruction of embryos for their stem cells and are uneasy about the harvesting of stem cells from already existing embryos. We likewise oppose euthanasia-on-demand and are grateful that the Supreme Court repudiated any national right to euthanasia in the 1990s. Centrists seek a full and open national debate on the best way to rewrite laws related to abortion that might respect the dignity of all affected by this tragic practice.

Centrist evangelicals also share the right's concern about the media. Slasher films, Internet pornography, obscene music lyrics, Howard Stern's radio antics, titillation-on-demand in evening sitcoms, cruel reality TV shows, and the like all speak to a disturbing moral malaise in American society. The evangelical right does not always articulate its opposition to such media in ways that we would agree with, but for most, the concern itself is legitimate.

I have sought to be fair and fulsome in describing what there is to like about the evangelical right. But there is also much not to like, *not from a secular perspective*, but precisely from within the evangelical Christian worldview. I will break this down into four primary concerns: partisanship, agenda, mood, and ecclesiology (understanding of the church).

When Jerry Falwell said in 2005 that the church won the 2004 election, he was implicitly identifying the interests and values of the church of Jesus Christ with the interests and values of the Republican Party or at least of George W. Bush. This judgment on my part does not hinge on debatable interpretations of one sentence in a Falwell speech. It reflects a theme constantly communicated in one way or another by the leaders, the documents, and the advocacy of most evangelical right organizations.[16] The American evangelical right functions as a political bloc within the Republican Party in the United States, just as organized labor has functioned within the Democratic Party. The connection is so tight that some Republicans are worried that the party has become the political arm of conservative Christianity, rather than the reverse.[17] I think that goes too far, as can be seen when one considers that the evangelical right is not the only major bloc within the Republican Party but instead competes aggressively with a small government libertarian bloc, a big-business bloc, a nativist bloc, a national security bloc, and others now struggling bitterly over the direction of the Republican Party.[18] But like these, the evangelical right (often called the "social-conservative wing of the Republican Party") organizes its activities essentially as a branch of the Republican Party, which seems to include both an overall commitment to advancing the Republican cause in electoral politics as well as an internal struggle to gain influence over against other blocs within the GOP itself.

So what exactly is wrong with this? Jesus said that no one can serve two masters. He also said that where your treasure is, there shall your heart be also. The Ten Commandments, of course, strike a related theme in declaring that "you shall have no other gods before me." I want to argue here that it is *impossible* both to represent "the church" and to function as a bloc within a national political party. Because no one can serve two masters, and because where your treasure is there shall your heart be also, one can predict that ultimately those Christians (and Christian organizations) that give themselves over to allegiance to a political party will lose the ability to retain their fundamental loyalty to Jesus Christ. They will meet various forks in the road in which it is either Jesus or the party; having chosen the party once and then again and then again, after awhile the choice of ultimate loyalty has already been determined, and it will set the course for all future decisions. The transition from faith-based advocacy group to branch office of the party becomes complete. This is wrong theologically. It is wrong morally. And it is at least at risk of running afoul of the constitutional boundaries between church and state.[19]

Many of the criticisms that can fairly be directed at the evangelical right reflect various aspects of this same problem. When their Web sites and spokespersons are clearly working from talking points that every Republican is using at a given time, that seem to come direct from the White House or GOP headquarters, it is clear that Christian conservative activists are being employed as agents of a party's agenda rather than as independent actors seeking to advance a particularly Christian agenda. When their Web sites include seemingly random bits of exhortation for agenda items that are not (and cannot be) grounded in a particularly Christian moral value—such as, say, support for Social Security privatization or John Bolton as UN ambassador—it is clear what is going on. Most egregiously, of course, when Web sites such as TMMC's talk quite directly about "helping to make President Bush's second term the most successful in history," clearly we see the abandonment of any pretense of political neutrality or grounding in a transcendent Christian moral vision.

I am claiming that the most important thing that is wrong with the evangelical right is that it has given up its fundamental allegiance to Jesus Christ in aligning itself so tightly with the Republican Party. This, in itself, is a huge error. But it also leads to other profound problems, some of which should be at least briefly named.

Worldly politics is an exalted, and at the same time, a grubby business. It involves the ordering of human communities under God's sovereignty, but it also involves an awful lot of no-holds-barred political campaigning, shady dealmaking, moral compromises, and temptations to misuse money and power. One reason why Christians must retain their political independence—because they are totally dependent on Jesus Christ as Lord—is so that they can retain their moral compass when they do venture into the political arena.

The ethical scandals of the late years of Republican government in Congress revealed a perhaps inevitable but nonetheless damnable spread of ethical misconduct in Republican ranks. Some of these scandals touched men who had developed their careers in part on their supposed Christian commitments. For Ralph Reed, former darling of the evangelical right, it was his involvement in the slimy dealings of Jack Abramoff that tripped him up. For Tom DeLay, it was both Abramoff and his raw abuse of political power in Texas and in Washington. Reed ended up defeated for a minor office in Georgia; DeLay ended up indicted and out of office. Both men proclaimed their loyalty to the Christian cause to the end. Remarkably, both found themselves defended more or less uncritically by leaders in the evangelical right even *after* the evidence of their shady behavior had been made known. It had become impossible for these religious leaders to "see" corruption when it tainted those who had been identified with their cause. This reminds me very much of how Jesus emphasized moral perception, our capacity to "see" what is in front of us, and how deeply that is affected by where our treasure is, and therefore where our heart is. Most of what we see comes from behind our eyes. It is rooted in the placement of our ultimate loyalties.

Right, left, or center, no Christian or Christian group should enter the public arena under the banner of Christ unless it is committed to a fierce political independence under the lordship of Christ. We love Christ, and we seek to bear faithful witness to his cause and his agenda in the world. We therefore enter the public arena in order to bear that witness, always, always remembering who we are and *whose* we are. If we enter the offices of Capitol Hill or the White House, we do so as emissaries of Christ and we leave as emissaries of Christ. We don't stay to become emissaries of Bush or Pelosi, of McCain or Obama. If we do, we have fallen prey to the oldest problem that there is among moral activists in politics—we went into politics to change politics, but in the end it was politics that changed us.

I propose a new litmus test for Christian engagement with politics: *whether we have the capacity to say no to our favored party or politician.* I would suggest that the way in which some evangelicals openly supported "war on terror" detainee policies that included torture, and cruel, inhuman, and degrading treatment—while many others simply refused to discuss the matter, let alone to condemn it (see chapter 5)—demonstrated the morally lethal result of the inability to meet this test.[20] Just as many Christian liberals of a previous generation were unable to say no to abortion-on-demand because they were more liberal than Christian, many Christian conservatives of this generation have been unable to say no to torture because they are more conservative than Christian. Torture, therefore, makes a great and terrible test case of whether any policy issue could emerge that might demand the moral separation of a Christian constituency from its favored Republican administration. Those who could not make that separation are at least vulnerable to the charge that their ultimate loyalty now rests with a political ideology rather than with Jesus Christ.

The second fundamental problem with the evangelical right is the narrowness of its agenda. It may be that the diagnosis I have offered here accounts sufficiently for this problem. One could argue that because the policy agenda of the evangelical right is essentially set at GOP head-quarters or in the quadrennial Republican Party platform, this accounts for its lack of interest in matters outside of a narrowly conservative band of concerns. They do not want to address issues that are not of interest to the party, or to take policy positions that would conflict with those of the party. This may be true, but I do not find myself satisfied with this explanation.

Consider this vignette. When centrist evangelicals and secular scientists gathered together in January 2007 to declare their shared commitment to addressing climate change and other creation care issues (see appendix 6), the reaction of the evangelical right organizations was entirely predictable: disdain. In a widely publicized letter to the NAE, twenty-five evangelical leaders of the religious right, including Dobson of Focus and Perkins of the FRC, decried creation care as shifting emphasis away from "the great moral issues of our time, notably the sanctity of human life, the integrity of marriage, and the teaching of sexual abstinence and morality to our children."[21] Granted, these are important and worthy items to worry over, as I indicated in the previous section. But who decided, and why, that these are the *only* moral issues worthy of evangelical attention? How did the evangelical public-policy agenda become so tightly constricted? What biblical basis could be offered for such a constriction?

I will make the case in future chapters for a broader moral agenda and for the specifics of that agenda. I think a broader agenda is clearly biblical; we ought to be addressing all of the major moral issues addressed in scripture. That is part of fidelity to divine revelation through the written Word of God. But what is puzzling to me about this particular narrowness is that it is not even logical. If the vast majority of credentialed climate scientists are right that we are gradually but inexorably raising the temperature of the planet, and that it is having, and will have, profound consequences, including considerable loss of life, especially in coastal or drought-stricken or hurricane-ravaged regions, how is that not a "life" issue? How is that not a matter of Christian moral concern? Another way to say it is this: All moral issues that one might take up assume the existence of a livable planetary ecosystem. No one will be talking about abortion, gay marriage, or any kind of marriage, if we destroy the conditions of livable human existence on the planet. A similar argument could be made about, say, nuclear weapons in the hands of terrorists and rogue states. Let's say that we were clearly and imminently threatened with nuclear annihilation from an Al Qaeda that had gotten its hands on twenty nukes from Pakistan. Would it still make sense that abortion and gay marriage should constitute the entirety of the moral agenda for evangelicals? Talk about fiddling while Rome burns!

The fact of the matter, as I have shown, is that the evangelical right *does* often weigh in on issues beyond abortion, stem cells, and gay marriage. Their Web sites are regularly laden with such bits and pieces of moral and political exhortation—tax cuts, immigration, the UN, the NEA, support for the troops, etc. My observation is that these materials are usually the most transparently partisan, the most clearly borrowed from the Republican playbook, the most thinly connected to any kind of coherent Christian moral vision. So the evangelical right seems to work like this: Confident in the moral rightness of their position on the life and marriage issues, they consistently and universally promote those causes (while the party finds various ways to absorb, deflect, advance, symbolize, manipulate, and deploy these evangelical right commitments). Then, the evangelical right addresses other moral and policy issues—such as war, government fiscal policy, immigration, the environment, racial issues, poverty relief, and others—most often by simply borrowing the party line rather than reflecting deeply on these matters from within the Christian tradition. Maybe they have not really noticed that they are doing this. But when other evangelicals (left and center) make precisely such an effort to address these kinds of issues, the evangelical right angrily rejects the very fact of such a move as a distraction from the life and marriage focus that they claim is appropriate for evangelicals—and that they themselves follow only inconsistently. This is simply an unacceptable state of affairs, and it is one of the reasons why the emergence of an evangelical left and center is a healthy corrective. It may force the evangelical right to offer a Christianly defensible treatment of issues other than abortion and gay marriage or lead to the growing dismissal of their relevance on the part of evangelicals who have a broader set of moral concerns.

I would suggest that the third primary problem with the evangelical right is, for lack of a better term, its mood of angry nostalgia.

As we have seen, conservative American evangelicals in recent decades have been deeply attracted to a narrative of cultural despair.

Normally the story begins with the rise of secularism in the 1960s, the abandonment of prayer in schools, and the *Roe* decision, all leading to an apocalyptic decline of American culture that must be arrested soon, before it is too late and "God withdraws his blessing" from America. The evangelical right pines for a lost world—strong, heterosexual nuclear families, culturewide moral clarity, more or less established Christianity, Jimmy Dorsey and Fred Astaire rather than 50 Cent or Madonna, *The Brady Bunch* rather than *The Simpsons*. As so often happens, this sad hunger for a lost past is frequently accompanied by deep anger at the perceived sources of its disappearance—liberals, feminists, secularists, homosexual activists, the NEA, abortion doctors, and so on. And one must not discount the role of fear in this potent brew: fear for one's children, fear about the future, fear of the loss of Christian hegemony in American culture, even fear of some kind of cataclysmic divine judgment. The solution offered is a return to a strong "Christian America" characterized by "traditional family values" gained through determined political action. No one who seeks to understand conservative Christians can dare to overlook these potent emotive sources of its passion and its appeal to so many Americans.

As a fellow evangelical, speaking within the family, I would begin by saying that neither nostalgia nor anger is the mood most appropriate or constructive for a Christian stance toward culture. We should look forward rather than backward, both because there is no way that twenty-first-century American society will ever turn the clock back to the 1950s and because the politics of nostalgia does not prepare us well to engage the realities of the moment. The cultural upheavals of the 1960s, which right-wing evangelicals so lament, brought good and not just bad, such as in the area of civil rights for African Americans—who are properly not interested in going back to days that were not so golden for them. Anger over the world left behind does not reflect Christ's spirit, does not get us anywhere, turns off those who do not share our anger, and probably alienates the majority of younger evangelicals, who simply do not share the same cultural reference points.

Our mythologizing of the founders as evangelical Christians, so much a part of the rosy glow we project back onto the past, is frankly embarrassing for its lack of historical realism. It is time we abandon it for a more nuanced picture of these people and their values. Our nostalgia for culturally established Christianity should be considered in light of what the First Amendment actually does say—and in view of our increasingly diverse neighbors, who come from every nation and religious tradition and whom we are called to treat with love and justice. We must come to terms with the fact of pluralism in our land—religious, civic, institutional, moral, linguistic, cultural, and political—and develop a far more sophisticated response than the current reactionary pining for homogeneous community.[22]

As for arrogant disdain for those who do not see it our way, angry culture wars rhetoric, slash-and-burn attacks on those who disagree with us, and lowball smear tactics to bring down hated politicians or even ideological enemies within the household of faith, there can be no place for such behavior among a people who acknowledge that Jesus Christ is the Lord of their lives. The church cannot and must not be represented in this way in the public arena.

This leads to a final note. It may be that the most important truth revealed by the rise of the evangelical right is the cost of the weak ecclesiology of evangelical Christianity. The ultimate source of our problem may be our misunderstanding (and malpractice) of what it means to be Christ's church.

Many have noted a general tendency in evangelical life toward a poorly developed ecclesiology. We do not share a particular denominational tradition, so we do not have that resource as a starting point, and therefore our understandings of the church are all over the place. We are not normally connectional or hierarchical, and so there is no bishop or other authority to hinder us from reading the scriptures any way we want or employing rhetoric about "the church" however we are so inclined. In many of our churches almost anybody can get ordained or become a preacher, with credentials and preparation varying dramatically—this pattern would extend to some of our most visible evangelical leaders, who emerge serendipitously. We tend to splinter into new denominations, nondenominational groups, and congregations, with such moves often accompanied by great and painful conflicts, and so we both get accustomed to conflict, and we all get to define for ourselves what Christianity is and what it might mean—for every aspect of life, including politics. We tend toward a pietistic individualism that often weakens any loyalty to the community of faith or any willingness to submit to a disciplined Christian vision. We are populists, and so we are often swayed by emotional appeals rather than careful, reasoned analysis. We reinvent ourselves every generation, and so—unlike, say, the Roman Catholic Church—we have no shared body of experience to draw from in relating to politics and government. We do not feel a sense of loyalty to the church universal and a responsibility to represent its cause well.

In light of all of these hindrances, it is a wonder that evangelical Christians ever get politics right. But we are learning some lessons in the crucible of current events. And under God's sovereignty there is always the possibility that the actual Christian faith of most who are attracted to the evangelical right will prove to be a resource for renewal. In other words, it is always possible that evangelical Christians will get convicted by God's Spirit of having gotten off track; that by the power of that same Spirit the full witness of scripture will begin to resurface; and that the moral witness of the church will be cleansed and reformed. Fragmentary evidence for this hopeful claim will be suggested in following chapters.

Chapter 3

THE EVANGELICAL LEFT

"The monologue of the religious right is over," says Jim Wallis.[1] This statement symbolizes the evangelical left's increasingly visible articulation of a values-oriented Christian political agenda that, in Wallis's estimation, has been too long dominated by the social conservatives of the evangelical right. Though there are various evangelical left voices, the white evangelical left has been led most visibly by Tony Campolo and Jim Wallis. Often they have developed coalitions with black religious leaders/activists, such as Jesse Jackson and his Rainbow/PUSH Coalition, with Asian Americans, Latinos, and leaders of the mainline Protestant and Catholic world, and sometimes with non-Christian faith groups in the progressive Muslim and Jewish communities and beyond. In recent years several Democratic politicians also have more or less affiliated themselves with the evangelical left, such as Jimmy Carter, and (arguably) Hillary Clinton, John Edwards, and Barack Obama.

By using the term evangelical left, I mean to make two distinctions. The first distinction differentiates politically progressive/liberal evangelicals from the kinds of politically conservative evangelicals discussed in chapter 2. The similarities and differences between these two groups will become quite clear in this chapter. The other distinction is between evangelical progressives/liberals and other left-leaning Christian,

Jewish, or secular groups. The evangelical left is not the same thing as the Catholic left or the mainline Protestant left or the secular left. It is true, however, that especially the religious groups often work together in coalitions on issues of common conviction, and conservative evangelicals often express concern that the evangelical left is more *left* than *evangelical*. (Of course, the evangelical right also works in coalition with the non-evangelical right and is vulnerable to the charge that it is more *right* than *evangelical*.) There is clearly considerable overlap between the evangelical left, the center-left of American Catholicism, and many of the scholars, activists, and denominational leaders in mainline Protestantism. Their policy positions and even their rhetoric are often indistinguishable. But still, in their methodology and history, the evangelical left generally retains its distinctly evangelical flavor.

WHO IS THE EVANGELICAL LEFT?

The evangelical left is *evangelical* in its self-identification, institutional location, and methodology. Left-leaning evangelicals, such as Wallis and Campolo *want* the evangelical label. They want to self-identify as evangelicals, and they resist vigorously any charge that they are anything other than evangelicals. If one mark of evangelical identity is a willingness to claim the label, then these activists and others like them qualify as evangelicals.

The evangelical left also emerges from within the "habitats" of the evangelical world, belonging primarily to evangelical denominations or serving in evangelical settings. Campolo, for example, has taught for decades at Eastern University, an evangelical university affiliated with the Council for Christian Colleges & Universities (CCCU), and has spent much of his career speaking in evangelical churches and conferences. Another left-leaning public evangelical scholar, Richard Pierard, spent the latter years of his career at Gordon College, a stalwart evangelical (CCCU) school outside Boston. Wallis, who attended the conservative Trinity Evangelical Divinity School, has long identified his organization, Sojourners, as an evangelical group—though he sometimes seems to prefer the "biblical" label today when describing both himself and his organization. Although some who could be identified with the evangelical left actually serve in nonevangelical contexts, such as Randall Balmer at Barnard College, the majority work and wor-ship in explicitly evangelical communities and are most eager to retain the label against those who would say that their progressive or justice-centered commitments move them beyond the evangelical pale.

The evangelical left generally reflects the heavily biblical methodol-ogy and theology of other evangelicals. Like most evangelicals, their primary source of authority is the Bible. At least in the popular writ-ings of the evangelical left, they do not often cite Christian tradition or natural law or social science or any other nonbiblical source. For better or worse, they tend to move directly from their interpretation of biblical passages and motifs to moral exhortation and policy advocacy. They do not stray from the categories of orthodox Christian theology. They reflect the characteristic evangelical emphasis on evangelism and con-version to faith in Christ, and they draw on evangelical piety by calling on their readers to "follow Jesus" in committed discipleship, with the particular lifestyle and ethical configurations that correspond with their reading of the scriptures.[2] They tend to be explicitly Jesus-centered in their use of scripture and their rhetoric.

The evangelical left is *left* because it reads scripture and interprets the demands of Christian discipleship to require what in our contem-porary American and Christian contexts are considered left-leaning moral commitments. Characteristically, the evangelical left argues that the teachings of the Bible, especially the prophets and Jesus, require Christians to be concerned about poverty, war, racism, sexism, and the environment. These are not the only salient issues for progressive evan-gelicals, but they are indeed at the center of their moral vision. They are most interested in pursuing peace and justice as these relate to race, class, and international conflict. They highlight issues that the evangeli-cal right generally downplays (race and class and ecology) or takes an entirely different approach to (gender and war). They tend to downplay issues (abortion and homosexuality) that the evangelical right high-lights. If they are attempting to remain within the evangelical camp, left evangelicals do not normally break openly with the right on the right's two core issues. But it is fair to say that they do not treat these issues as central in the way that the right does. We will consider this pattern when we talk about Wallis in more detail.

ORIGINS OF THE EVANGELICAL LEFT

Michael Cromartie has traced the evangelical left (he calls them "radical evangelicals") to the protest voices of the 1960s.[3] In 1965 the radical evangelical magazine *The Other Side* was founded; six years later, the *Post-American* (later called *Sojourners*) was launched. Both reflected the social battles of the 1960s between cultural progressives and conservatives. Most evangelicals lined up on the conservative side, with its opposition to "free love," rejection of the women's movement and the Equal Rights Amendment, queasiness about the civil rights movement, enthusiasm for American capitalism, and support for the Vietnam War. But this other group of evangelicals took the culturally "liberal" position on each of these issues (other than sexual ethics—if they abandoned traditional sexual ethics, they stopped being evangelicals, usually by their own declaration). Thus was born the evangelical left. In some ways its agenda has not changed much in forty years; nor has its institutional configuration. Wallis did not come into existence ex nihilo after the 2004 election, when his book *God's Politics* was released to such fanfare. He had been saying essentially the same thing since 1970. But in the interim, a large evangelical right movement had coalesced and had begun to exercise significant political clout and get massive attention in the national press. Wallis filled a niche—an evangelical who did not share the agenda of Jerry Falwell or Pat Robertson. He found a fresh hearing for his message in this new context. And his message (along with Campolo's) now included a quite explicit rejection of much of the agenda, spirit, and politics of the evangelical right. Thus one might say that the culture wars came *into* the evangelical world, with a vengeance.

VOICES FROM THE EVANGELICAL LEFT

It is easy to see that the evangelical left does not have the massive institutional infrastructure of its right-leaning counterpart. The money and grass-roots support simply have not been available to build such an institutional apparatus, despite the fundraising efforts of such groups over many decades. In recent years there has been some development of funding support for evangelical left groups from outside the evangelical world, as the rest of the culture worries over the visibility and clout of the evangelical right and seeks to fund alternative voices. (This, of course, raises the accusation from the right that the evangelical left is functioning as a smokescreen or front for the secular left, a charge vehemently denied by these evangelicals.)

Like the right, evangelical left organizations tend to be built around charismatic founder-leaders, but the dearth of resources means that they tend to be much smaller, often institutionally shaky, and heavily reliant on interns, volunteers, and low-paid staff. (Thus enforcing the moral obligation to live simply!) The agenda of such groups gets out through books, lectures, magazines, and an increasingly savvy use of public relations operatives and skills. Academia provides a niche for some on the evangelical left, more than on the right. For a closer look inside the white evangelical left, we will consider three particular individuals and their organizations in this chapter: Tony Campolo, Jim Wallis, and Brian McLaren. We will also look at several voices from the black evangelical left, including Jesse Jackson and Obery Hendricks.

Tony Campolo

Tony Campolo, professor emeritus of sociology at Eastern University, is an ordained American Baptist minister and itinerant speaker who has always traveled in evangelical circles. Besides his teaching, writing, and relentless speaking ministry, much of Campolo's effort has focused on practical ministry to the urban poor. As founder of the Evangelical Association for the Promotion of Education (EAPE), Campolo's mission has been to "help build the Kingdom of God by combining evangelism and social justice in the name of Jesus."[4] According to his Web site, Campolo also currently serves a Baptist church in (predominantly black) west Philadelphia. Like many on the right, he also hosts a weekly radio program, but this one (*From Across the Pond*) is broadcast in England.[5] Campolo briefly enjoyed (if that is the right word) broader national exposure when he became one of Bill Clinton's spiritual advisors in the wake of the Lewinsky scandal. Critics described his role more as an apologist than a confessor.

Campolo's EAPE organization has been involved in supporting several other ministries, both internationally and domestically. The former include Beyond Borders (focusing on literacy in Haiti), Compassion

International, and Oasis/Zimbabwe, which provides housing, school-
ing, and care for hundreds of children who have been orphaned, and
in many cases, personally afflicted by the terrible AIDS epidemic in
Africa.

Domestically, EAPE works with several programs. Cornerstone
Christian Academy provides an academically challenging environment
for west Philadelphia's poorest children. Urban Promise targets at-risk
teens and children in order to provide tutoring, extracurricular activities, job training (for young entrepreneurs), and Bible study. Perhaps
the best known EAPE program is Mission Year, which recruits young
adults to live and work as full-time missionaries in inner-city neighborhoods for one year. This program is quite popular among evangelical
college graduates. Despite his "retirement," Campolo's mission is still
felt at Eastern, where the teacher now has left behind the Campolo
School of Social Change, which seeks to develop "Christian profession-
als who will use their skills to transform urban communities around the
world."[6] Campolo may well be best remembered for the energetic and
engaging lectures that he offered in thousands of churches, colleges, and
seminaries over his many decades of public ministry. In a sense, this was
his primary grass-roots strategy, and it left a mark on many lives. More
contemporary forms of communication for Campolo include his extensive use of podcasting and other emerging communication strategies.

In his several dozen books, almost all written for a popular audience, Campolo has struck a consistent set of themes. He has emphasized
the centrality of the church and the need to maintain its intellectual
and political independence. He has stressed finding the courage to tell
the truth even when such "hot potatoes" are uncomfortable to touch.[7]
Echoing a theme common to all progressive evangelicals since the
1960s, he has decried any split between the commitments to evangelism
and social action/justice/service, a problem going back into the origins
of the modern evangelical movement in early-twentieth-century fun-
damentalism. (These days, the issue within evangelicalism should not
really be framed as "combining evangelism and social action" because
many are doing that; it is about what *kind* of social vision one should be
acting upon. That is what the debate is really about.) Campolo has both
taught and embodied an incarnational Christian response to some of

the worst social problems—that is, he has shown that Christians need to go where the need is the greatest and serve there in Christ's name. His issue agenda has included strong focus on poverty reduction, foreign aid for the poorest countries, support for the public schools, women's equality, Christian environmentalism, and gun control. He has attacked gay-bashing, the killing of abortion doctors, racism, television, smoking, the tobacco industry, harsh immigration legislation, Christian talk radio, the blurring of church-state boundaries, the emergence of conservative Christians as a bloc within the Republican Party, and American/evangelical nationalism, militarism, and xenophobia.[8] His books are generally packaged as the work of a "radical evangelical prophet" who tackles the tough issues, reminds the nation that socially liberal positions on many issues are compatible with the teachings of Jesus, and (especially in recent years) stands up to the evangelical right.

Jim Wallis

Jim Wallis has now succeeded Campolo as the most recognizable personality from the evangelical left, largely as a result of the success of his best-selling book *God's Politics*, his more visible political engagement, and his more ardent cultivation of a national media presence. As indicated previously when talking about the origins of the evangelical left, Wallis may be best understood as a product of the 1960s, representing a Christian version of the progressive face of that era. His ministry began its germination in 1971 when as a relatively new Christian who had been involved in the student movements of the 1960s, he enrolled at the conservative Trinity Evangelical Divinity School (TEDS) in Deerfield, Illinois. There he entered into community with a small group of like-minded evangelicals who were concerned about social justice and opposed to the Vietnam War—at a time when most evangelicals (including at TEDS) were quiescent about social justice and in favor of the Vietnam War. Their first publication was the magazine provocatively named *The Post-American*, a title which has infuriated and inflamed Wallis's adversaries long after its abolition.

The communitarian group moved to take up residence in inner-city Washington, D.C., in 1975, where the name of Sojourners was chosen for an intentional community, its local ministry, and its publication. Rooted in a mission to "articulate the biblical call to social justice, inspiring hope and building a movement to transform individuals, communities, the church, and the world," Sojourners has in various ways over the last thirty years combined residential communitarian living with neighborhood service and national activism.[9] Wallis and at least a remnant of his community have remained in Washington to this day, though it is clear that the intentional communitarian embodiment of the Sojourners mission has faded over the decades, with Sojourners now existing more as a traditional advocacy organization. Sojourners' current activities include the magazine and a mix of other publications, a strong cyberspace presence, grass-roots and net-roots organizing, and volunteer service. Wallis clearly serves as the face of the organization and leads its work of preaching, teaching, activism, and writing; other staff members have tended to be less visible. Like many other evangelical groups, Sojourners essentially functions as the embodiment of the leader's vision and the platform for his activities. And yet Sojourners has proven to be a more sturdy and visible institutional presence than most of the initiatives or organizations that others on the evangelical left have founded. It is worth studying as an organization before we consider Wallis's own writing in some detail.

Sojourners tackles a wide range of issues, both international and domestic. Adversaries describe it as dovish, populist, and statist; Sojourners rejects such a characterization; instead it defines itself as biblical, and therefore pro-peace and pro-social justice. The international agenda of Sojourners in recent years has included opposing the Iraq War (actually, all wars) and American "imperialism," fighting for more just Israeli policies in the Middle East and an end to the occupation of Palestinian land, supporting "fair trade" (and opposing trade deals such as Central American Free Trade Agreement [CAFTA]), advocating African debt relief, decrying world hunger, pushing for an end to the Darfur genocide, opposing torture, and pressing for nuclear disarmament. (It was strongly in favor of the nuclear freeze and other arms-control strategies and agreements during the Cold War.) Domestically, Sojourners tends to emphasize economic justice issues, such as ending childhood poverty, supporting quality public education, advocating for the small family farm, raising the minimum wage, and widening access to quality health care. Sojourners has been opposed to capital punishment, for environmental regulation and care of creation, and suspicious of big business.

Both Wallis and Campolo belonged to Call to Renewal (CTR), a national network of churches, faith-based organizations, and individuals founded in 1995. The original stated purpose of the group was to fight poverty through a "search for common ground untainted by partisan ideology" in American public life.[10] One hundred Protestant, evangelical, Catholic, and Orthodox religious leaders met on May 22, 1995, to "addres[s] the need for a renewed political vision" that included people of faith who were (purportedly) not dominated by ideology or political partisanship.[11] CTR emerged from the leadership of Wallis, and after more than a decade with Sojourners and CTR as separate organizations, CTR was folded back into the Sojourners tent in 2006 as the organization took the official name Sojourners/Call to Renewal.

CTR's founding document, "The Cry for Renewal," briefly became prominent in the mid-1990s. Besides decrying the nastiness of partisanship and the politics of personal destruction, CTR promoted seven planks of a good society:[12]

1. Full participation by people of all races
2. A living family income for all who responsibly work
3. Affordable, quality healthcare for all, regardless of income
4. Schools that work for all our children
5. Safe, affordable housing
6. Safe and secure neighborhoods
7. Family friendly policies and programs in every sector of society.

CTR for a time amounted to a form of evangelical left coalition building along the lines of the coalition that developed on the evangelical right. Having attended at least one CTR meeting in the 1990s, I can recall a level of denominational and ethnic diversity that I had not previously encountered in my travels in evangelical America: Catholics, Pentecostals, mainliners, white evangelicals, Latinos/as, Asian Americans, and African Americans were broadly represented, though all tended to lean left politically. Apparently this group eventually became indistinguishable from the Sojourners group that founded it, and it receded back into the Sojourners fold.

Wallis seized the moment after the 2004 election with his best-selling book *God's Politics* and a major media campaign that went with it. Despite the subtitle *A New Vision for Faith and Politics in America*, Wallis actually said very little that was new (for him) in this widely publicized book. It struck similar themes to his earlier *The Soul of Politics* and the weekly material in his magazine.[13] What was really new was the context—the massive cultural debate about the role of the evangelical community and its "values voters" in helping to elect George W. Bush. Wallis's book was timed perfectly to hook into the antivalues-voter backlash and represent a contrasting alternative evangelical view.

Wallis positions himself and his vision in *God's Politics* as an alternative to both the evangelical/religious right and the secular left. The evangelical right, he argues, is beholden to the Republican Party, focuses entirely too much on "sexual and cultural issues," and neglects the "weightier matters of justice" such as war, poverty, and the environment. The secular left is filled with "liberal secularists who want to banish faith from public life," have contempt for religious people and their values, and just "don't get" the spiritual and social power of "genuinely evangelical . . . historic biblical faith."[14]

Contrary to the labeling I am offering in this book, Wallis explicitly rejects the idea that he represents the "religious left." He seeks to rise above such a label by identifying himself with the biblical prophetic tradition and by pointing out issues on which he is conservative, such as the sacredness of life and the value of parenting and strong families.[15] Even on the issues in which he is described as "left," such as his focus on poverty and war, Wallis describes these as simply *biblical* concerns that challenge the indifference and many of the policy prescriptions of both liberals and conservatives. He emphasizes, just as Campolo has also done, that "God is not a Republican or a Democrat," a slogan that became a popular bumper sticker for a time during and after the 2004 elections and which tends to infuriate the evangelical right.

Beyond the prophets, Wallis focuses his theological attention on Jesus himself. This is an important move, and not just when Wallis makes it. Peter Heltzel is probably right in his book when he claims that each major strand of evangelical public theology is operating from a different understanding of Jesus.[16] Wallis appeals to the teachings of Jesus in the Sermon on the Mount as justification for a stance that is pro-peace, pro-poor, and pro-justice. Jesus taught enemy love, transnational loyalties, humility, self-reflection, truth telling, respect for human rights, and fearless trust in God. For Wallis, all of these contrast sharply with reckless war making, torture of detainees, tax cuts for the rich, strident nationalism, subliving-wage jobs, deceptive rationales for the Iraq War, and anxiety-riddled efforts to ensure our national security through an endless preemptive war on terror.

Wallis offers extended discussions of three particular issue clusters in the remainder of *God's Politics*: international relations, economic justice, and social issues, the latter including abortion, capital punishment, race, marriage, and homosexuality. The ordering of these issues signals Wallis's attempt to reprioritize and rename the true "moral values" issues of what he understands to be genuine biblical faith. In the teeth of an evangelical right that often reduces moral values to abortion and homosexuality, Wallis symbolically moves those near the bottom of his list. His passion is found on the war and poverty issues. Thus is born a titanic struggle between the evangelical right and left, which is likely to continue indefinitely.

On war, Wallis begins with the terror attacks of September 11.[17] He sees the trauma of this terrible event as having become a missed opportunity to rethink both our domestic and international priorities and considers the response waged by the Bush Administration to have been almost entirely wrongheaded. He suggests that we need to take terrorism quite seriously but not be so distorted by fear as to lose our own moral bearings. We need humility about our national virtue rather than self-righteousness. He suggests a "root causes" strategy for understanding terrorism and a peacemaking, policing, and prevention approach to fighting it. He urges a multilateral and international-law-governed, rather than unilateral and force-governed, U.S. response to the terrorist security threat.

Elsewhere in this section of *God's Politics*, Wallis offers a scathing condemnation of the war in Iraq as a "preemptive war of choice, rather than necessity, fought against overwhelming world opinion" and with disastrous consequences of many types.[18] Long before American public opinion began turning against the war, indeed, in the runup to the war itself, Wallis opposed it, and many of his warnings (along with those of other critics) have been borne out. Wallis suggests that one of the most pernicious developments of the war has been a creeping Pax Americana, an open affirmation of the United States as a righteous empire, with President Bush adding a Christian theological dimension that edges in the direction of the long-rejected Christian crusade theology. Such themes have been sounded repeatedly by many on the religious left since 2001, and especially since the war in Iraq.[19] Setbacks in Iraq and Afghanistan, and the reverses in the 2006 elections, though, seem to have tamed some of the "Captain America" rhetoric and sidelined many of the rhetoricians that caused this concern.

Wallis traces some of the hostility in the Arab world toward our nation to our uncritical support for unjust Israeli occupation policies. He decries suicide bombings and other immoral Palestinian responses to Israeli policies, but clearly his heart is with the Palestinians. Long before Jimmy Carter got in trouble for saying so, after a visit to the Palestinian territories Wallis wrote, "the more I saw, the more it reminded me of apartheid in South Africa."[20] He claims that "Israeli violence is enormously disproportionate to Palestinian violence," and that neither is morally justifiable. He names and sides with Jewish activists who also decry Israeli occupation policies, such as Michael Lerner and Arthur Waskow, as well as Israeli human-rights organizations. In the American context, these are indeed "left" positions, as is the claim that a more evenhanded U.S. approach to the Israeli-Palestinian conflict will help drain the swamp of Arab hostility toward our nation. Indeed, he is to the left of many in the Democratic Party on this one.

When Wallis turns to poverty issues, he begins with the overwhelming biblical witness on this issue—over two thousand verses.[21] He suggests that American Christians have simply dismembered their Bibles by misusing, ignoring, and abusing this profound biblical witness to God's concern for the poor and demand for economic justice. Following Matthew 25, he argues that Christians will be held eternally accountable for how they treat "the least of these."

In light of this biblical witness, Wallis decries poverty, both in the United States and around the world. He sees a drastic misshaping of federal government spending priorities, and dramatic underfunding of basic poverty programs, public education, and health care for the poor. To address these problems "we must seek a comprehensive plan for change, involving every sector of society." Here, Wallis says, left and right really can come together. The right is right in emphasizing the way poverty is linked to family breakdown and other bad personal moral choices, many of which are best addressed at the personal, family, church, and civil society level. The left is right in emphasizing continuing structural problems like the lack of a living wage for many jobs, the lack of affordable housing, the ongoing effects of racism, and the impact of a "cutthroat global economy" that pushes down wages, cuts health benefits, and lays off workers before finally sending all the jobs overseas.[22] Wallis emphasizes the spiritual impoverishment that often accompanies great wealth and calls for a spiritual turn toward personal and social responsibility and service. He attacks corporate greed and scandals, such as those that hit Enron and Adelphia, and uses these cases to illustrate the corrupting relationship between big business, money, and politics in America.

Turning to the international arena, Wallis applauds the emergence of the Jubilee debt-relief campaign, which aimed at debt cancellation for poor countries and has won a number of successes. He urges a "fair trade" rather than free-trade model, in the process joining in the antiglobalization attack on the international monetary and trade regime led by the World Trade Organization (WTO), the World Bank, and the International Monetary Fund (IMF). He rejects the major free-trade deals of the 1990s, such as North American Free Trade Agreement (NAFTA). Wallis articulates strong support for the UN's Millennium Development Goals, embraced in 2000. These include the following targets toward which serious progress is to be made by 2015: eradication of extreme poverty and hunger, universal primary education, gender equality, reduction of child mortality, improving maternal health, combating HIV/AIDS and other infectious diseases, ensuring environmental sustainability, and developing a global partnership for development.

Having devoted 122 pages to a discussion of war-related issues and 88 pages to economic concerns, Wallis turns in his final section to "social issues."[23] Besides a brief discussion of capital punishment and a good but surprisingly thin chapter on race, he gives just four pages to abortion and seven pages to gay marriage, clearly signaling both directly and by his brevity where his moral priorities lie.

Wallis links abortion and capital punishment, opposing both under the rubric of a consistent ethic of life. He does not offer a detailed stand on abortion. Instead, he focuses on what he says is the practically fruitless but politically fruitful Republican antiabortion rhetoric, which is paired with what he considers to be electorally unwise Democratic rigidity on abortion. He urges the Democrats to open the door to a range of opinions on the matter and thus win the hearts and votes of many who are with them on most other issues. He emphasizes strategies that could reduce the demand for abortion. On the death penalty, Wallis opposes capital punishment in principle and favors a moratorium on executions. On race, Wallis speaks from a lifetime of urban experience to argue for truthful speech about "America's original sin." He supports a national apology for slavery, urges a proper understanding of the link between racism and poverty, decries the Republicans' Southern Strategy, initiated in the 1960s to win the southern white vote through coded appeals to white racism, worries over the mindset and lifestyles of young black men, and supports aggressive church-based racial reconciliation efforts.

Turning at last to "family values" issues, Wallis reframes the debate to emphasize finding ways to support parents as they are squeezed by economic and social pressures that make it difficult for them to survive (economically and relationally) and to raise their children well. He decries the high divorce rate, abuse rate, and out-of-wedlock birth rate and names these as major problems and causes of other problems, such as poverty. When he finally turns to the homosexuality issue, Wallis seeks to position himself as an arbiter for peaceable dialogue. He decries antigay crusades, supports gay civil rights and civil unions but expresses his personal current opposition to gay marriage. Beyond this, he wants to deemphasize the issue and allow it to be resolved by the citizenry and the churches through civil dialogue.

Brian McLaren and the Emerging Church Movement

The so-called emerging churches understand themselves as a movement born in reaction to the dying culture-religion of the baby boomers. Eddie Gibbs and Ryan K. Bolger see the emerging churches as new Christian communities that are adapting to postmodernity. "Because cultural understanding has always been essential to good mission practice," they say, "because Christendom and Modernity are in rapid decline, because the church is in decline, because the majority of current church practices are cultural accommodation to a society that no longer exists, because a new culture means that new organizational structures are required, and because boomers are the last generation that is happy with modern churches," the emerging movement has been born.[24]

One of the most influential leaders of the emerging movement is Brian McLaren, author, pastor, and chair of the Emergent Village organization/Web site. McLaren and Wallis are allies who respect each other and often work together. Having served as board chair for Wallis's Sojourners and working closely with Wallis, Campolo, and other leaders of the evangelical left, McLaren and the emerging movement share their basic tenets, while focusing on the younger generation and its disenchantment with what modern American churches have to offer.

> In English, the word 'emergent' is normally an adjective meaning coming into view, arising from, occurring unexpectedly, requiring immediate action (hence its relation to "emergency"), characterized by evolutionary emergence, or crossing a boundary (as between water and air). All of these meanings resonate with the spirit and vision of Emergent Village.[25]

In McLaren's writing and preaching, he frequently stresses Jesus' words, "Do unto others as you would have them do to you." The emerging churches' interpretation of this passage leaves no room for war, disproportionate wealth, or racial discrimination of any sort. McLaren seeks to offer a third alternative to "liberal" and "conservative," critiquing both for the weaknesses and pitfalls to which they are prone. He, too, wants to transcend left and right.

When dealing with the right's key issues of homosexuality and abortion, McLaren remains ambivalent. He acknowledges the importance of issues of sexuality (among which McLaren includes abortion and homosexuality), but he sees other "nonsexual" issues as more pressing. He offers global warming, and the consequences of unchanged environmental policies, as an example of what might be a higher priority issue than the struggle over homosexual marriage.[26]

McLaren has voiced deep concerns over the war in Iraq. Freedom and peace are not achieved through war. War is a "nightmare" to Jesus. Although he does not call himself a pacifist, he does say that he is a sympathizer and says that as followers of Jesus, we should long for pacifism. Whenever we talk of war, he asserts, and if we must go to war, we should do so with sadness and grieving. For every dollar we spend on war, we should spend two in rebuilding the ravaged war-torn area once the war is over. There is a high cost to war, and McLaren says he would gladly pay twice what he pays in taxes now so that he could see reparations undertaken on behalf of the destroyed people and land.[27]

Loving one another means caring about those who are victims, in need, and suffering from injustice. The victims of exploitation and oppression are the most central figures in Jesus' ministry, and McLaren and emerging churches seek to live and preach that commitment. McLaren says that "evangelism and social justice and ecology and the creation of good art and serving the poor and forgotten are deeply integrated facets" of the emerging movement.[28]

THE BLACK EVANGELICAL LEFT
Jesse Jackson and Obery Hendricks

A number of voices from within the black community could be identified as representing the black evangelical left. Here I select one visible and one less well-known figure: Jesse Jackson and Obery Hendricks. Their messages are similar and can be found widely in the black religious community, though some might dispute their evangelical credentials.

Perhaps the single most recognized (and controversial) black leader in the United States over the last thirty-five years has been Rev. Jesse Jackson, Martin Luther King Jr.'s young follower and colleague who attempted to help carry forward the civil rights movement after the murder of King.

Jackson founded Operation PUSH (People United to Serve Humanity) in Chicago in 1971.[29] The goals of Operation PUSH were "economic empowerment and expanding educational, business and employment opportunities for the disadvantaged and people of color." In 1984, Jackson founded the **National Rainbow Coalition**, a national social-justice organization with a more political emphasis, devoting its resources to political empowerment, education, and changing public policy. In September 1996 the Rainbow Coalition and Operation PUSH merged into Rainbow/PUSH Coalition, which is now an international human rights organization, committed to economic development, voter registration and participation, healthcare, jobs, peace, education, and justice. Its motto is "Fighting For You Is What We Do!"

For Jackson and the black evangelical left, slavery and segregation created an environment in America in which a strongly Afrocentric and activist church was the only kind of black church that could survive. Jackson is acutely aware of the lingering effects of slavery, and his coalition addresses racism and poverty on many fronts. When hurricane Katrina ravaged New Orleans, Jackson saw the following days as evidence that the victims of Katrina, impoverished people of color, were not regarded as equal. He wrote, "Katrina is a metaphor for the neglect, abandonment, and insensibility that is the norm in America as it relates to the treatment of people of color."

Jackson has spoken out adamantly in opposition to the war in Iraq, calling it "likely the worst foreign policy catastrophe ever." He pushes for a health care system in which all members of society, regardless of income, have access to quality healthcare. He has made the claim, as other black leaders have, that illegal immigrants are suffering under a form of slavery. He joined the immigration struggle in 2005, saying,

> People of color are brothers and sisters under and of the skin, whether we are called undocumented 'Latino' immigrants or 'African Americans.' . . . Today the hands that picked the cotton are joining with the hands that picked the lettuce, connecting barrios and ghettos, fields and plantations—working together for a more just and open society.

Jackson treats the problems of the criminal justice system, the prisons, education and opportunity in urban areas, healthcare access and quality, and the condition of the black family in America, as signs that black suffering and even a kind of slavery have not ended. Blacks in America today are fighting what Jackson calls the fourth stage of slavery. The first three stages were fighting for the end of bondage, for the end of segregation and "legal degradation," and for the right to vote. "And now," he says, "we are fighting for access to capital, economic security, industry, technology and trade."

In his book *The Politics of Jesus*, Obery Hendricks, an African American professor of biblical interpretation at New York Theological Seminary, calls for a serious reconsideration of the values that guide our decisions.[30] Jesus' radical example, he asserts, focuses on justice for the poor. To Hendricks, the death penalty, war, and economic and racial injustice are in blatant opposition to Jesus' teachings. As Hendricks looks at the politics of Jesus compared to the politics of certain administrations (Ronald Reagan's and George W. Bush's in particular), he finds the Republican Party sadly lacking in Christian virtue. Jesus' ministry placed a radical emphasis on social and economic healing. Few leaders in America, he asserts, have reflected a Christlike, radical passion for justice. In his mourning for the victims of hurricane Katrina, of war, and of poverty, he stingingly condemns the Bush administration, and has little respect for those on the evangelical right who support or advise him.

As McLaren has done, Hendricks applies the "golden rule" as an avid rejection of any type of social or economic injustice. However he finds many conservative evangelicals falling woefully short of this. He says that conservative Christians, although adhering to a strong commitment to sexual purity, show no real signs of concern for the poor and oppressed. Justice, Hendricks claims, has been replaced by many with a narrow, "hyperspiritualized" religion that turns a blind eye to realities outside the walls of the church. Although he sees sexual immorality as a deeply offensive sin, he argues that social and economic justice issues are much more pressing. He presents President Clinton's sexually immoral conduct with a young intern as despicable, but not as devastating and repulsive as the suffering and costs of the war in Iraq—a war Hendricks sees as existing as a result of untruths presented by Bush.

Hendricks' views on the war and on the Bush administration in general are evident when he makes statements on "Bush's lack of concern for human suffering," "Bush's lack of respect for human life," and his "macabre" actions. He decries the behavior of politicians, especially Bush, as being hypocritical, neglectful, and indicted by scripture. "They have chosen to forget that Jesus was more concerned with the needs of the poor than the desires of the rich."

WHAT'S RIGHT WITH THE LEFT

One's response to the evangelical left is undoubtedly deeply affected by one's own ideological positioning. In this book I am attempting to move toward the most fully biblical and morally responsible evangelical political engagement that I can imagine. I want to evaluate the left, as I did the right, on that basis.

I think that the left is best at what might be called its indigenous agenda—what it is for, rather than what it is against. This indigenous agenda goes back to the very origins of the evangelical left in the 1960s. Martin Luther King Jr., who in some ways might be seen as a founder and certainly remains an icon of the evangelical left (as he is for so many others), often grouped together as "triple evils" the triad of poverty, racism, and war. He linked them all in his famous April 1967 criticism of the Vietnam War, but they appeared as a group in his writings before that time.[31] These three issues remain at the heart of the moral vision of the evangelical left. Quoting Wendell Berry, for example, Wallis also connects poverty, economic injustice, and war: "The most alarming sign of the state of our society now is that our leaders have the courage to sacrifice the lives of our young people in war, but have not the courage to tell us that we must be less greedy and less wasteful."[32]

Certainly the evangelical left agenda has expanded to include other causes beyond these triple evils. These other causes most often also originally emerged from what would be considered the left—women's rights and the environment are two notable examples. So the trajectory might be seen this way: Some evangelical Christians became convinced that poverty, racism, war, sexism, and environmental destruction were not secular issues and certainly not just progressive concerns—they were biblical priorities. The evangelical left then swung into action, seeking to rescue such moral priorities either from being captured by the secular left or being ignored by the evangelical right.

They were right to do so. The evangelical left is to be warmly commended for forcing such issues as these onto the agenda of Christian public witness. This has been their fundamental project for almost forty years, through most of which their voices were lonely and obscure. Considered biblically, concern for the poor, rejection of racism, and care for God's creation are unequivocal biblical teachings and thus at a moral level essentially nonnegotiable. The Bible's witness on the use of force is more complicated, but the evangelical left has made a valuable contribution in simply articulating the peace strand, centered in Jesus, as opposed to the war strand, centered in certain historical books of the Old Testament. The same could be said on the women's issue; the left has highlighted the egalitarian strand of the New Testament in a historic Christian subculture best known for noticing the patriarchal or male leadership strand of that same New Testament. Discussion of the substance of these moral issues goes beyond the scope of this chapter, but suffice it to say here that the inclusion of poverty, war, race, gender equity, and the environment is at least biblically defensible, and in some cases biblically obligatory, and the evangelical left deserves the credit for saying so.

When the evangelical left turns to what (and who) it is against, the primary target is clearly the evangelical right. I am among those Christian thinkers/activists who have had unpleasant encounters with adversaries on the secular left. Wallis has also clearly had such encounters. But just as there is no rivalry like sibling rivalry, sometimes it seems to me that there is no conflict now raging that can compare to the internecine war between the evangelical left and right. So even though Wallis positions himself as a mediating voice between the secular left and the evangelical right, his rhetorical energy and polemical agenda clearly are directed against the right. This is generally true of the evangelical left as a whole.

I believe that most of the critiques that Wallis and others direct against the evangelical right are appropriate. Many have already appeared in the previous chapter. No one says more clearly than the evangelical left that the evangelical right has become essentially a branch office of the Republican Party. No one is clearer in saying that the evangelical right has narrowed the moral agenda of the scriptures well short of a holistic biblical perspective. The evangelical left has also been wise in noting those areas in which the right has come close to—or crossed the line into—blurring appropriate church-state boundaries. This critique has more credibility from the evangelical left than from secularists or other strict church-state separationists. That is because evangelical left voices have been much more friendly to such programs as President Bush's faith-based initiative, which most of them (and centrists, too) believe reflects a proper understanding of the First Amendment Establishment Clause, even if they are not happy with the motivations or implementations of the program on the part of the Bush Administration.[33]

The evangelical left has also been willing to critique the right's use of sensitive wedge issues like race and homosexuality to swing voters in the direction of the GOP. Wallis's discussion of the GOP Southern Strategy is bold, though it is important to add now that the evangelical right (as opposed perhaps to some on the secular political right) has generally come a long way on the race issue. Most white evangelical leaders of all types want to avoid any taint of racism and do seek racial reconciliation. This probably results from a combination of a guilty conscience over white evangelical quiescence and resistance during the civil rights movement, together with the effects of the biblical message itself, with its clear emphasis on the image of God in all, on justice, and on reconciliation and inclusive love. It remains to be seen, however, whether the new, primary "other" of our time, the homosexual, will also find a place in the soft, loving gospel heart of conservative Christians. Too often, at least for now, the tone of evangelical right activism on issues related to homosexuality is quite harsh (see chapter 6).

Another strength of the evangelical left, at its best, is its Jesus-centered radicalism. The left notices, studies, celebrates, and seeks to follow the socially radical Jesus of Nazareth, who proclaimed God's reign, resisted social injustice, included the outcasts (women, Gentiles, Roman soldiers, tax collectors, prostitutes, children) at his table, attacked greed and miserliness, fed the hungry, and rejected the violent Zealot option. This Jesus also lived and preached the absolute sovereignty of God over every area of life and every aspect of the personhood of his followers. This "radical" call to commitment rules out divided loyalties and false idols of race, class, party, and nation.

I think it is this Jesus-centered radicalism that may be most responsible for a distinctive strength—and for some an infuriating object of
scorn—in the evangelical left. This group simply refuses to embrace an
uncritical pro-American nationalism. This internationalism, or critical
patriotism, fits with a gospel-centered message of Christ's sacrificial
death for "every nation and tribe and language and people"(Rev 14:6),
as well as a creation-centered message of the intrinsic dignity and value
of every human life, made in the image of God (see Gen 1:26-28). It
is argued by some that the evangelical left never has a good word to
say about America—that they are, indeed, post- (or anti-) Americans,
that they are "blame America firsters." My view is that while balance is
needed in considerations of the complex layers of responsibility for what
is wrong in the geopolitical order or any particular situation, a willingness to look with a critical eye on one's own people, tribe, and nation
is of fundamental significance both to moral and relational health, and
reflects key teachings of Jesus himself (cf. Matt 7:1-5). It may be that
the evangelical center, to be considered in the next chapter, can help
us move beyond either a reflexive anti-American left or pro-American
right stance.

One final note. A particular strength of the (white) evangelical left
is its intentional commitment to an inclusive table in its own organizational life and in its ministry. Related to this is a deep commitment
to urban America. The evangelical left has planted its flag in racially
diverse, often predominantly black and Hispanic, urban America, in
cities like Philadelphia, Chicago, and Washington. They have lived
there, they have ministered there, and they have written and agitated
for change from within a moral horizon created by their incarnational
presence in some of the most blighted communities of American life.
This also means that they know and relate to black, Latino/a, Asian,
and other religious leaders, and they seek to work in coalition with such
leaders where they can. This goes well beyond the nods in the direction
of racial reconciliation that have been made, even with all good intentions, in much of the rest of the evangelical world.

This purposeful decision to locate in urban America and stand in
solidarity with the moral concerns generated there really does help the
outside observer make sense of the moral agenda of the evangelical

left. It helps explain why Wallis devotes eighty-eight pages to detailed discussion of poverty-related issues, and why he and others on the left often push for healthcare reform, good public schools, criminal justice and police reforms, affordable housing, voter rights enforcement, union protections, job-training programs, environmental justice, and so on. They are listening to voices coming from urban, predominantly racial/ethnic minority churches and are familiar with the policy priorities articulated in black-authored works, such as *The Covenant*, by Tavis Smiley, which articulates the agenda items just mentioned in the previous sentence. It also helps us make sense of why an issue like abortion or gay marriage might not resonate as deeply for the evangelical left. Their attention rests elsewhere, especially in the daily struggle for survival and dignity that defines life in our most neglected urban communities.

WHAT'S WRONG WITH THE LEFT

The evangelical left is perhaps most vulnerable to critique (at least from within the evangelical community itself) for its stances on abortion and homosexuality. I have already alluded to these issues but now must consider them a bit more definitively.

I have shown that evangelical left leaders strongly resist the reduction of morality to abortion and homosexuality. Indeed, they often seem reticent to take on these issues at all. Considering Campolo and Wallis here, their starting point on abortion tends to be their dismay that *Roe v. Wade* became a major "rallying point" for the rise of the Moral Majority and the evangelical right. They critique the use of the issue in political campaigns as merely a symbolic gesture toward an ethic of life, primarily used by Republicans to rally the troops but of little or no practical impact.[34]

It is striking that in *God's Politics*, Wallis never actually articulates a position on what the legal status of abortion should be. Elsewhere, in at least one interview, he has indicated that he is open to incremental, abortion-reducing measures, such as waiting periods, parental notification and bans on late-term abortions.[35] But there is no evidence in his writings that he would support the overturning of *Roe v. Wade*. He does emphasize the significance of offering the kind of practical help needed to women facing crisis pregnancies. He calls on the Democratic Party to work with Republicans on acceptable versions of such measures while generally making room for pro-life voices. But that is about as far as he will go on the issue. And the matter receives little attention in his main book or on the Web site.

I would have to suggest that this is not an adequate expression of an evangelical Christian public ethic in relation to abortion. It does not signal that it takes fully seriously the sanctity of *all* human life, including those lives developing in the womb. It is not just that the left is far softer on its preferred abortion policy measures than the right (or the center) would be, but that the matter simply does not seem to rise very high on their moral agenda. It does not get serious and sustained attention even in book-length treatments of major moral issues facing the church and the nation. There is no visible analysis of the complex but significant issue of the moral status of fetal life. There is little if any steam, energy, or expression of outrage at the routine practice of abortion that has been woven into American life and ends at least one-fifth of all pregnancies. Evangelical left authors proclaim that they are pro-life, but this does not seem to cash out in a real significant way on the abortion issue. This leaves evangelical left thinkers vulnerable to the charge that their stance on abortion is essentially a nod in the direction of the pro-life camp, to placate critics and be able to hold on to the evangelical label, rather than evidence of committed participation in the struggle against abortion.

The homosexuality issue is quite different in many ways, but in terms of both culture wars politics and internal evangelical politics it presents similar dynamics. So far, the evangelical right and center have proven unwilling to move away from the ancient Christian position that homosexual behavior is banned by scripture—along with other sexual acts that fall outside of monogamous, heterosexual marriage. Indeed, this view of the morality of homosexual acts is one of the key dividing lines in American religious life between evangelicals of every denomination (including the Catholic Church) and most progressives/liberals. Consider the conflict that is tearing apart the Episcopal Church as just one example.

Those who are unwilling to budge from this position increasingly evoke the wrath of not just the homosexual community, but also the secular and religious left. If it is important to you to remain in good standing with these branches of the left, but you also want to remain in good standing with the evangelical community, this presents a significant (indeed, excruciating) problem. It is not at all clear that the camel can go through the eye of that needle.

I think that these dynamics help to explain the positioning of the evangelical left on homosexuality.

Tony Campolo, for example, does take the traditional evangelical view that "same-gender eroticism cannot be reconciled with Scripture." (He notes that his wife, Peggy, has decided that she no longer believes this.) Jim Wallis never quite makes an affirmation either way. But both men are clear that they want to deemphasize the issue, and both are heated in their opposition to gay bashing. Campolo calls the church to stop treating homosexuality as some kind of "supersin" and to cease and desist from demonizing gays and lesbians.[36] Wallis says similar things, as we have seen.

Campolo breaks with the evangelical right and undoubtedly many in the center by arguing that as a result of his understanding of the separation of church and state, he would rather the *legal issue* of gay marriage be separated from the church's *moral* opposition to gay marriage, thus allowing committed gay couples to apply to the state for legal recognition in some form. Campolo wants in this way to protect the rights of gays, while ultimately leaving the religio-moral issue of *blessing* the union up to local congregations.[37] Wallis supports civil unions while expressing hesitation about gay marriage.

Unlike Campolo, in print Wallis mainly talks about the process of talking about homosexuality. Wallis notes that *Sojourners* "has not taken a 'position' but rather an 'approach' to civil dialogue" among Christians who seek justice and reconciliation, rather than condemnation.[38] Wallis's overall approach to the issue is a reorienting of the debate to place it within the broader context of the pressing matters of the day (i.e. war, poverty, etc.), while never fully expressing his thoughts on the basic question of the morality of homosexual acts. He calls for reconciliation and civil dialogue but speaks mainly in a procedural voice rather than a normative one—beyond the call for gay civil rights. One wonders if he risks forfeiting the prophetic voice he desires by backing away from statements of moral conviction (one way or the other) on this issue. It seems to be a matter of great discomfort for him.

Although the homosexuality issue will always be a sensitive one because of the sacred human beings whose lives we are talking about here, and who have so often been mistreated, the evangelical center (and of course the right) still affirms on the basis of biblical authority that God's intended design for sexuality is one man and one woman, in lifetime marriage. It is easy to see how the evangelical left can be perceived as essentially drifting away from that position without really saying so. It is possible that one reason for this is the huge price that would be paid by Wallis on the left if he were to be more forthright on this issue or on the right, if he were to abandon clearly any moral objections to homosexual behavior.

The evangelical left receives considerable criticism from the right for its dovish position on war. Campolo, McLaren, and Wallis, for example, are at least functionally pacifists, though only Campolo says so directly. Campolo qualifies his stance as a "troubled" pacifism, citing his opposition to the rule of tyrants as being a possible exception.[39] (In other words, he has trouble opposing humanitarian military intervention.) Wallis tends to use just-war language in his public argumentation, for example, to argue that Iraq did not qualify as a justifiable war in 2003. But it is hard to imagine a war that Wallis could support because there is no evidence that he has ever supported one.

A great contemporary test on this issue of war was whether one could support the military effort to remove the Taliban regime in Afghanistan after September 11th. Given that regime's connections with and support for Osama bin Laden and Al Qaeda, including providing a safe haven to train, equip, and send forth the terrorists who murdered thousands, it is hard to imagine a more clearly justifiable war. Certainly the overwhelming majority of the world community supported the legitimacy of our attack on Afghanistan, as did the evangelical right and the evangelical center. Yet Wallis, at least, has never been willing to offer explicit support for that invasion or to declare it as a just war. In God's Politics, he frames any mention of the U.S. offensive in Afghanistan in terms of civilian casualties. He suggests that an international legal response would have been preferable to the use of military force.[40]

The fact of the matter is that in terms of coalition politics, the evangelical left includes a goodly number of pacifists. It also includes many others who are not pacifists but whose hearts and convictions incline strongly against war as a result of an immersion in the moral witness of Jesus, or perhaps on the basis of a strict version of just-war theory, in which the tests of just-war theory are applied rigorously rather than loosely (see chapter 8). The creative work of Glen Stassen and others in developing a just-peacemaking theory has also been quite influential on the evangelical left.

I have often been involved in drafting processes for various documents in which we were attempting to keep a coalition together that included this mix of positions. Language was usually selected that could somehow be generic enough to gain the support of pacifists and nonpacifists alike. It is quite possible to argue that the results sometimes strain the limits of full intellectual coherence.

Pacifists who want to be actively involved in public debate about peace and war sometimes do not want to own up directly to their pacifist convictions for fear that their views will be rejected out of hand. So they find just-war-type objections to every conceivable military action. I am coming around to the conclusion that building a winning activist coalition is less significant than offering an intellectually coherent stance on war. If one is a pacifist, one should simply claim one's commitment to this grand Christian tradition and oppose all wars on principled grounds, rather than seeming to find prudential or just-war grounds to oppose each and every specific military conflict initiated by the United States.[41] If one is a just-war thinker and opposes a war on those grounds, one should say this as well. And if one is a just-war thinker who generally opposes war but believes that a particular war must be supported, one should say so, regardless of who might be offended. The goal is to think rightly, to bear sound Christian witness, not to keep the coalition together.

In short, one clear difference between the evangelical left and the center (not to mention the right) is that the left's reluctance to ever support war is not shared by the center. This is a major point of distinction between the two camps that will be considered further in chapter 8.

One last critique of the evangelical left seems appropriate here. It has to do with the matter of political independence.

I have already made the claim that the evangelical right has erred badly in aligning itself as a bloc within the Republican Party. The question can legitimately be asked whether the evangelical left has steered fully clear of becoming a bloc within the Democratic Party.

There is an interesting moment in God's Politics in which Wallis perhaps reveals a bit more than he intended about where his political loyalties lie. In writing about abortion, he counsels the Democratic Party on how, for pragmatic reasons, it should loosen up its rigid pro-choice party orthodoxy. He says,

> Such a respect of conscience on abortion and a less dismissive approach to conscientious dissenters to Democratic orthodoxy would allow many pro-life and progressive Christians the 'permission' they need to vote Democratic. Again, there are millions of votes at stake here.[42]

As a prophetic Christian voice rather than a political strategist, why should Wallis care whether this "pragmatic" move on the part of the Democrats would help them gain millions of votes? Is this a relevant concern for Christian moral witness or for the mission of the church?

After God's Politics came out, Wallis was much in demand as a speaker at Democratic Party consultations and events.[43] He seemed to be positioning himself as one who could help the Democrats learn to speak the language of faith and thus win back moderate to progressive religious voters. For a time at least, he indeed began to sound like a political strategist, as in the previous quote about abortion, rather than a radical Christian prophet, as in his books and magazine. My critique is that you cannot be both a party strategist and a Christian prophet. In biblical terms you cannot wear both the king's mantle and the prophet's robe. These are separate callings that are only damaged when they are mixed. This mixture is precisely what has happened to the evangelical right. Christian witness will not be benefited if it also happens to the evangelical left. But it requires incredible vigilance to maintain such boundaries. One way the Catholic Church has done so is to prohibit its clergy from serving in public office. Evangelicals might benefit from working out similar guidelines related to our entire public witness. I offer such guidelines in appendix 7.

The two major political parties in this country are like two suns in the same cosmic neighborhood that fight to pull the in-between planets into orbit around them. The power of party identity is so profound that otherwise thoughtful people can lose the capacity for independent reflection. Christians then move on to confuse that party loyalty with our loyalty to Christ and biblical moral values.

We need a transcendent moral vision that can serve as its own kind of "sun," powerful enough to function as the center of our own moral solar system and to help us resist the pull of worldly competitors. We also need a strong enough theology of the church and its distinctive mission and witness that we do not end up getting seduced by the politicians who so much want us to serve their agendas rather our own.

In the next chapter, we will consider whether there is emerging today a distinctive evangelical center that is finding more success than either left or right in pursuing such a vision.

Chapter 4

THE EMERGING EVANGELICAL CENTER

I want to propose that a center is emerging in significant institutions of American evangelical life. This evangelical center is gaining in momentum and has the potential to function as a centripetal force. On some issues, such as immigration, genocide in Sudan, and religious liberty, it has the ability to pull together a muscular coalition that includes the leading voices from the evangelical right and the evangelical left. On other issues, such as creation care and torture, it demonstrates a growing ability to bring left and center together and thus stake and hold ground despite the opposition of the evangelical right. This chapter will argue that the center is now firmly entrenched in many of the leading institutions in evangelical life. I will also suggest that this evangelical center (and to a lesser extent the left, but not the right) is winning the hearts and minds of younger evangelicals and thus represents the likely future of evangelicalism far more than the graying evangelical right.

Provocative assertions all, but there is a prior question to address at this stage of our discussion: How do we know who or what should be defined as *evangelical centrist*? How do we know the center when we see it? This is a legitimate question, and especially important in light of the fact that most centrist evangelicals do not really label themselves as such. (At least not yet, not until they finish reading this book!) Given my clear preference for the centrist evangelical label and what I am defining as its perspective, it is imperative that I offer some boundaries for what will count as defining this perspective.

I think that earlier discussions of the evangelical right and evangelical left have prepared the way for at least a working definition of the characteristics and convictions of the evangelical center. Let's begin there and then move ahead to consider the variety of individuals and organizations that might be viewed as constituting the emerging evangelical center. In the second part of the book, I will offer essays on several different policy arenas in an effort to illuminate at least one person's vision of a centrist evangelical moral witness. And in the appendixes, I will offer and comment on the key policy documents of the evangelical center.

NOT RIGHT, NOT LEFT, BUT CENTER

Pulling together all that has been said thus far in this book, the evangelical center can be defined as having the following characteristic emphases that make us *similar to* the evangelical right:

* Shared, visible, central concern about the decline of marriage and its impact on the well-being of children
* Clearly articulated opposition to abortion and euthanasia
* Opposition to the creation-for-destruction of embryos and majority opposition to the harvesting of stem cells from existing embryos
* Strong concern about the moral content of mass media
* Rejection of the morality of sex outside of heterosexual, monogamous, marriage
* Rejection of gay marriage.

I have argued that the evangelical center tends to be *different from* the evangelical right in at least the following ways:

* Commitment to political independence and avoidance of partisan entanglements and their negative consequences
* A broad and holistic moral agenda rather than a narrow focus on abortion and homosexuality

- Rejection of the mood of angry nostalgia and aggrieved entitlement about the Christian role in American society

- Realistic appraisal of the role of religion in the founding generation of the United States rather than the right's romanticized story of American origins

- An effort to be more deeply biblical and ecclesiological in our formulation of Christian public moral witness

- Greater sensitivity to American pluralism and to the full constraints of the First Amendment in our rhetoric and policy agenda.

The evangelical center has the following characteristics that tend to make them *similar to* the evangelical left:

- Emphasis on the plight of the poor as central to a biblical moral agenda, and willingness to support at least some government-based policy solutions

- Emphasis on racism as a moral and policy issue of continuing significance

- Opposition to the routine resort to war and willingness to dissent from at least some U.S. wars

- Articulation of a constrained, critical patriotism rather than a nationalist "God and country" stance

- Friendliness toward an internationalist vision and cooperative strategies to address global problems

- Gradual embrace of a just-peacemaking ethic as a way to prevent war and to address its root causes

- High priority to creation care and acceptance of the seriousness of the global warming problem

- A commitment to human rights, which includes opposition to the use of torture and cruel, inhuman, and degrading treatment of detainees in the war on terror .

The evangelical center is *different from* the evangelical left in at least the following ways:

- On race, the center tends to speak of racial reconciliation (like the right) rather than racial justice, like the left. (I do not consider this a strength of the center—not even the center is "always right," nor are the various centrist voices always in agreement with each other.)

- On economic ethics, the center has not embraced the antiglobalization, anti-free trade, economic populism of the left. Its economic ethic remains more sympathetic to the current practice of global capitalism but is in many ways underdeveloped. With the exception of Ron Sider, it does not really speak the language of economic simplicity or voluntary poverty.

- On war, the center does not accept the working pacifism of the left and is more willing to support wars that meet a careful rendering of the just-war theory. The center was not united in opposition to the Iraq War, unlike the left.

- On gender, in comparison with the left, the center tends to be relatively quiet, reflecting divisions within the center on this issue.

- On the issue of America's role in the world, the center tends to be much more muted in its overall criticism than the left. It does not generally accept or employ the language of "American imperialism."

- The (white) center offers less attention to public education issues than does the left and in general seems somewhat less focused on the particular needs of the urban poor. (Again, this is not a strength.)

- The center does not resonate with the left's tilt toward the Palestinians in the Israeli-Palestinian conflict.

- The center so far has retained more political independence than the left has retained in its drift toward the Democratic Party.

- The center is divided on the issue of capital punishment, thus it does not share the general opposition found on the left.

- The center is willing to treat issues such as abortion and gay marriage much more openly and extensively than is the tendency on the left.

- The center usually tries to avoid polemical engagement with the right, whereas some on the left now seem to define themselves in part by that engagement.

Some issues and perspectives are essentially consensus positions across every point on the evangelical political spectrum. When evangelicals unite on matters such as these, our voice is especially powerful. These issues generally include:

—*Commitment to the constitutional structure of American democracy*, with a "substantive neutrality" rather than "strict separationist" reading of the First Amendment's Establishment Clause

—*Involvement in the democratic process* of a nation that we love and support in the form of active, engaged citizenship.

—*Global compassion and justice concerns*, such as sex trafficking, forced slavery, AIDS funding, debt relief, U.S. foreign aid, world hunger, and genocide in Sudan.

—*Domestic compassion and justice concerns*, such as immigration, universal access to healthcare, conditions in U.S. prisons, and prisoner social reentry policies.

—*Global religious liberty issues*, such as free exercise of Christian and other religious beliefs in every part of the world, but especially the Muslim world.

—*Domestic religious liberty issues*, such as the free exercise rights of evangelical churches and schools to hire/admit according to religious and moral conviction tests appropriate to our faith tradition and equal access of faith-based organizations to government funds if their programs are effective in meeting social needs. These views are rooted in broad embrace of the "substantive neutrality" interpretation of the First Amendment.

—*A broad commitment to a human-rights agenda* and support for human rights conventions and laws. (Though, sadly, the right has been unwilling thus far to clearly reject the use of torture in the war on terror. This is a huge blind spot, as noted earlier.)

—*Rejection of any kind of explicit racism* and a stated desire to heal broken relationships between racial groups.

—*Explicit rooting of all such moral and policy convictions* in appeals to biblical teachings and Christian faith, with a related appeal for the freedom to articulate both our values and the reasons for them in public debate.

In what follows I hope to be able to show that there is indeed emerging today a robust evangelical center across the landscape of evangelical America. I think this emergence is one of the most promising (and underreported) developments in evangelical life today—and therefore in American public life. I want to be honest here in claiming my own support of this evangelical center, and my own growing involvement in making some of the history described in this chapter over the last few years. (I will offer the relevant disclaimers and personal notes throughout this chapter.) The evangelical center is certainly where I land. To stake a claim to this center and hold this ground is why I am writing this book. But I hope that I can be an advocate for this center while also offering critical engagement with it, just as it is, right now. The reader will judge if this is so.

To the Center from the Left
Ron Sider and Evangelicals for Social Action

One way to begin this discussion is to consider the way organizations have moved toward the center both from the left and from the right. Having already considered the evangelical left vision, it is instructive to consider the subtle difference offered by a leader frequently identified with the evangelical left—Ron Sider, author of the groundbreaking *Rich Christians in an Age of Hunger*.[1] Sider's thirty-year-old organization is called Evangelicals for Social Action (ESA). Even though this organization has never grown large and is dwarfed in size by such evangelical right groups as Focus on the Family, ESA has been an important point of identification for an influential minority of evangelicals. (Disclaimer: I served on the ESA staff for three years, have written numerous articles for their magazine, and continue to remain in contact with the organization and with Sider. Other than my teacher and coauthor Glen Stassen, no single figure in the evangelical world has had more impact on my own thinking than Sider.)

Sider's story is relatively well known. Born in Canadian Mennonite country, Sider earned a Ph.D. in historical theology at Yale. A pacifist with an activist streak, Sider became involved in the 1970s in attempting to wrench American evangelicalism away from its embrace of quietism, privatism, otherworldly evangelism-alone approaches to missions, and conservative politics. He was an organizer and key player in a 1973 conference that produced the Chicago Declaration of Evangelical Social

Concern, which called evangelicals to confront racism, injustice, and discrimination against women.[2] Sider's 1977 publication of *Rich Christians* put him squarely in the public eye; his striking, biblically based attack on Christian complacency in a world with "a billion hungry neighbors" won him both plaudits and enemies and launched his career with a flourish. He has remained closely focused on economic-justice issues ever since.

Quite early, Sider embraced the "biblical egalitarian" position on the role of women, a view that sharply differentiated him and his organization from those on the evangelical right, especially at the time when he embraced those positions in the 1970s. Sider led ESA to oppose the first Gulf War in 1991, and in general ESA's antiwar stance has been nearly indistinguishable from that of Jim Wallis and others on the evangelical left (which is the main obstacle to counting him in the evangelical center).

With the help of some significant grant funding, ESA launched the Evangelical Environmental Network (EEN) in the early 1990s; this organization has partnered with an ecumenical and interfaith consortium of like-minded groups over the past fifteen years and has made visible progress in raising environmental awareness and lowering resistance to environmental regulation and in promoting acceptance of global warming science and ecofriendly lifestyle change among evangelicals.[3] EEN was the organization that put together the Evangelical Climate Initiative (ECI), a 2006 declaration that claimed that tackling global warming was a Christian moral imperative. I was the principal drafter of this statement, which has been signed by over one hundred evangelical leaders, including such luminaries as Rick Warren, Bill Hybels, and thirty-nine Christian-college presidents (see appendix 5). *This was a defining event for evangelical environmentalism and for the consolidation of an evangelical center.* It also evoked furious opposition from the religious and political right.

EEN, under its gifted leader, Jim Ball, has also been skillful in building internal evangelical coalitions involving such mainstream evangelical relief and development organizations as World Relief and World Vision, thus in an indirect way contributing to the growth of an evangelical center anchored in long-standing evangelical charitable and parachurch organizations, as I will suggest further in this chapter.

Poverty, war, ecology, and women's rights sound like the profile of an evangelical left organization, and yet—like Wallis and Sojourners, but perhaps with more credibility—ESA and Sider have resisted being pigeonholed on the left and seem to have also retained greater political independence. Like Wallis, Sider has long embraced a "consistent pro-life agenda"—in this he was deeply affected by the example of Senator Mark Hatfield (R-OR) and by Catholic thought in the 1970s and 1980s.[4] He has followed through in his pro-life commitment with clear opposition to abortion, which he has not hesitated to write about in his magazines or books. He has not equivocated on this point, even while (like those on the left) emphasizing the various fairly radical steps that would be required to actually welcome over a million at-risk children into our nation each year. Sider has also refused to waver on homo-sexuality, believing that homosexual behavior cannot be reconciled with biblical teaching—though he and his organization have joined voices like Campolo's and Wallis's in strongly resisting the demonization of homosexuals and in calling for civil discussion of public policy issues related to homosexuality. Moreover, Sider has moved to the center-right on church-state issues, having been persuaded by the argument that the courts since World War II have mistakenly embraced a kind of estab-lished antireligion secularism and need to move toward the "substantive neutrality" position in church-state jurisprudence.[5] This helps to explain his support for school vouchers and President Bush's faith-based initia-tive. Sider has also not hesitated to critique the evangelical community for its internal moral failings in certain "family" issue areas, such as divorce, premarital sex, and pornography.[6]

For some years, Sider envisioned the development of a consensus statement of evangelical social ethics that could heal the gap between the evangelical left and right.[7] He was a key force behind the drafting of what ultimately became the "For the Health of the Nation" statement, offered in 2004 by the National Association of Evangelicals (NAE) and widely quoted prior to the 2004 election. This sophisticated statement and a book including and expanding on it (*Toward an Evangelical Public Policy*) can be seen as a major breakthrough toward the emergence of an evangelical center in American public life.[8] I will examine it closely in appendixes 1 and 2.

TO THE CENTER FROM THE RIGHT
NAE, CCCU, CT, IVP, and Baker

Those familiar with the history of the National Association of Evangelicals
(NAE) surely had to be a bit surprised by the organization's embrace
of "For the Health of the Nation." It marked a significant departure for
the sixty-year-old organization, which functions essentially as a consortium of evangelical denominations, missions organizations, and other
church and parachurch bodies, together representing over 30 million
members.[9] The NAE moved toward a decisive expansion of its public
policy engagement in 1978, when it enlarged its Washington office and
enlisted Rev. Robert Dugan to be its leader. Dugan and the NAE seized
on the election of Ronald Reagan as an opportunity for an expansion of
evangelical influence in Washington, and today the NAE Web site still
celebrates the "unprecedented access to the White House" that the organization came to enjoy during that period. Reagan himself addressed
NAE conventions in 1983 and 1984. NAE's modest legislative successes
at that time included passage of drunk driving legislation, church audit
procedures, and equal access to public school facilities for religious
groups. NAE also established a Peace, Freedom, and Security Studies
initiative that took a quite conservative line on the U.S.-Soviet standoff
during the time when the religious left was pushing for a nuclear freeze.
It was during this period that the NAE sent George Weigel to Union
Seminary to stiffen the spines of wavering evangelicals like me.

In essence, then, the NAE's public policy agenda in the 1980s was
relatively limited but clearly conservative, and one might have expected
NAE's stance today to have situated it unequivocally within the evangelical right.

However, to the great joy of some and chagrin of others, a new wind
is blowing in the NAE. Despite the clear theological conservatism of
the organization, NAE was willing not just to sign on to but to help
sponsor the "For the Health of the Nation" statement, which gained
the unanimous support of its board of directors in 2004. Its governmental affairs office in Washington, led by Rich Cizik since 1995, has
taken on not only conservative Christian issues such as abortion and
embryonic stem-cell research but also global warming, human rights in

North Korea, global democratization, African aid and debt relief, HIV/ AIDS, immigration, human trafficking, international religious persecution, U.S. detainee policy, Muslim-evangelical dialogue, and genocide in Sudan.[10] The robust, human-rights-oriented internationalism of this NAE agenda has won unlikely admirers across the political spectrum and several important legislative victories in the past decade.[11] Cizik himself played a key role in drafting "For the Health of the Nation" and has his finger in the pie of evangelical political activism pretty much wherever it occurs. In light of these developments it seems appropriate to situate the NAE, especially its governmental affairs office, as a (if not *the*) major voice in the newly emergent evangelical center.

Precisely because of his visible embrace of a broad, centrist agenda, Cizik and the NAE have weathered increasingly intense attacks from the evangelical right in recent years. The focus of many of these attacks has been Cizik's embrace of the global warming issue. His "conversion" on this issue came gradually, through the good offices of Ball and EEN especially, but once Cizik was convinced about this issue he did not waver. Cizik's support for ECI in 2006 was strong, but it did not include his signature, as he did not have the full support of the NAE board for that signature. Still, he has remained visible and engaged on this issue. He took the next step on global warming by helping to organize an innovative partnership between evangelicals and secular scientists. NAE provided the sponsorship on the evangelical side; the Center for Health and the Global Environment at Harvard Medical School led on the scientific side. A private meeting was held at Melhana Plantation in early December 2006, and it was followed by a major national press event in January 2007. The group—of which I was a part—released a declaration of mutual commitment on climate change, biodiversity, and other ecological concerns and pledged to continue to work together to press for aggressive national action on these issues (declaration printed in appendix 6).[12]

Perhaps this was the last straw for the evangelical right. As discussed previously, in late February 2007, James Dobson and two dozen other like-minded evangelical right leaders sent an open letter to the NAE board, requesting that it rein in Cizik, either pulling him off of the global warming issue and back to the "real" issues, or dismissing him. The NAE responded at its March 2007 board meeting by essentially ignoring the Dobson letter, affirming the broad policy agenda established by their own "For the Health of the Nation" statement and endorsing a lengthy human rights/antitorture declaration called "An Evangelical Declaration Against Torture" (which I led in drafting—see appendix 3 for text and signatory list). This polite but firm response to Dobson helped to establish, perhaps once and for all, that there is an independent evangelical center with its own vision that cannot be bullied or dictated to by the evangelical right.

Another institutional expression of this evangelical center as it has emerged from the right can be found in evangelical insitutions associated with the Council for Christian Colleges & Universities (CCCU).[13] Both the schools themselves, considered individually, and to a lesser extent, the CCCU as an organization, offer considerable evidence of an emerging evangelical center. For brevity, I will focus on the CCCU itself. (Disclaimer: I have worked in a CCCU-affiliated school and have lectured widely on the CCCU circuit.)

The CCCU describes itself as "an international higher education association of intentionally Christian colleges and universities." With a budget of $11 million, the CCCU represents 105 member institutions in the United States and Canada, as well as an additional 75 affiliated institutions in over 20 countries. Student membership in CCCU member institutions is 300,000, with 1.55 million alumni. The mission of the CCCU is "to advance the cause of Christ-centered higher education and to help our institutions transform lives by faithfully relating scholarship and service to biblical truth." The CCCU is a kind of trade association of schools whose mission and identity fit with the criteria established by the CCCU. Member schools must offer an accredited, comprehensive, liberal arts undergraduate education, have a public, board-approved, Christ-centered mission statement, offer programs that integrate scholarship, faith, and service, and "hire as full-time faculty and administrators only persons who profess belief in Jesus Christ." Among the most visible CCCU schools are Wheaton, Calvin, Gordon, Westmont, Messiah, and Union. In essence, these schools are the one hundred most theologically conservative, explicitly Christian, accredited four-year universities in the nation.

Given this profile, one might expect the public stance of the CCCU leadership, based in Washington, to lean to the political right. It should be noted that CCCU leaders, including Robert Andringa, who served as president from 1994 to 2006, have not primarily positioned the organization as a political activist group. Most of the engagement of the CCCU in Washington concerns the institutional self-defense of CCCU schools, in light of the precarious condition of church-state jurisprudence as it affects explicitly Christian colleges and universities. Thus the primary public policy agenda of the CCCU is to retain the space for its member schools to practice their faith-based missions and to hire and teach on the basis of their faith and values.

However, at least under Andringa, in subtle ways the CCCU quietly positioned itself with or near other organizations and individuals in the evangelical center. One interesting mark of this was found in two decisions to change the name of the organization from the Christian College Coalition to the Coalition for Christian Colleges & Universities (1995) and then finally to the Council for Christian Colleges & Universities (1999). One reason for these name changes was "to set the association more clearly apart from . . . the Christian Coalition," at the time perhaps the most visible evangelical right group.[14]

The CCCU's program agenda includes considerable interest in racial and ethnic diversity (generally called intercultural competency by the CCCU), gender equity, and "culture-crossing" initiatives in many parts of the world. This internal commitment was matched by an external move in January 2003, when the CCCU joined fourteen other higher education associations in backing "race-conscious admission practices" such as those at the University of Michigan. The statement took the form of a letter to President Bush backing affirmative action, the 1978 *Bakke* decision, and the importance of conscious efforts to maintain diversity in higher education.[15] Support for race-based affirmative action is certainly not common on the evangelical right. It was a clear marker of delineation between the two camps.

The CCCU's social change agenda is also signaled by its commitment to "culture-shaping" initiatives, such as programs to place students in Hollywood, in journalism, in music, and in government, rather than a strategy of attacking such arenas of culture for their godlessness, which is traditionally more common on the evangelical right. Other interesting marks of the CCCU's approach include the CCCU's organizing of dialogue sessions on the issue of homosexuality that involve a variety of voices, including psychologists such as David Myers of Hope College who want Christian colleges to drop their objections to consensual, loving, homosexual relationships. Although most CCCU leaders and schools remain conservative on this issue, the tone being set by the CCCU differs sharply from that which is found farther right. The CCCU's spirit on this issue is reflected in a comment from Andringa to his board: "I am trying to figure out how to sit down with leaders of the gay rights movement so we can relate to people, not just to fears and threats in this arena."[16]

The CCCU leadership generally supported the initiative driven by the EEN to tackle the global-warming problem. Dozens of CCCU presidents signed the statement. As well, Bob Andringa offered a private letter of congratulations and thanks to John McCain and the other senators who brokered the compromise in summer 2005 to keep the U.S. Senate from collapsing in acrimony over judicial filibusters. (By way of contrast, James Dobson was livid about this compromise agreement and said so publicly.) The council has aligned itself with peace efforts in the Sudan, takes initiatives to support HIV/AIDS efforts in Africa, has opened up dialogue between Christians and Muslims, and attempts to help its campuses deal with social justice issues generally. And overall, it is clear that the CCCU is attempting to retain its political independence, to speak to leaders of both parties while being beholden to none, and to do so in a civil manner. Andringa informed his Board: "I am trying in many small ways to keep the dialogue civil and work in as much of a bipartisan manner as possible."[17]

The diversity of the CCCU membership, along with the focused mission of the CCCU, likely means that the organization's leaders will only dip their toes in political waters on an occasional basis. But as of now, they appear to be doing so in a way that aligns them with the emerging evangelical center. And while a survey of the leading scholars and teachers at CCCU schools is beyond the scope of this project, my experience on many of these campuses gives me confidence that the grass roots reflects the leadership in terms of the move toward a centrist evangelical vision.

Another remarkable development in recent years has been the shift in positioning of evangelicalism's leading magazine, *Christianity Today*. (Disclaimer: I have written for *Christianity Today* for ten years.) Founded in 1956 by Billy Graham and his father-in-law, L. Nelson Bell, and first edited by the leader of postwar evangelicalism, Carl F. H. Henry, *Christianity Today* is now Christianity Today International, a thriving enterprise and, in fact, an online community whose Web site attracts 11.8 million visitors monthly, and a publishing company now delivering ten print periodicals that combine to attract over a million subscribers, resources for ministers and local churches, college and seminary guides, a media guide, classified ads, and so on—it's a one-stop shop for the card-carrying evangelical crowd.

Still, at the heart of this far-flung enterprise is *Christianity Today* magazine, edited by David Neff since 1990. Those who know *Christianity Today's* history at all know that under its most (in)famous executive editor, Harold Lindsell (1968–1978), *Christianity Today* was a hard-right magazine pressing for a quite conservative evangelicalism. This vision differs dramatically from the editorial stance of the magazine now. Observers attribute this shift to Neff's leadership as well as to the ethos created by former editor Kenneth Kantzer and longtime "corporate editor" Harold Myra. Those evangelicals who want a magazine more like Lindsell's *Christianity Today* now prefer *World*, which fills that niche on the evangelical right.

Christianity Today remains, indisputably, evangelical. It profiles evangelical leaders, is filled with reams of evangelical advertising, and articulates recognizably evangelical perspectives on world affairs, missions, and theological and ethical issues. It has taken consistent editorial stances against gay marriage, abortion, easy divorce, and so on. *Christianity Today*, however, has also implicitly and explicitly distanced itself from the evangelical right in recent years. It has done so in a number of editorials on specific issues; for example, it has taken the EEN line in expressing concern about climate change in a time when many conservative evangelicals remain hostile to such concerns. It has tackled the same kinds of issues, such as human rights, genocide, and global debt relief, that have been taken on by Rich Cizik and the NAE. It recruited me to write a major antitorture cover article for the February 2006 issue.

And *Christianity Today* has been increasingly willing to take the gloves off and explicitly confront the evangelical right. In a striking July 2005 editorial, *Christianity Today* begins by saying: "George W. Bush is not Lord. The Declaration of Independence is not an infallible guide to Christian faith and practice. . . . The American flag is not the Cross. The Pledge of Allegiance is not the Creed. 'God Bless America' is not the Doxology. Sometimes one needs to state the obvious—especially at times when it's less and less obvious."[18] The article goes on to reject statements made by Family Research Council Action, Ted Haggard (then NAE president), the evangelist D. James Kennedy, and others. This article rejected the equation of biblical truth with American values, the evangelical right narrative that treats the founders as biblically minded Christians, and the apparent belief that finding the right (strict constructionist) judges is the key to the moral renewal of the United States. It called the church back to a focus on Jesus as Lord and to the centrality of worship rather than politics as the main thing Christians are to be doing in the world. Implicitly, it warned evangelicals about a dangerous kind of political idolatry in which God and country, the church and the state, and Jesus and George W., are conflated and confused.

It should also be noted, in keeping with my emphasis on people and organizations in this study, that Neff has come to function as a leading evangelical statesman in recent years. He wrote the initial draft of "For the Health of the Nation." He has played a key role in evangelical activism related to the environment through EEN. He helped to draft "An Evangelical Declaration Against Torture," the statement mentioned earlier that was approved by the NAE board in March 2007. In other words, he has come to occupy a major place in the emerging evangelical center, along with such voices as Sider, Cizik, and others. The organizations these men lead hold considerable influence, especially when taken in the aggregate, and point to the significance of an emerging evangelical center with a growing sense of its own distinctive vision and enough clout to begin to throw its weight around.

The evangelical book publishing world has also shifted from the right to the center. Certainly this is not universally true, but any review of the titles, let alone the content, of stalwart evangelical publishers such as Intervarsity Press and Baker Books reveals a definite shift to the evangelical center in the last decade or more. It seems clear to me—as one who has published with both of these houses—that their rejection of the evangelical right agenda and spirit is indisputable. They are seeking to represent and to shape the emerging evangelical center.

To the Center from a Suffering World
The Evangelical Compassion Agencies

In a November 2006 article in the *Washington Post*, evangelicals Joe Loconte and Michael Cromartie wrote, "churches and faith-based organizations are growing enormously in their international outreach.[19] Groups such as World Vision are often the first responders to natural disasters. The Association of Evangelical Relief and Development Organizations, founded in 1978, now boasts forty-seven member groups in dozens of countries. As anyone familiar with these organizations knows, they help people regardless of creed, race or sexual orientation—another democratic (and evangelical) ideal." Loconte and Cromartie help us to pay attention to another major sector of evangelicalism: the plethora of what might be called "compassion agencies" that work here and around the world on behalf of suffering people.

It is my contention that many of these organizations embody the kind of broad, holistic moral agenda that fits within my paradigm of the emerging evangelical center. They are service organizations rather than lobbying agencies or political agencies, and so they do not focus on defining themselves as centrist evangelical groups. Many of them began as strictly charitable or missions organizations but through the years have come to attend to a broad range of concerns that affect the people to whom they minister. I think that a look at several of these organizations helps to suggest ways in which these well-regarded institutions in evangelical life are in their own way a part of the emerging evangelical center.

Consider what is perhaps the classic evangelical relief organization, World Vision (WV).[20] Founded in September 1950 by Dr. Bob Pierce in response to the needs of Korean War orphans, WV today defines itself as a "Christian relief and development organization dedicated to helping children and their communities worldwide reach their full potential by tackling the causes of poverty." With a worldwide staff of over 23,000, supported by 4.7 million U.S. donors and total revenues of just under $1 billion in 2006, WV serves in nearly one hundred countries, including the United States, and claims to reach 100 million people. They require no religious allegiance or conversion from those who receive their services. They organize their work into three primary areas: disaster relief, community development, and global issues. This latter category includes educating the public "on poverty and justice-related issues and advocat[ing] on behalf of the poor and children in crisis." WV has a massive child-sponsorship program, offers food aid, clean water initiatives, HIV/AIDS care and prevention, especially in Africa, and rapid response disaster relief in some of the hardest hit regions of the world. Their forays into longer term economic development work now include microfinancing of more than 440,000 initiatives in forty-six developing countries; these created or sustained over 900,000 jobs in 2006.

WV in recent years has turned its attention to environmental issues, including global warming. In December 2006, David Schieman, U.S. director of WV's Africa programs, declared, "World Vision's experience in field operations in Africa points to climate change as a major factor in reducing crops and livestock herds. Every farmer we talk to says there is either not enough rain, or it's very erratic, or both. They can't feed their families anymore and the situation is getting worse. Ten years ago that kind of concern [environmental preservation] was associated with 'tree huggers,' but now we are all thinking much more in these terms and looking at ways to protect the land, trees and vegetation." This ground-level experience of the actual effects of climate change may be one reason why Rich Stearns, president of WV, signed the ECI statement in February 2006. It is harder to deny global warming when you actually serve among those whose lives are already being affected by it.

If one way to define the evangelical center is its embrace of a broad moral agenda that includes the well-being of children and families, active efforts to address poverty and its causes, and concern for the global environment, it seems that WV makes an excellent example of a centrist evangelical organization.

Another, quite different organization with a richly holistic vision is the International Justice Mission (IJM), founded in 1997 and directed by Gary Haugen. This hugely innovative and courageous organization is immensely popular with evangelical college students. Anyone who wants to understand contemporary evangelicalism needs to attend to IJM, a rapidly growing organization with a budget over $10 million and operations in a dozen countries.

The mission statement of the organization is as follows: "International Justice Mission is a human rights agency that rescues victims of violence, sexual exploitation, slavery, and oppression."[21] IJM actually goes into global contexts of sex slavery and forced labor and rescues men, women, and children from those who are exploiting them. They also take on unprosecuted rape and sexual defilement cases, as well as instances of violations of citizenship rights, illegal police detention, and police brutality. A member of the Association of Evangelical Relief and Development Organizations (AERDO), IJM's fourfold purpose includes victim relief, perpetrator accountability, structural prevention, and victim aftercare. It stops abuse, documents crimes for later prosecution, cares for victims, and seeks to change the social conditions that lead to such horrific crimes around the world. To paraphrase Martin Luther King Jr., this is an organization both tough-minded and tender-hearted. Surely its ground-level work requires considerable courage.

The Archbishop of Canterbury, the Rt. Rev. Rowan Williams, has aptly described IJM in this way: "This organization, founded on Christian principles, combines the efforts of missionaries, lawyers, criminal investigators and government relations experts to work for the prevention of injustice in our world." It is this combination that makes the organization such a winning one. It is rooted in the long-standing evangelical international missionary impulse. Indeed, that is how it began, as a result of conversations with thousands of missionaries and relief workers. And yet it does not proselytize. Instead it bears witness to Christ through deeds of love and justice on behalf of some of the most pitiable human beings in the world—human slaves. Meanwhile, it makes the enormous contribution of triggering an interest in the concept of justice and the work of human rights in American evangelical communities for which this is not our native language. Evangelism, prayer, and love, yes; justice, rescue, and rights, no; IJM succeeds in bringing these together. And it is bringing these concerns to Christian college campuses around the nation through its campus chapter program.

Haugen and his organization are tightly focused on their mission. And yet because there is a certain seamlessness about moral concern, especially about concern for human rights, Haugen has ventured into one of the most sensitive moral issues of our time, decrying the use of torture in the U.S. war on terror in the February 2006 issue of *Christianity Today*. I have to say quite honestly that Haugen is among a small handful of evangelicals who have "gone out there with me" by offering published work on the torture issue. Perhaps it is difficult to close one's eyes and heart to the cries of those in Guantanamo and Bagram and Abu Ghraib when your work involves hearing such cries in Thailand, Peru, and Cambodia.

To the Center from the Margins
Black and Hispanic Evangelicals

I have already said that it is difficult to "fit" black and other nonwhite evangelicals into the right-left-center paradigm that we are employing in this book. But to omit such evangelicals, from our discussion for this reason would be to perpetuate their marginalization. I want to suggest in this section that John Perkins and Tony Evans might fairly (if loosely) be classified as center-left and center-right black evangelicals respectively, and that reflection on their messages and ministries is important for our project here. I also want to dip a toe in this section into the Latino/a evangelical world in the United States as well.

Perkins was among what might be called the founding generation of "card-carrying" black evangelicals in the United States, which emerged in the 1960s and 1970s. He grew up in small-town Mississippi and personally endured the brutal injustice and miserable suffering of those engaged in the civil rights struggle in that state. Along with the late Tom Skinner, who came from Harlem with a different persona and background but a similar message, Perkins became one of the earliest champions of aggressive efforts to achieve racial justice and racial reconciliation in American evangelicalism—and through evangelicals, in the broader society. It is hard to overstate his significance as a dialogue partner for white evangelical leaders such as Ron Sider, who reveres Perkins.

Perkins created a significant institutional legacy with his Christian Community Development Association (CCDA), founded in 1989 to embody at a national level the vision that he and his wife, Vera Mae Perkins, had been pursuing for decades. The mission of CCDA is "to inspire and train Christians who seek to bear witness to the Kingdom of God by reclaiming and restoring under-resourced communities." Specific purposes of CCDA include the following:

- To strengthen existing Christian community-development organizations
- To encourage new Christian community-development efforts
- To promote Christian community development through regional training
- To educate and mobilize the body of Christ at large to become involved in Christian community development in their area
- To sustain, enable, and inspire those individuals doing Christian community development.

Fundamentally then, CCDA is about Christian investment in community transformation efforts, especially in predominantly minority, poor, urban America. Perkins and CCDA emphasize the holistic theological and human vision that motivates their work:

> Many in ministry get passionate and involved in one area of need and think if they solve this particular problem that all else will be resolved. Christians, of course, often focus this area on a personal relationship with Jesus Christ. Of course, the most essential element to Christian Community Development is evangelism and discipleship. Yet solving problems with lasting solutions is more than evangelism and discipleship. . . . There is never a simplistic answer to the problems in poor communities. Often, people will say that the problem is spiritual, social or educational. Of course these are problems, but they are only part of the larger problems. Solving the housing problem does not solve the emotional struggles that a person has. Christian Community Development has a wholistic approach to ministry that deals with the spiritual, social, economic, political, cultural, emotional, physical,

moral, judicial, educational and familial issues of each person. . . . It is being completely pro-life for a person, not only eternally, but also as the person lives on this earth.[22]

Notice how this statement reflects the characteristic effort in the center and left of the evangelical spectrum to avoid body/soul, earth/heaven dualisms, thus bringing together evangelism and social ministry into one holistic package. Perkins also here articulates the "completely pro-life" language that is common in both the center and the left and tends to be resisted by the evangelical right.

One final note about CCDA concerns the astonishing diversity of its staff and board. The twenty-five-member CCDA board is indeed a rainbow coalition of black, Hispanic, white, and Asian members, with nine women, some of them ordained ministers. They are almost exclusively urban based, and most are themselves involved in ministries that include community development. Its five-person staff is similarly diverse. One of the unique strengths of black evangelical organizations is that they often thoroughly integrate their leadership teams in a way that white evangelicals have only begun to do. They set a standard here that among white evangelicals has been most closely approximated on the evangelical left, in groups such as Sojourners.

Turning to what might be called the black evangelical center-right, let us consider the ministry of Tony Evans, the African American senior pastor of Oak Cliff Bible Fellowship in Dallas, Texas, a congregation of over seven thousand members. Evans is also president of The Urban Alternative (TUA), which seeks to address issues such as family disintegration, crime, racial division, drug addiction, immorality, and injustice. His ministry through his church and through TUA focuses on spiritual transformation, because Evans believes all problems are, at root, spiritual concerns more than social concerns. His outreach programs focus on a "Kingdom Agenda."[23] His vision is one that blends strong personal piety/morality with a passionate concern for social justice and restoration. Because he bases his arguments in scripture and his interpretation of the kingdom of God, he does not fit neatly into either the right or the left. He maintains that his agenda is not political but spiritual.

In his 541-page book *What a Way to Live!*, Evans presents what he calls his "comprehensive world view and philosophy of ministry." More characteristic of right than center, Evans maintains a traditionalist understanding of the roles men and women should play, adhering to a strict hierarchy of men and women, not only in the home, but in the church as well. Basing his views of the criminal justice system in scripture, Evans does not rule out capital punishment for murder or corporal punishment for other serious crimes. But he also acknowledges the faultiness of America's prison system. "As long as the best idea we can come up with for dealing with crime is to warehouse criminals in prison, we won't get anywhere."[24]

While Evans offers quite conservative prescriptions in some areas, his experiences as an African American pastor battling racism and economic injustice lead him to a more complete set of values than the standard "life and marriage" agenda of the right. Although Evans has a strong disdain for abortion and homosexuality, he does not belabor the point. The few times he alludes to homosexuality in his book, he actually is stressing the fact that it is *not* the only moral agenda of the church, nor the most important. "If the church would have treated racism like it did the sins of adultery, homosexuality, and abortion, racism would have been addressed a long time ago."[25]

Racism has deeply affected Evans' own life, and he echoes Billy Graham's convictions when he says that "the racial division of its members and the resulting classism is the greatest problem facing the kingdom of God."[26] He strongly attacks racist theories and practices that are supposedly grounded in scripture and presses for action in reconciliation and restoration. Because racism is a sin and not just a social issue, he urges his readers and congregants to deal urgently with racism.

Evans does not see affirmative action as a viable (or a biblical) solution, because there are no fixed standards of compensation. Since no one can know when the "debt" has been fully paid, he argues that affirmative action leaves the two sides arguing about what is just and fair in undoing the negative effects brought on by slavery and segregation. He offers an alternative solution. Because slavery was an evil against a group of people that has had enormous repercussions, he calls for the federal government to issue an apology, seeking forgiveness for the sin of slavery and for the effects it has had on the nation. He also advocates for a memorial to be built in "a strategic location in Washington, DC, to serve as a permanent reminder of the evil of slavery and to honor its victims."[27] In order to prevent future cases of racism and to compensate the victims if such cases arise, he would like to see a restitution system for future incidents, and to provide incentives for institutions and organizations that practice and promote diversity and empowerment.

As Evans explores economic issues, he speaks out against greed, irresponsibility, and the injustices of the taxation system. Overtaxation is a "systematic evil," and to Evans that means anything more than 10 percent. However, Evans asserts that heavy taxation is partly the fault of the people. "We have asked the government to do things that government was never meant to do," and "[o]nce we ask the government to take over things like charity, medical care, and education, government is going to tax us excessively to pay for all of those systems." Evans places a heavy emphasis on personal responsibility, generosity, saving, and investing wisely. At Evans' church, numerous outreach programs exist to help end the economic desperation in the surrounding urban area. Biblical economic seminars, study programs for the GED, college courses offered by a local university on the church's campus, job skill training, a food pantry and thrift store, and entrepreneurial programs to help develop the plans of those wanting to start their own businesses are a few of the ways Evans and his church act on Evans' belief that "the church is the answer to welfare."[28] Evans believes empowerment is achieved through education and spiritual renewal.

Considered as a whole, Evans' ministry offers the kind of breadth of moral vision that I have situated in the evangelical center, while his treatment of the conservative hot-button issues of abortion, gender roles, and homosexuality clearly differentiates him from the evangelical left. He helps to demonstrate the claim made previously that even quite conservative black evangelicals tend toward a more holistic vision, with an attention to racial and economic issues that is often missing among white evangelicals whose daily experience does not demand attention to such concerns. (Another example of a black megachurch pastor who can be described similarly is the nationally known T. D. Jakes, based in Dallas.)

Turning to the massive and growing Hispanic community in the United States, one can find a quite clearly centrist evangelical organization in the National Hispanic Christian Leadership Conference

(NHCLC), founded in 1995 and today led by Sam Rodriguez. This organization describes itself as the preeminent organization for born-again/evangelical Latinos in the United States, representing approximately 15 million Hispanic evangelicals (roughly one-third of the overall Hispanic population in the United States). Its mission is to serve as a voice for Latino evangelicals and Latino-affiliated NAE churches and denominations. It explicitly identifies itself as a sister organization to the NAE.

Like the NAE but also distinct in its way, the NHCLC purposefully embraces a broad religious agenda that extends well beyond the public-policy arena that we are discussing in this book. In the area of policy, the organization articulates an agenda that includes "the family, immigration, economic mobility, education, political empowerment, and societal transformation." One can clearly see overlap with the agenda of black evangelicals in the areas that one might predict: economics, education, and political empowerment. A distinctive concern of Hispanic evangelicals, as of seemingly all Hispanics who engage in U.S. public life, is the immigration issue. As of the time of this writing, U.S. immigration policy remains a hugely controversial and unresolved issue. There are signs that the leadership of the white evangelical community in almost all of its expressions will attempt to unite with Hispanic leaders in pressing for some version of immigration legislation that resembles the humane approach taken by President Bush but not yet successfully pushed through Congress. This could be a breakthrough moment in both the white evangelical community and in bridge building with Latino evangelicals.

I have to acknowledge as a white centrist evangelical that, on the whole, the Latino evangelical world in the United States remains largely unknown to me, and I imagine, to most like me. I have heard of such academic stalwarts as Jesse Miranda, Eldin Villafañe, Justo Gonzales, and Albert Reyes, and on the ministry side Rudy Carrasco and Luis Cortés, the latter serving as leader of the influential organization Esperanza USA. But still we occupy different worlds. We will know that true racial/ethnic reconciliation and true Christian community are emerging in the evangelical world when these worlds of white, black, and Latino/a evangelicalism (and Asian American, and others) begin to interpenetrate much more than they do now. And for those interested especially in the public witness of the evangelical world and its effectiveness, one can only imagine the impact of a united moral witness offered by the leaders of all of the ethnically diverse evangelical communities in the United States.

TO THE CENTER FROM THE REFORMED TRADITION
The Center for Public Justice

One of my favorite people in the evangelical world is Jim Skillen, the political scientist who serves as head of the Center for Public Justice (CPJ).[29] I have known this rigorous, gentle scholar for about fifteen years, our paths first crossing in the early 1990s when I served with Ron Sider at ESA. (Since then I have been involved occasionally in making presentations at CPJ programs.) Skillen's CPJ is probably the most intellectually substantive evangelical policy organization of any type—right, left, or center. I would argue that it belongs in the evangelical center and that it has been occupying that center for decades. It has a broad policy agenda that includes religious freedom, education, welfare, security and defense, homosexuality, and human life issues, among others. It retains its political independence and does *not* tack with the political winds. This is probably because it is firmly rooted in a meaty intellectual tradition—the Dutch Reformed tradition as developed in the life and writings of Dutch Christian statesman Abraham Kuyper— that keeps it grounded in its own particular methodology for addressing public-policy questions. One of its printed brochures describes the organization as "the only national civic organization that grounds its research, publications, training, and advocacy in a comprehensive Christian political foundation." This is probably an accurate statement; I can think of no exceptions.

CPJ was founded in 1981, with Skillen named its director and serving continuously in that role since the organization's inception. Today the organization seeks to "equip citizens, develop leaders, and shape policy in pursuit of our purpose to serve God, advance justice, and transform public life" in the United States. Specifically, it offers succinct, high-quality policy analysis of current policy issues, identifies promising younger scholars/leaders in whom to invest time and training through policy institutes and the like, and advocates for specific policy positions in Washington. Its small staff of policy researchers and analysts focuses on both domestic and foreign policy concerns. Probably no organization has been more persistent in advancing a "substantive neutrality" position on church-state issues, with consequent support for school vouchers for religious and other private schools, for the faith-based initiative, for freedom-to-hire protections for religious groups, and for all related measures that permit maximum space for religious people and bodies to participate without handicap in American public life. CPJ played a key role in crafting the successful welfare reform efforts in the mid-1990s, and especially in that legislation's breakthrough recognition of the key social contribution made by faith-based economic relief and empowerment organizations. On foreign policy, CPJ operates out of a just-war framework while consistently demonstrating an admirable imperviousness to partisan loyalty or uncritical support for any government's policies. Meanwhile, of at least as much interest to Skillen and CPJ are deeper concerns that go beyond the daily fare of public debate. These include political community and authority, the responsibilities of Christian citizens and officeholders, representative government, civil society, and the nature of freedom.

To the Center from the Megachurches
Rick Warren, Joel Hunter, and Rich Nathan

Within Protestant Christianity, the vibrant center of American religious life is now clearly found within evangelical churches rather than in mainline Protestantism. And no churches have proven more successful at attracting massive numbers of attendees than the megachurches. These amazing institutions now attract as many as 20,000 every weekend to an array of worship services, usually in astonishingly large facilities that seem to extend for miles.

Predominantly white evangelical megachurches vary considerably in their engagement with American public life. Many are entirely disengaged and focus on classic evangelical concerns such as personal salvation, evangelism, doctrinal teaching, individual morality, and child-rearing. Some are engaged politically but are explicitly conservative and become platforms for the evangelical right. This has certainly been the case with many of the large Southern Baptist congregations that dot the cities of the American South.

Many eyes, however, are now turning to a few key megachurches that are clearly landing in the evangelical center and in doing so are creating considerable consternation on the evangelical right.[30] These include Rick Warren's Saddleback Church in Southern California, Joel Hunter's Northland Church in central Florida, and Rich Nathan's Vineyard Church in Columbus, Ohio. All deserve more space than they will get in this chapter but can at least be introduced here.

Rick Warren has become the most influential pastor in the United States. His two *Purpose Driven* books (on churches and personal life) have sold tens of millions of copies and created Warren disciples all over the American landscape.[31] Tens of thousands stream into his Saddleback Church every weekend. He is constantly in the news. By now it is probably fair to say that if Billy Graham has a successor in American religious life, it is Rick Warren.

Thus it is no small matter that Warren has moved his ministry and his message squarely into the evangelical center. Warren has embraced the broad, holistic public-policy agenda that I have suggested is a key characteristic of the evangelical center. He is pro-life and pro-family but also pro-foreign aid, pro-debt relief, and pro-AIDS funding in Africa. His church is investing deeply in a ministry in Rwanda (P.E.A.C.E.) that is addressing poverty, disease, AIDS, and illiteracy, and he is seeking to enlist millions of Christians in such efforts. He has also publicly rejected the moral legitimacy of torture and signed the ECI global warming statement, both actions clearly differentiating him from the right.

Joel Hunter also has emerged in recent years as an articulate advocate of a centrist evangelical agenda. Hunter is the pastor of a unique, multisite nondenominational megachurch in central Florida that serves 12,000 people every weekend. Like most Americans, I first learned of Hunter in late 2006. He had just been named president of the Christian Coalition (CC), the fading evangelical right group described earlier in this book. I knew that Hunter was a signer of the ECI global-warming statement, and so I was happily surprised to learn that he had been named president of CC. We spoke on the phone, and I wished him Godspeed as he attempted the historic task of, as I put it, turning an evangelical right organization into a centrist group. I was therefore disappointed but not quite surprised when the news broke shortly thereafter that he and the board of CC had not been able to move forward together. There are few more apt symbols of the difference between the evangelical right and center than Hunter's abortive presidency of the Christian Coalition. Hunter's explicit political independence, his concerns about global warming, his signature on "An Evangelical Declaration Against Torture," and his support for antipoverty programs all clearly situate him in the evangelical center.

With Rich Nathan and the Vineyard churches we are dealing not just with an individual church or pastor but what may be emerging as a centrist evangelical network of churches that essentially amounts to a denomination. There are 650 Vineyard churches in the United States and over 1500 worldwide. Founded in 1983 under the primary leadership of John Wimber, Vineyard churches are theologically evangelical with a charismatic twist, and they reflect an organizing theological emphasis on the kingdom of God that is actually rather unusual in evangelical circles, while being highly congenial to someone like me who has cowritten a book called *Kingdom Ethics*.[32]

The Vineyard churches seem to be emerging as evangelical centrists. I do not know the movement well enough to know why this is the case. Perhaps it is the central emphasis on the kingdom of God, God's reign over all the earth and all that happens here; if so, it would not be the first time this has happened. Vineyard pastor Rich Nathan certainly sounds all of the notes that have come to characterize the evangelical center or even the left: He has opposed torture, emphasized peacemaking and concern for the poor, and addressed racial and gender discrimination. His church supports fair-trade coffee and offers free legal services to anyone needing help—including, for example, illegal aliens. Vineyardites keep turning up in the evangelical center. The national director of all Vineyard churches, Berten Waggoner, signed the "Evangelical Declaration Against Torture." A Vineyard pastor, Ken Wilson, has been deeply involved in evangelical environmental efforts. I think I am noticing a broader tendency for at least some in the charismatic and Pentecostal branches of the evangelical world (beyond the Vineyard churches) to trend in a more centrist direction on a number of social issues. It could be that part of the emergence of the evangelical center will be a growing voice for centrist/progressive charismatic Christians, a community that represents the fastest-growing edge of evangelical Christianity both here and around the world.

TO THE CENTER FROM THE NEXT GENERATION
What Young Evangelicals Are Singing

As a college professor, I notice the kinds of music my students are listening to. At Christian colleges, that music tends to be explicitly Christian. It emerges from that vast "undiscovered country" (to the middle-aged) of music that young people find significant in their lives. Perhaps at no other time in life is music as important to most people as it is when they are teenagers and young adults.

A few years ago a student suggested that I listen to a Christian musician named Derek Webb. I discovered a young man whose lyrics fit almost perfectly with what I am calling the evangelical center.

Webb, who is in his early thirties, began his career as part of a mainstream Christian music band called Caedmon's Call. But in an interview, Webb implies that he grew weary of the apolitical and unprophetic music that he and most Christian artists had been producing.[33] Indeed, anyone who spends much time listening to (white) contemporary Christian music knows that it is dominated by praise and worship motifs and rarely offers much moral content at all—especially not moral content of a holistic variety. It also rarely demonstrates any awareness of the broader social and political landscape in which evangelical Christians sing their praise and worship songs. Sadly, it is music by comfortable white people for comfortable white people.

Webb set out to change that, and his music—especially his CD called *Mockingbird*, does so. In one song, "A King and a Kingdom," he attacks the identification of Christ as "a white, middle-class Republican." In an interview, he explicitly rejects the identification of Jesus' moral concerns with those of, well, white middle-class Republicans. "The people he loved most lavishly were often socially stigmatized, and he reserved some of his harshest language for law-keeping church leadership." Webb's songs are morally sophisticated in a quite striking way. Even in just the one song already mentioned, "A King and a Kingdom," he alludes to a biblical inclusiveness in relation to immigrants, the lordship of Christ the king over against all worldly or national loyalties, and the danger of our enemy-making when the real enemy may reside within our very souls.

In "My Enemies Are Men Like Me," Webb somehow manages to see the fundamental gospel problematic of war and to oppose it without taking the pure pacifist line—which is also where the evangelical center lands:

> how can i kill the ones i'm supposed to love
>   my enemies are men like me
> I will protest the sword if it's not wielded well
>   my enemies are men like me

Later in the song he links war and poverty in a memorable line:

> when justice is bought and sold just like weapons of war
>   the ones who always pay are the poorest of the poor.[34]

On the whole, Webb manages to keep together a theologically orthodox evangelical commitment with a rejection of the knee-jerk political conservatism that so often goes with it. Like many of my own students, he wants to break the often seemingly unbreakable connection between the one and the other. One might say that these are the birth pangs of the evangelical center (and left) in the next generation.

Music reflects the artist's life experiences and passions. Those who suffer misery and injustice will often sing about it. Those who do not know such experiences cannot sing about them. Christian rap and hip-hop, just like some secular versions of the same kind of music, often resonates with the experiences of the streets. A song like "Cry No More" by rap artist KJ-52, tells the wrenching story of the songwriter's victimization by a stranger who raped him when he was just seven years old, a kid trying to walk down the street. The song concludes movingly with affirmation that God has healed him and left him able to forgive the one who abused him. There is no political agenda here. But songs like these do call the Christian listener's attention to a world of sorrow and the need to address its problems and love its victims. This helps us see once again how the religious and moral agenda of the urban, the poor, and the nonwhite in America will *never* be able to be oblivious to these kinds of social-justice issues. They are the daily bread of the least fortunate in our land.

Alternative strands of Christian music also point to a range of moral and social-justice themes. I don't dare to say whether these bands are more clearly left or center. But the lyrics and the lifestyles of groups such as the psalters, mewithoutYou, Five Iron Frenzy, Stretch Arm Strong, the Seeds, and others reflect many of the themes we have considered in this chapter. They appeal to young people, including young evangelicals who, quite frankly, do not care what Dobson or for that matter Cizik or Wallis, really think. (They probably don't care what anybody over forty thinks—so I'm irrelevant too!) It is a commonplace to say that the future rests with the young. The young people that I know generally would agree with (evangelical centrist) former Bush speechwriter Michael Gerson when he says, "There are lots and lots of young people . . . who are very impatient with older models of social engagement like those used by the Religious Right. They understand the importance of the life issues and the family issues, but they know that concern for justice has to be broader and global."[35] This comment was quoted approvingly in a 2006 article in *Relevant* magazine, widely read by twentysomething evangelicals.[36] Their favorite organizations, their music, and their magazine offer just a few of the signals indicating that younger evangelicals may be primed and ready to join the emerging evangelical center.

PART II

FINDING THE CENTER
Key Issues for Evangelical Public Engagement

Chapter 5

TORTURE AND HUMAN RIGHTS

Amazingly, the evangelical community in America remains grotesquely silent about [torture].
Silence in a court of law implies agreement, and the court of world opinion watches and waits
for an evangelical response.

—*Christianity Today* reader Dan Karns, 2005

I became involved in addressing the torture issue only after a request from the editors of *Christianity Today* in late 2005. I regret that I had not really focused on the issue before that time. But other evangelicals had been paying attention, and apparently the sentiments of readers like Dan Karns struck home with the editorial team at evangelicalism's flagship magazine. They asked me to write what became a cover article, released in February 2006. (A version of it is adapted in this chapter.) At about the same time, I was asked to speak to a conference at Princeton Seminary hosted by the new National Religious Campaign Against Torture (NRCAT). I was one of two evangelicals to address the conference; the other was the evangelical stalwart Gary Haugen of International Justice Mission (IJM), whose impressive ministry I discussed in chapter 4. The interreligious gathering was hungry for evangelical involvement and certainly knew the significance of evangelical opinion in this country.

These two requests for involvement—one from inside the evangelical community and one from outside—pushed me toward commitment to a moral issue on which evangelicals remain largely silent.

Actually, it is worse than that. It's worse than silence. After I wrote my article for *Christianity Today*, I discovered that there is indeed an evangelical constituency for torture. Their opinions were quite visible on the *Christianity Today*, Web site, on the blogs and message boards, and in some quite nasty personal letters I received. Among a people who are marked by their supposedly Christ-centered worldview are some who find no conflict between Jesus and waterboarding, as long as it is purportedly in the interests of national security. I was astonished by this. I remain astonished by this.

But this is not the last word on evangelicals and torture. In the late summer of 2006 a small group of evangelicals was approached by NRCAT to talk about what more could be done to encourage evangelicals to think seriously about the issue of torture as it had emerged in the "war on terror." Working with seed money provided by NRCAT, a steering committee (with me as chair; and Ron Sider, Glen Stassen, Rich Cizik, and staffer Mary Head) began work.

In September 2006, this group, which eventually took the name Evangelicals for Human Rights (EHR), pulled together a distinguished drafting committee to write a major evangelical statement on torture. The drafting committee revised and polished multiple drafts of the document until the group felt that they could improve it no more.

In March of 2007, "An Evangelical Declaration Against Torture: Protecting Human Rights in an Age of Terror" (see appendix 3 for full text, plus signatories) was endorsed by the National Assocation of Evangelicals (NAE) board, bringing much attention to the declaration and initiating its public release. During that same month, a Web site (www.evangelicalsforhumanrights.org) was launched to provide resources for churches and organizations, as well as up-to-date news and legislation, essays, articles, and reports related to human rights, torture, and U.S. detention centers.

The media coverage was impressive; the Associated Press, Reuters, *The New York Times*, the *Washington Post*, and ABC News are only a few examples of those who covered "An Evangelical Declaration Against

Torture." The statement was also featured in countless blogs, was passed along through networks of influential evangelical educators, pastors, lawyers, writers, and leaders, and was used in a number of churches. The full twenty-page declaration was presented in a summer 2007 edition of the *Review of Faith and International Affairs*. The number of EHR resources on our Web site for churches and organizations continues to grow. The organization, which I continue to lead as president, will continue as a voice of conscience at least through 2008.

Of course, all of this activity has not gone unchallenged. My analysis would be that the evangelical left and center are coalescing around a total rejection of torture and of the other human rights violations (like indefinite detention without habeas corpus or other legal recourse) that have occurred in the war on terror. We are willing to acknowledge and face up to the wrongs that were done at Abu Ghraib, Bagram Air Base in Afghanistan, Guantanamo Bay, and apparently in CIA "black sites" in various unknown locations. We have seen the evidence that these were not just the acts of a few "bad apples," but instead (at least in part) reflections of tragic shifts in government policy that can be documented by their paper trail. We recognize that both executive branch decisions and certain legislative provisions intended to facilitate prosecution of the war on terror have crossed moral and probably constitutional boundary lines.

One could wish that the evangelical right would come along with us on this one, but so far they have not budged. There is (apparently) always some problem with every statement made and every article written by any evangelical who is opposed to torture. We are charged with failing to define torture clearly enough. Or we are not concerned about national security. Or we are not adequately addressing the possible ticking-time-bomb scenario, where a terrorist has a bomb in New York and someone might need to be tortured to stop it. Or this is a new kind of war requiring new kinds of means. Or we should simply employ just-war criteria, which allow the use of the maximum necessary coercion, which might include torture.

Sometimes the attacks are ad hominem—this is just a "religious left" slam on the Bush administration; a bunch of pacifists got together who do not care anything about military strategy and needs; we are a front group for the Democrats. And so on. I believe that the substantive criticisms are addressed adequately on the EHR Web site and in my published writings about torture. The guilt-by-association and ad hominem attacks are worth no response. And one purpose of writing this book is to say that to oppose the hard right is not to be "religious left"; it might mean to be "center," or even simply "moral" or "constitutional" or "Christian." It is my fond hope that the evangelical right will come to see that remaining silent in the face of torture, or quibbling over definitions while doing nothing to oppose torture, or even justifying torture, marks a disastrous Christian moral failure that deeply wounds our public witness in every way. My ongoing efforts on this issue within the evangelical community are grounded in this goal: *to help delegitimize torture within the entire evangelical community*, eventually making opposition to torture a consensus evangelical position.

To make that case, I offer the following moral analysis of torture.

VIGNETTES OF TORTURE

"Three marines in Mahmudiya used an electric transformer, forcing a detainee to 'dance' as the electricity coursed through him."[1]

"On another occasion DETAINEE-07 was forced to lie down while M.P.'s jumped on his back and legs. He was beaten with a broom and a chemical light was broken and poured over his body. . . . During this abuse a police stick was used to sodomize DETAINEE-07 and two female M.P.'s were hitting him, throwing a ball at his penis, and taking photographs."[2]

"A dog was allowed in the cell of two male juveniles and allowed to go 'nuts.' Both juveniles were screaming and crying, with the youngest and smallest trying to hide behind the other juvenile."[3]

"They threw pepper on my face and the beating started. This went on for a half hour. And then he started beating me with the chair until the chair was broken. After that they started choking me. . . . And then they started beating me again. They concentrated on beating me in my heart until they got tired from beating me."[4]

A detainee "had been hooded, handcuffed in the back, and made to lie down, on a hot surface during transportation. This had caused severe skin burns that required three months' hospitalization."[5]

"In November 2002, an inexperienced CIA case officer allegedly ordered guards to strip naked an uncooperative young detainee, chain him to the concrete floor, and leave him there overnight without blankets. He froze to death, according to four U.S. government officials."[6]

"al-Qatani was forced to perform dog tricks on a leash, was straddled by a female interrogator, forced to dance with a male interrogator, told that his mother and sister were whores, forced to wear a woman's bra and thong on his head during interrogation, and subjected to an unmuzzled dog to scare him."[7]

A former Iraqi general "died of asphyxiation after being stuffed head-first into a sleeping bag . . . at an American base in Al Asad."[8]

UNDERSTANDING TORTURE

The word *torture*, tellingly, comes from the Latin *torquere*, to twist. While definitions are contested, Webster's Dictionary can get us started in its claim that torture is "the inflicting of severe pain to force information and confes¬sion, get revenge, etc." Our concern here, though, is not just with any purposeful infliction of severe pain, but with that severe pain inflicted by someone who acts on behalf of a state and in its perceived interests.

According to international law scholar Lisa Hajjar, the governmental context is the key to understanding torture.[9] It involves "purposefully harming someone who is in custody—unfree to fight back or protect himself or herself and imperiled by that incapacitation." For Hajjar, the definition of torture hinges not so much on the specific details of various kinds of harm that human beings can do to one another, but on the fact that the tortured are prisoners in the custody of a government. They are people on whom suffering is inflicted for some public purpose.

This helps us understand our current situation. The unresolved debate in our nation concerns whether various kinds of harm can be inflicted by those serving our government upon prisoners who are in our custody. Most particularly, the debate focuses on what kinds of measures legitimately can be taken to extract information from prisoners held by us in the "war on terror" and/or the wars in Afghanistan and

Iraq. As such, it is a debate about the proper use of government power in a liberal democracy.

As to the exact kinds of acts that constitute torture, there is no single precise definition—they seem to fall along a continuum, but this does not signify that the meaning of the term is infinitely elastic. International agreements that deal with torture provide some clues. The 1948 Universal Declaration of Human Rights simply states that "no one shall be subjected to torture or to cruel, inhuman, or degrading treatment."[10] Article 17 of the Third Geneva Convention (1949) asserts that "no physical or mental torture, nor any other form of coercion, may be inflicted on prisoners of war," but instead, "persons taking no active part in the hostilities . . . shall in all circumstances be treated humanely."[11] The 1985 UN Convention Against Torture defines it as "any act by which severe pain or suffering, whether physical or mental, is intentionally inflicted on a person."[12]

The United States is a signatory to all of these international declarations and historically has incorporated their principles into military doctrine. For example, the U.S. Army Field Manual tells soldiers that "[Geneva] and U.S. policy expressly prohibit acts of violence or intimidation, including physical or mental torture, threats [or] insults . . . as a means of or aid to interrogation."[13] These boundary lines were clearly crossed in the years just after 9/11, but fortunately the Pentagon has rethought its position. The most recent revision (2006) of the Army Field Manual, "Human Intelligence Collector Operations," specifically rules out acts that we know occurred during the four years after 9/11.[14] These now-prohibited acts are enumerated as follows: forcing the detainee to be naked, perform sexual acts, or pose in a sexual manner, exposing an individual to outrageously lewd and sexually provocative behavior, intentionally damaging or destroying an individual's religious articles, placing hoods or sacks over the head of a detainee; using duct tape over the eyes, applying beatings, electric shock, burns, or other forms of physical pain, "waterboarding," using military working dogs, inducing hypothermia or heat injury, conducting mock executions, and depriving the detainee of necessary food, water, or medical care.

Mark Bowden, a military scholar and author of *Black Hawk Down*, reminds us that torture is "a crude and ancient tool of political oppression," practiced by governments for various reasons through the centuries and by many still in our own time.[15] The kinds of acts most often classified as torture make for a dreary catalog of pain. They include slicing tongues out, beatings with clubs, use of electric cattle prods, employment of mind-altering drugs, sticking pins under or through fingernails, cutting off fingers, hands, ears, noses, or other body parts, and so on. There is no end to inventive ways of harming the bodies and minds of other human beings.

When President Bush says of the United States that "we do not torture," perhaps these latter kinds of acts are what he has in mind. But it is now clear that after September 11th, elements within the Bush administration, chafing under the perceived constraints of the ban against torture, attempted to carve out room for acts that brushed up against the boundary line separating aggressive interrogation from torture without (they believed) crossing over it. Called "enhanced interrogation techniques," "professional interrogation," "moderate physical pressure," or even (by outside analysts) "torture lite," these included a variety of measures, some approved as policy by our government and others not publicly acknowledged or approved but found by both independent and government investigators to have occurred in our detention facilities. They included many of the acts now banned by the Pentagon.

The abuses appear to have been particularly prevalent in military intelligence interrogations, among private U.S. contractors serving the military, among the underprepared and poorly trained military police at places like Abu Ghraib, and apparently in some CIA interrogations. Though the Pentagon has now explicitly rejected many of these precise techniques and practices, no such ban has been applied in relation to the "high value" detainees that may or may not still be held by the CIA. And there is considerable evidence of mistreatment of prisoners "rendered" to other countries (many known to practice torture) by our government. Lack of any independent access to such sites or prisoners makes it impossible to know what is happening in these cases. It cannot be said with certainty that the practice of torture or acts tantamount to torture by our government or with the implicit consent of our government has ended.

WHERE AND HOW IS TORTURE PROHIBITED?

The ban on torture in international law, as Hajjar notes, "is stronger than almost any other human right because the prohibition of torture is absolutely non-derogable and because the law recognizes no exceptions. What this means is that no one—ever, anywhere—has a 'right' to torture, and that everyone—always, everywhere—has a right not to be tortured. It also means that anyone who engages in or abets torture is committing a crime."[16]

The prohibition on torture has been understood since the late 1940s as both a matter of fundamental human rights and a right accorded to prisoners of war. In other words, no human being may be tortured, just because they are human. And no prisoner of war may be tortured, not just because they are human but particularly because they are prisoners of war and as such are covered by various protections in international law. Both understandings were deeply affected by the atrocities that occurred against civilians and POWs during World War II.

This ban on torture has roots deep in the emergence of liberal democracy because, as Michael Ignatieff has written, "liberal democracy stands against any unlimited use of public authority against human beings, and torture is the most unlimited, most unbridled form of power that one person can exercise against another."[17] Therefore it is one of the strongest international legal prohibitions in existence; once ratified and codified by states, it becomes part of each nation's law as well. Hajjar points out that at least in legal terms the right not to be tortured is actually stronger than the right to life: "There are many circumstances in which people legally can be killed, but none under which people legally can be tortured."[18] For example, it is perfectly legal (however tragic) to kill an enemy combatant in wartime, but not at all legal to take that same person into custody, disarm him, and then torture him.

And this prohibition on torture in international law quite explicitly admits no exceptions. The United Nations Convention Against Torture puts it this way: "No exceptional circumstances whatsoever, whether a state of war or a threat of war, internal political instability or any other public emergency, may be invoked as a justification for torture."[19]

The United States ratified this convention in 1994, before September 11th, before our launch of the war on terror. Now many Americans believe that acts at least tantamount to torture are indeed morally permissible in the exceptional case posed by Islamist terrorism. As State Department official Cofer Black famously put it: "All I want to say is that there was before 9/11 and after 9/11. After 9/11 the gloves came off."[20] Here is why I believe that, regardless of September 11th, the absolute prohibition of torture remains a moral and legal norm that should not be weakened.

A Moral Analysis of Torture

Let me begin by granting the obligation of government to preserve public order and protect the security of its population. This principle is recognized in international law, moral thought, and public opinion. For Christians, it is clearly stated in Romans 13:1-7, which is an important text for evangelicals. Government deters violations of peace and order, punishes wrongdoers, and does all it can to advance the common good within the limits of its mandate. This work of government does involve the sword; that is, coercion, and in necessary cases, violence. Various legal and moral restrictions are placed on government as it exercises this fearsome power. It is generally understood that government officials must use the minimum force necessary to accomplish their missions.

Let me also grant that the terrorist attack of September 11th was one of the most heinous acts ever visited on this nation and a clear violation of the laws of war and of any kind of civilized moral code. Terrorist acts around the world since then remind us that our nation, along with many others, faces the threat of enemies who do not adhere to the kinds of moral scruples that we are considering here.

Finally, I also grant the point that Bowden makes in arguing that there is a built-in tension between what he calls the "warrior ethic" and the "civilian ethic."[21] For the warrior, the goal is to accomplish the mission. For the civilian, the goal is to preserve the rule of law. Even if we grant that well-intentioned warriors also recognize the importance of the rule of law and that well-intentioned civilians recognize the importance of accomplishing the mission, their passions and priorities tend to differ. They will always stand in some tension with each other. Managing this tension is a major challenge in any civilized society. I acknowledge that I write from the civilian side.

So I do not write to demonize those who believe that protecting our nation's security and preventing the horror of another September 11 requires the use of interrogation techniques that could be classified as at least borderline torture. But I do believe that the case against this move is far stronger than the case for it. Here is why:

Torture violates the intrinsic dignity of the human being, made in the image of God. As evangelicals constantly profess, the human person is a creation of God. Every inch of the human body and every aspect of the human spirit come from God and bear witness to his handiwork. We are made in the image of God (Gen 1:26-28). Human dignity (value, worth) comes as a permanent and ineradicable endowment of the creator, to every person.

Recognition of the intrinsic dignity of the human being requires a corresponding restraint in our behavior toward all human beings. Christians, at least, should be trained to see in every person the imprint of God's grandeur. This should create in us a sense of reverence or even sacredness. Here, we say—and we say it even of detainees in the war on terror—is a human being sacred in God's sight, made in God's image, someone for whom Christ died. No one is *ever* "subhuman" or "human debris," as Rush Limbaugh has described some of our adversaries in Iraq.[22] An inchoate sense of the proper reverence due to every human being makes its way even into secular and public codes, such as international legal documents. These texts may not be able to say why human beings should be treated with respect, but they know that this is in fact a binding obligation. Christians can say why: because this "detainee," even this "terrorist," if he is one, is a child of God, made in God's image.

A moral commitment to the dignity of the human being is sometimes fleshed out in terms of human rights. Just because they are human, on this view, people have rights to many things, including the right not to be tortured. Christians sometimes debate the legitimacy of "rights talk," partly because it is a language often overused in modern debate and partly because we think about how Jesus gave up all of his "rights." Just because someone claims a right does not mean that it is a right. But I believe that at least an implication of a biblical understanding of human dignity is the existence of a set of human rights. Among the most widely recognized of these in both legal and moral theory is the right to bodily integrity; that is, the right not to have intentional physical and psychological harm inflicted upon oneself by others. The ban on torture is one expression of the right to bodily integrity.

The absoluteness of such human rights can be debated. Following the categories of Catholic moral reasoning, Robert G. Kennedy has argued that even the most widely recognized human rights, such as the right to life or the right not to be tortured, are absolute in *existence* but not *extent*. What this means is that while the right not to be tortured applies to all people, like all rights it can, at least in theory, be qualified by other rights and by the requirements of justice. Kennedy argues that "defensive interrogatory torture" (and only this kind of torture) may be morally legitimate under very carefully qualified conditions. And yet he goes on to argue that "it is quite likely that most instances in which interrogatory torture is employed would not conform to these principles and so would be immoral."[23]

Whether we open the door to torture just a crack, as Kennedy suggests, or keep it firmly shut as an absolute ban, as I believe, the principle of human dignity and its correlated rights remains a transcendently important reason to resist the turn toward torture. And because rights correspond with obligations, all of us who recognize the human right not to be tortured have an obligation to protect that right. This is an obligation—I say it with sorrow—that as Christians, and as Americans, we have not been meeting.

*T*orture *mistreats the vulnerable and thus violates the demands of public justice.* Lisa Hajjar points out that torture, by definition, is something that a government does to a person in its custody.[24] Imprisoned people are vulnerable people. Whatever they did, or may be suspected of having done, once in our hands they are completely vulnerable to us.

Justice has many meanings and can be defined in many ways. But it is clear in the scriptures that God's understanding of justice tilts in the direction of the vulnerable. "Do not mistreat an alien or oppress him, for you were aliens in Egypt. Do not take advantage of a widow or an orphan. If you do and they cry out to me, I will certainly hear their cry" (Exod 22:21-23 NIV). As this text suggests, primary forms of injustice include the violent abuse and domination of the powerless by the powerful and their exclusion from participation in a community that cares about their rights and needs. Evangelicals purport to care about justice and the vulnerable. Here is a good test case of the extent of that care.

One reason why there are so many layers of procedures and protections given to accused and imprisoned people in our legal system (and to prisoners of war in international law) is precisely their powerlessness at the hands of government authority. Justice requires attempting to balance the scales so that defenseless people are not overpowered or abused by governments. This is especially important in any legal system, which has the power to deprive people of their liberty, and sometimes their lives.

The tens of thousands of people who have been detained by our government and military in the last four years are, by definition, as prisoners, vulnerable to injustice. Those of them who have been abused or mistreated by representatives of our nation—as in the examples cited in this chapter—are victims of injustice, however carefully we may define or excuse the treatment that we have meted out to them. They were in our hands and we abused our power over them. They were dominated, harmed, abused, and sometimes violated physically, even murdered. Christians must learn to care about justice; more, we must develop a deep passion for justice, the kind of passion for justice that God has, the one who hears the cries of the oppressed and dominated (see Exod 2:23-25). Torture is an injustice and must be protested as such.

Authorizing any form of torture trusts government too much. Human beings are sinful through and through (see Rom 3:10-18). This is a critical claim of biblical faith and is deeply believed among evangelicals. We are not to be trusted. We are especially dangerous when unchecked power is concentrated in our hands. This applies to all of us.

So certainly it is likely that authorizing even the "lightest" forms of torture risks much abuse. As Richard John Neuhaus puts it, "We dare not trust ourselves to torture."[25] Or as Gary Haugen wrote, "Because the power of the state over detainees is exercised by fallen human beings, that power must be limited by clear boundaries, and individuals exercising such power must be transparently accountable."[26] This conforms entirely to the logic of the entire mission of IJM.

Haugen rightly emphasizes both the procedural and substantive regulation of detainee interrogation. Given human sinfulness, it is not just that people should be told not to torture, but also that structures of due process, accountability, and transparency must buttress those standards to make them less likely to be violated and subject to redress if violated. This is what is so dangerous about the use of secret CIA prisons and other unreachable and unaccountable sites. As Manfred Nowak, UN special rapporteur on torture said at the time the CIA's secret prisons were revealed, "Every secret place of detention is usually a higher risk for ill treatment, that's the danger of secrecy."[27] Just because U.S. government officials say that we can be trusted to act "in keeping with our values"—without due process, accountability, and transparency—does not make it so. No government is so virtuous as to be able to overturn the too often verified laws of human nature or to be beyond the need for democratic checks and balances.

Torture invites the dehumanization of the torturer. In reflecting on torture, Mark Bowden concludes that sometimes it is the right choice. But even so, he worries, "how does one allow it yet still control it? Sadism is deeply rooted in the human psyche. Every army has its share of soldiers who delight in kicking and beating bound captives. Men in authority tend to abuse it—not all men, but many. As a mass, they should be assumed to lean toward abuse."[28]

Loosening long-standing restrictions on physical and mental cruelty toward prisoners risks the dehumanization not just of the tortured but the torturers. What may be intended as carefully calibrated interrogation techniques easily tempt their implementers in the direction of sadism—pain infliction for the sheer fun of it—especially in the heat of military conflict, in a climate of fear and loathing of the enemy, and in the context of an endless war on terror. How many of us could be trusted to draw the line consistently between the permitted grabbing, poking, and pushing, on the one hand, and the banned punching, slapping, and kicking, on the other? How much self-control can we reasonably expect people to exercise? And once the line has been crossed to torture, as Michael Ignatieff claims, it "inflicts irremediable harm on both the torturer and the prisoner."[29]

Frederick Douglass commented famously on how holding a slave slowly ruined the character of the woman who owned him. Martin Luther King Jr. frequently talked about how in a sense the greatest victims of segregation were the white people whose souls were deformed by their own hatred. Aleksandr Solzhenitsyn, reflecting on the Soviet Gulag, said that "our torturers have been punished most horribly of all: they are turning into swine, they are departing downward from humanity."[30]

War threatens the dehumanization of all sides and all parties. This is why there are so many limits placed on how wars may be fought. The ban on torture is one of those limits, and for good reason.

Torture erodes the character of the nation that tortures. A nation is a collective moral entity with a character, an identity across time. Causes come and go, threats come and go, but the enduring question for any social entity is who "we" are as a people. This is true of a family, a church, a school, a civic club, or a town. It is certainly true of a nation. Evangelicals across the board profess to care about character.

Senator John McCain, who has consistently opposed the drift toward torture, has said, "This isn't about who they are. This is about who we are. These are the values that distinguish us from our enemies."[31] In a *Newsweek* article, he put it this way:

> What I . . . mourn is what we lose when . . . we allow, confuse, or encourage our soldiers to forget that best sense of ourselves, that which is our greatest strength—that we are different and better than our enemies, that we fight for an idea, not a tribe, not a land, not a king . . . but for an idea that all men are created equal and endowed by their Creator with inalienable rights.[32]

McCain is saying something very important here. His worry is that any move toward torture threatens our national character, our shared values, and our goodness as a nation. He rightly acknowledges that our Islamist terrorist enemies do not share our commitment to the rule of law, to human rights, to procedural justice, to limits on what can be done for the cause, however holy. This is tragic, even evil, and it makes them a particularly lethal and insidious threat, but it does not somehow settle the question of how we as a nation should respond.

We often say in evangelical circles that people of integrity respond to life on the basis of scriptural principles, not preferences, feelings, or circumstances. We act on the basis of who we are, not who others are. If someone is ruthless to us at work, this does not authorize biblical people to be equally ruthless in return. If people violate their covenant with us, it does not authorize us to do the same to them. Mature people, and nations, know what their core values are and seek to act in every circumstance in a manner consistent with those values. If they abandon those values when severely tested, it raises real questions as to how deeply such values were ever held.

*T*orture *risks negative consequences at many levels.* Those who know anything about moral theory know that the argument for torture is essentially a utilitarian one. Some are willing to torture because they believe it is the best means available to protect the 300 million people who live in this country. Hundreds—thousands—of (foreign) detainees suffer as the price of protecting millions of us. Thus we achieve the greatest good for the greatest number of people. Many protorture evangelicals have made such arguments, despite the general conservative evangelical abhorrence of utilitarian thought. It is a sad contradiction.

Utilitarianism (as evangelicals once knew) is a deeply flawed moral theory. In emphasizing intrinsic human dignity and concerns about both personal and national character, I have implicitly rejected any purely utilitarian argument for (or against) torture. Indeed, because I believe that torture is intrinsically wrong, it poses a risk to the argument I am making even to entertain utilitarian considerations. But because many policymakers and citizens at least implicitly operate from a utilitarian framework, it must be addressed here.

The greatest gain promised by the resort to torture is that it might extract information from suspects that would otherwise be unavailable. In the most sensational and widely discussed scenario—the so-called ticking-bomb case—utilitarians argue strongly that the torture of one terrorist at a pivotal moment could in turn save thousands of lives, and thus it must be permitted.

In a brilliant utilitarian analysis of what an institutionalized torture regime might look like and what its consequences might be, Jean

Marie Arriga has suggested a number of difficulties even for a utilitarian approach to torture.[33]

For example, and as many others have noted, there is abundant evidence that people will say anything under torture, just to stop the pain. It is not just that they will be intentionally deceptive, but even more that after sufficient torture they may lack the mental ability to distinguish between truth and falsehood or to convey the truth. If the goal of torture is to extract critical information, these problems are obviously profound. Several news agencies have reported that information apparently gained from torture has proven false—after being announced as an important intelligence score by the U.S. government. The overall reliability of intelligence gained from torture remains the subject of great controversy.

The ultimate goal in gaining this information is to protect national security. However, there is good reason to wonder whether the use of torture more deeply motivates extant terrorists and turns more people from concerned bystanders into hardened terrorists than any intelligence benefit that might be gained. An editorial in the *Vancouver Sun* put it well: "Those subjected to physical torture usually conceive undying hatred for their torturers."[34] One must therefore also consider the greater likelihood that American civilians (here or especially abroad) and American troops overseas will be subject to torture (or terror) by aggrieved enemies.

Further, as has already happened, sometimes the consequences of torture are worse than intended, as when victims die prematurely as a result of the physical or mental toll. From a utilitarian perspective the main problem here is that a dead person cannot give you any information whatsoever. And, of course, as news of deaths trickle out, moral outrage scandalizes the torturer's own people, the families and communities of the people who have died in custody, and general world opinion.

Arriga's most original insights concern the unintended but likely institutional consequences that can and often do flow from a torture regime. For example, medical and psychological practitioners become involved in enhancing and medically managing torture techniques, thereby risking the corruption of these institutions, which are supposed to serve as agents of healing—or evoking their opposition. Biomedical specialists are recruited to study and develop torture, and torture resistance, techniques. Special torture interrogation units are established, with training in especially sophisticated methods of torture and a consequent demoralization and negative effect on other governmental and security institutions. The use of rogue torture interrogation services, such as organized crime, covert U.S. torture agencies, and brutal foreign intelligence services also poses severe problems in terms of command and control of torture operations and the empowerment of rogue elements here and abroad.[35] Arriga's article was published in 2004; one wonders how many of her concerns already are uncomfortably close to hitting their mark in our own case.

The ticking bomb case is theoretically important but in actuality, a red herring. It has been wisely said that "bad cases make bad law," and this is true here. The percentage of such ticking bomb cases among the tens of thousands we have detained must be less than infinitesimal. It is just as foolish to legitimize the practice of torture because of this rare possible exception as it would be, say, to legitimize the practice of adultery because of the possibility that someone might have to commit adultery to save their child's life from a criminal who demands sex in exchange for the child's survival.

Much ink has been spilled considering how to handle these rare ticking-bomb cases. Perhaps the most widely discussed proposal has been Alan Dershowitz's suggestion that we permit torture only through a "torture warrant" signed by a judge or a very high government official, such as the president himself, who would therefore bear full legal, political, and moral responsibility.[36]

This would certainly be better than what we have been doing. But I think that any potential resort to torture in rare, ticking bomb cases would be better handled within the context of an outright ban. The grand moral tradition of civil disobedience, for example, specifies that there are instances in which obedience to laws must be overridden by loyalty to a higher moral obligation. These instances usually involve unjust laws, but this is not always the case. Dietrich Bonhoeffer participated in an assassination plot against Hitler but did not argue for the rewriting of moral prohibitions of political assassinations. He was prepared to let God and history be his judge. If a one-in-a-million instance were to emerge in which a responsible official believed that the ban on torture must be overridden as a matter of necessity and emergency response, let him do so knowing fully that he would have to answer for his action before God, law, and neighbor. This is a long way from an authorized-torture regime.

AGAINST TORTURE

Long ago, German philosopher Immanuel Kant wrote about the perennial human tendency to find exceptions to binding moral rules when those obligations bind just a bit too tightly on *us*. "Hence there arises a natural . . . disposition to argue against these strict laws of duty and to question their validity, or at least their purity and strictness; and, if possible, to make them more accordant with our wishes and inclinations, that is to say, to corrupt them at their very source, and entirely to destroy their worth."[37]

I believe that this is the best explanation for what has happened on the issue of torture in our nation. *Our current crisis represents our succumbing to the temptation to waive moral rules that we have every reason to know are applicable to us.* They are part of international law, military law, and moral law. They reflect clear biblical teaching widely embraced by evangelicals, a group that claims to adhere strictly to God's Word. We would certainly not want our troops or our "detainees" or ourselves to be tortured were the shoe on the other foot. We know that torture is wrong, but just not now, not in our exceptional case, not in this global war on terror. We are tempted to follow the logic of a *Time* magazine article when it says, "In the war on terrorism, the personal dignity of a fanatic trained for mass murder may be an inevitable casualty."[38]

And yet we are queasy enough about even this "inevitable casualty" that we do not want to call *torture* torture. We do not want to expose our policies or our prisons or our prisoners to public view. We deny that we are torturing, or we deny that our prisoners are really prisoners, or when pushed to the wall, we remind one another of how evil the enemy is. We give every evidence of the kind of self-deception so characteristic of the descent into sin. Why can't every evangelical identify this pattern for what it is?

It is past time for evangelical Christians to settle this issue and to offer a clear, united public voice against torture. We must shake free *now*, without any further delay, from our sluggish inattention to this issue, from any complicity with torture, and from our overall tendency toward comfortable partnership with (Republican) American government. We must speak truth to power here. We say we care about moral values and that we vote on the basis of such values. Many of us say that we care deeply about human rights violations around the world. Our concern about human rights violations directed and permitted by our own government must be just as deep.

This is a call to say a clear and unequivocal no to torture, ultimately on the grounds of evangelical faith, but not on the basis of any kind of idealistic withdrawal from realistic engagement with the world. It is time that we raise our voices and make ourselves heard in our churches, in Congress, in the judiciary, in the executive branch, and in public opinion.

Evangelical Christians have dual loyalties that do not always easily cohere. We are loyal to our nation but also, and always more fundamentally, to Jesus Christ. Sometimes these loyalties conflict. In this case, though, rightly understood, they do not.

We serve a tortured, crucified Savior. In the politics of a long ago empire, reasons of state appeared to require his torture and death. "It is better for you that one man die for the people than that the whole nation perish" (Jn 11:50).

I have sought to show that a proper understanding of our national well-being requires the rejection of torture. Now I want to close by saying that for evangelical Christians a proper understanding of our ultimate loyalty—to Jesus the tortured one—makes any support of torture unthinkable.

Chapter 6

MARRIAGE AND THE LAW

The hallmark of the evangelical right has been its stated concern about the well-being of the family. We have already seen that efforts to broaden the right's moral agenda beyond "family values" have been resisted strongly. The evangelical left seems to shrink from family issues as an aspect of their resistance to and distaste for the rhetoric of the evangelical right and maybe also because of their collegial relationships with left-leaning folks who resist the very notion of a God-given design for the family. The center, not fundamentally driven by resistance to the evangelical right or the secular left, ought to be able to articulate a fresh perspective on family issues. But so far little has been offered.

One place to start might be to do something that few have actually done—think seriously and comprehensively about marriage and divorce law. The evangelical right was launched in the 1970s and 1980s by its practical concern about family well-being—this was James Dobson at his best. Dobson and others taught couples how to date, mate, stay married, and raise their children well. Certainly there were elements of this teaching that did not reflect an evangelical consensus (gender roles, discipline stratagems), but the majority of evangelicals found this kind of profamily material quite helpful, and many still do. Even so, the broader trend was that evangelicals kept being miserable in marriage, kept divorcing, and kept producing dysfunctional kids, at about the same rate as everyone else in society. The constituency for the Christian right grew to include millions of divorced people, especially divorced women who were often single mothers. Efforts to stop the divorce runaway train seemed largely ineffectual. The public witness of evangelicals on divorce began to quiet, even while the therapists and dating services churned out books and programs designed to help couples.

Meanwhile, the press for full social acceptance of homosexuality, including gay marriage, began to intensify. Conservative evangelicals in the 1990s shifted their focus to the homosexuality issue. Most profamily activist efforts on the right now seem to involve stopping gay marriage or, really, preventing any social gain for homosexuals. Concrete proposals related to preventing heterosexual divorce or dealing with its aftereffects have become increasingly rare. Family values gets reduced to opposition to homosexuality or even homosexuals, which sometimes ends up seeming little better than a cover for antigay ostracism and discrimination. This is hardly a satisfying moral agenda for evangelicals in relation to the family.

Here is where the evangelical center has an opening. What if we stepped in to consider seriously the best way to craft marriage, divorce, and family law? And what if we made the well-being of children the focus of our concern? I suggest that this is the way forward. Evangelical centrists can lead a fundamental rethinking of marriage law, including the gay marriage issue, from this child-focused perspective. Perhaps this can enable right, left, and center evangelicals to find more common ground and therefore a common voice. Perhaps it can also lead to a demotion of the gay marriage issue to its proper (less central) place in evangelical public engagement on the family. It might also take a bit of the venom out of the culture wars on this issue.

This chapter—based partly on work previously published in my 2004 book on marriage—offers a top-to-bottom rethinking of marriage and divorce law. Its length reflects the seriousness of the task and the lack of much precedent for it.

❈ ❈ ❈

Evangelical Christians, like most traditional religious believers in the West, believe that marriage is a God-given institution intended to meet the needs of human beings made in the image of God. It is designed to be covenantal in its structure—a binding, sacred agreement between a man and woman who pledge their lives to each other, made in the presence of God and the gathered community (both religious and civic). This covenantal structure is also a provision made by God for our good, and it is equally essential to the proper functioning of the institution itself. Marriage belongs to the entire human family and is not an exclusively Christian institution. Therefore the health of marriage should be of concern to all thoughtful people. The obvious current decline of marriage in Western societies affects people of all faiths and no faith, especially the most vulnerable among us—our children.

For all of these reasons, it is appropriate for evangelical Christians to consider strategies to strengthen marriage that extend far beyond the boundaries of the church. Certainly our first task is to get our own house in order. Our divorce rate is appalling, and our overall paralysis in responding to divorce and its victims is equally appalling. So we begin at home. But we must also articulate a vigorous public witness about marriage in every venue we have available to us.

As a part of this effort, it is appropriate for us to press our representatives in government to take steps that might have the potential to strengthen marriage as an institution. The law undoubtedly matters a great deal in establishing the community context in which people undertake marriage and consider divorce. The law guards entry to, and exit from, marriage, either strengthening marriage as an institution or undermining its very foundation.

The reader may be surprised at the many proposals to strengthen marriage already being considered and implemented in the states. Evangelical Christians have played a role in advancing some of these. Others we have generally ignored. Careful examination of the options can help us catch a vision of what a centrist evangelical public witness on the family may look like in the years ahead.

ENTRY POINTS FOR LEGAL REFORM

Some evangelical Christians who are interested in the reform of divorce laws have tended to concentrate their fire on no-fault divorce. This focus is much too narrow. No-fault divorce, as we will discuss in more detail later, has to do specifically with the issue of how and on what grounds an individual or couple may enter into divorce. *Yet if we want to think coherently about addressing the divorce problem through legal means, we must look at the entire marriage and divorce law system.* The fundamental issue is marriage, not divorce.

Marriage is a relationship primarily governed by state law. Each of the fifty states offers a comprehensive system of laws governing the full range of activities related to marriage. The federal government relates to marriage primarily through welfare and tax policies, though in 1996 it did take a major step beyond this role in defining marriage as a relationship between a man and a woman (the Defense of Marriage Act). Still, the most important arena for actual policy change remains with the states. In each state:

- The *entry into marriage* is regulated. Laws govern who has the capacity to marry, what makes a marriage legally valid, and how licenses are obtained.
- The *conduct of marriage* is regulated. Laws govern the status of premarital agreements ("prenups"), property rights, legal liability, and the treatment of spouses and children (violence, abuse, etc).
- The *entry into divorce* is regulated. Laws address residency and jurisdiction, grounds for legal separation and divorce, the process of divorce, mandated counseling or waiting periods, and the handling of property and child-related issues during the divorce process.
- The *post-divorce relationship* is regulated. Primary issues include child custody and visitation, family support duties, and final terms for any financial and property settlement.
- Finally, in its shaping of laws related to each particular pressure point in the marriage and divorce process, and in its broader approach to marriage and divorce, government com-

municates values that cannot help but have an impact on public attitudes and practices. This "bully pulpit" dimension of public policy response must also be considered when thinking about divorce-law reform.[1]

Public Policy Levers

Laws have logic to them, hard as that may be to believe sometimes. Think of it as a system of levers and pulleys. Policymakers try to accomplish certain social goals. They embed these goals in laws and regulations. Political debate involves not only argument about which goals to pursue, but also how strenuously to pursue them. The more strenuously a goal is pursued, the more pressure is put on people to adjust their behavior. Levers and pulleys are attached to laws in order to increase the pressure to conform to them.

Essentially, with regard to any particular social practice, whether marriage or fly-fishing, policymakers can do one of the following:

Remain Neutral

Policymakers can decide that there is no governmental interest in either encouraging or discouraging a particular action. Or alternatively, they can conclude that any attempt to interfere with this action would exceed the boundaries of their jurisdiction or limit freedom too much.

Create (or Permit) Options

Policymakers can choose to open up a range of options to citizens for the accomplishment of a particular social goal, while remaining essentially neutral concerning which options citizens avail themselves of. For example, government has a legitimate interest in seeing that its citizens receive an adequate education. But government permits and sometimes creates a diversity of options for accomplishing that goal.

Offer Incentives or Disincentives

Government can create incentives and disincentives by which it can encourage or discourage behavior. The "incentive set" that government has available to it is impressive. Most compelling is the power of the purse. Government can create incentives by offering money to those who perform the behavior government seeks. These dollars can be delivered via the tax system, in the form of direct cash grants, or through the reduction or waiver of licensing fees. Government can create financial disincentives in similar ways.

Government also has the ability to create and offer nonfinancial incentives or disincentives. It can offer public honor or dishonor, praise or blame. It can, for example, publish a list of the fifty companies in the state that are doing the best job of putting former welfare recipients to work and then hold a press conference that honors them. This kind of approach is a major feature of the most recent state initiatives to strengthen marriage.

REGULATE ACCESS (OR EXIT)

Another policy lever available to government is its ability to regulate access to some product or benefit, or to regulate the exit from a status or responsibility. Thus, while cigarette smoking is permitted in our country, access to cigarettes is limited to those over a certain age. The same holds true of access to alcohol or R-rated movies. These examples immediately bring to mind the limits of law, for each of these is routinely violated. Yet access regulation is an important policy mechanism. It is especially important with marriage and divorce because both are "products" that you actually get from the government, even though evangelicals believe that government does not create marriage, it only recognizes "what God has joined together."

MANDATE OR PROHIBIT

Finally, policymakers can decide that an action is of sufficient importance that it must be either prohibited or mandated. Because mandating or prohibiting certain behaviors limits personal freedom, a higher burden of proof must be met to justify it. The social benefit gained must exceed the cost to personal freedoms. This is something evangelicals often forget (perhaps especially conservative evangelicals, though all of us are vulnerable to this problem), because we tend to be fixated on a moral vision drawn from scripture and are less focused on respecting freedom. This is so even though freedom itself, at least in the New

Testament, is a biblical moral value. Most often, the move to this highest level of law involves a prohibition rather than a mandate, with a punishment attached. We are required not to kill, not to rape, not to steal, not to torture (let's hope), and so on. However, it is easy to think of things we are required to do, such as wear our seatbelts or pay our taxes.

Public policy signals its level of seriousness on such matters through the harshness of the consequences of violations. The same principle holds true with all policy mechanisms: they can be employed with varying degrees of intensity depending on their public significance.

In the ongoing debate about marriage and divorce law reform, variations of each of these public policy levers have been proposed. Those who are passionate about particular issues tend to move immediately to the "mandate or prohibit" level. Quite frequently, however, such demands are inappropriate to the issue under consideration, politically unrealistic, or a violation of personal freedoms or church-state boundaries. We must remain open to less dramatic measures.

ENTRY INTO MARRIAGE
Reform Options

Let us turn now to particular legal reform proposals and possibilities, as well as two proposals that might be viewed as systemic reforms. We begin with the entry into marriage.

Most states currently regulate the entry into marriage very lightly. Those seeking marriage must obtain a license by filling out a brief form and paying a small fee. There is sometimes, though not always, a very brief waiting period, which the American Bar Association legal guide says is intended "to give a brief cooling-off time during which the parties can change their minds if they wish."[2] (College students laugh when I tell them about this. They understand.) This might be viewed as a modest access regulation strategy—as are provisions restricting the marriage of close blood relatives. Those marrying must have the legal capacity to do so, in terms of mental and psychological competence. Most states also regulate access to marriage by age, generally requiring both parties to be eighteen years old (sixteen with consent of parents). Some states lower the age if the woman is pregnant and parents consent. Sometimes judges are brought in to help determine competence to marry. Currently all states except Massachusetts prohibit same-sex marriages, and Vermont, Connecticut, New Jersey, and New Hampshire permit gay "civil unions." Probably more states will have adopted gay civil unions or even marriage by the time this chapter sees the light of day.

One reform option is to attack the problem of marital quality and divorce through more vigorous regulation of the entry into marriage. A number of different strategies have been proposed.

First, some are proposing either the *requirement or the encouragement of a program of premarital preparation, including some combination of testing, counseling, and education.* Such an initiative could be undertaken in tandem with another measure, *the strategic use of extended waiting periods and fees related to obtaining a marriage license.*

In 1998 Florida became the first state in the nation to pass a law—the "Marriage Preparation and Preservation Act"—with precisely this approach. Couples who take a four-hour marriage preparation class can get a $32.50 discount on their marriage license and can marry with no waiting period. Those who choose not to do so must wait three days and pay the full fee.[3] Tennessee passed similar legislation in 2002 that added $62.50 to existing county license fees, which is waived if the couple can certify that they have taken a four-hour marriage preparation class. Minnesota legislators passed a similar bill involving twelve hours of premarital counseling, but it was vetoed in April 2000 by then-governor Jesse Ventura. Maryland's governor Parris Glendening signed a bill similar to Florida's into law in 2001. No state has *mandated* premarital counseling; only voluntary or incentive-based approaches are currently under consideration. Florida procounseling lawmakers discovered that any mandated plan ran into bipartisan opposition on libertarian grounds.

Another strategy related to the entry into marriage is to address the *age* issue more carefully. States could choose to use one or another lever to try to increase the age at which couples marry, reasoning from all relevant data that teen marriages are likely to be less stable and enduring than those begun later. In March 1998 a Missouri legislator proposed an incentive-based law along these lines. Representative Pat Kelley's bill would have the state offer a $1,000 bonus to any couple that delays marriage until both are at least twenty-one.[4]

Close kin to this kind of approach would be a strategy aimed at encouraging *longer courtships*.[5] States could offer incentives to those who have known each other at least six months and thus discourage impulse marriages. One minimal way to move toward this goal would be to impose a longer waiting period from the day of application for a marriage license; this could perhaps be waived on proof of receipt of premarital counseling.[6] Again, such an approach would reflect the recognition that marriages are more likely to succeed if preceded by a significant courtship period.

How Are Evangelicals to Evaluate These Kinds of Proposals?

There are practical administrative concerns, but in my view these are solvable. Such policies could require states to create a new or expanded bureaucracy. If the state actually provides premarital counseling, there is the question of the expansion of state payrolls to accommodate hordes of official marriage preparers. There is the issue of whether state funding would be provided for those couples unable to pay for counseling. There is the question of possible abuse through the filing of false affidavits.

More deeply, some argue that premarital counseling is ineffective because such couples rarely view their relationships realistically. Coerced premarital counseling might be even less likely than voluntary counseling to have a positive impact on the couple involved. And yet these arguments have been answered by solid data indicating that well-designed premarital inventories and counseling programs have had a positive impact both in strengthening marriages and in preventing certain foolish marriages from taking place.[7]

Some see this kind of regulation as an intrusion of the state into the private sphere. This libertarian-type objection will likely doom any mandatory measures. As Illinois Republican James Durkin said, "It's not our place to dictate how people will enter into the sanctity of marriage.For the state to mandate premarital counseling is just going too far."[8] This was essentially Governor Ventura's objection as well—even to a *voluntary* plan!

Even those of us who support the basic concept here must be aware of the "iron law of unintended consequences." Given the rising rate of cohabitation in our society, it can be argued that nothing should be done to increase its frequency but that putting "speed bumps" in the path of marriage could lead some couples simply to live together instead, thus making the cure worse than the problem.

Despite these concerns, I think all evangelicals should support an incentive-based, voluntary approach focused on significant premarital preparation tied to a waiting period. Even taking proper care to protect personal liberty and limit the power of the state, such an approach does not violate the boundaries of the state's jurisdiction. The administrative time and costs are worth the trouble and can be limited through the use of streamlined procedures.[9] The state should not be in the counseling business itself, instead, it should accept the counseling offered by any certified counselor. This includes religious-based counselors—church-state issues on this front should not be seen as a problem, and the state must not restrict the "religious" content of such instruction. Evangelicals should play a key role here; I have had the privilege of offering such counseling to several dozen couples myself over the last fifteen years. County clerks could keep a list of providers on hand and would make this list available to all applicants for marriage licenses (or divorce petitioners).[10]

To sharpen the incentive all the more, states should offer tax breaks for couples who undergo premarital counseling in any given year, unless the counseling was free. States should not establish some kind of entitlement to premarital preparation, but they could use surplus funds from the federal Temporary Assistance to Needy Families (TANF) program (popularly known as "welfare") to provide vouchers for low-income couples to take marriage-preparation classes. This approach was pioneered by Arizona in 2000.

Evangelicals should support broadening the difference in the way counseled and noncounseled couples are treated: to be bold, how about a sixty-day waiting period and a $200 fee for those not receiving counseling? This would certainly raise the level of incentive to undertake the premarital program. It would require experimentation to see exactly how high a fee and how long a wait could be employed without negative side effects. A state could defend higher fees and longer waiting periods by spelling out the stark social costs of divorce and the state's legitimate interest in discouraging it, as many states are now doing. All fees could be officially designated for the massive divorce-related government expenses that are a daily reality. Tennessee's legislators did this by designating all extra license money to the Department of Children's Services and other agencies whose time and money are spent dealing with divorce-related issues.

Evangelical leaders, congregations, or denominations could contribute mightily to the rate of participation in a state-encouraged premarital preparation process simply by offering high-quality programs themselves *and by refusing to marry anyone who refuses to participate in them.* This should be the stance of evangelical ministers and congregations with regard to premarital preparation in any case, regardless of state law.[11] But where states move in this direction, the churches can happily partner with government.

THE CONDUCT OF MARRIAGE
Reform Options

Current state laws regulate the conduct of marriage in three basic arenas: finances, children, and domestic violence.

In terms of finances, a maze of regulations covers all aspects of the financial partnership that is marriage: property, debt, and taxes are among the issues that garner most attention. The decision concerning whether or not to have children is left to the couple, as are most decisions concerning how to raise children. The rights of children themselves are also the subject of law. Domestic violence statutes rightly prohibit murder, assault, rape, or robbery between spouses or against children.

Besides this, the states tend to demonstrate no particular interest in the well-being of the marriages within their jurisdiction. This section of the law is almost always the briefest in state codes. The state remains neutral, or as Milton C. Regan puts it, "agnostic," about behavior within families.[12] Although it is certainly true that states must not micromanage relationships between husbands and wives, it is no less true that states have a compelling interest in marital harmony and permanence. This abdication of any promarriage stance should trouble all evangelicals.

States should move from neutrality to a clear public stance of encouraging high quality, just, and lasting marriages. As (liberals!) Sylvia Ann Hewlett and Cornel West have put it, "government should get back into the business of fostering the value of marriage as a long-term commitment."[13]

I suggest the following modest initiative: *States should use incentives to encourage married couples to undertake marriage enrichment and marriage counseling activities.* There would be no need for states to develop such activities or programs themselves. They would simply offer a modest tax incentive to couples that could certify their participation in such a program (as proposed in New Mexico in 2001). Church-state and funding issues raised by this kind of approach were discussed above. The only real policy debate here is not whether such programs would benefit marriage but instead whether public will exists for investing tax dollars for this purpose.

At a much broader level, states need to consider a wide range of measures that would offer public policy support for stable and permanent marriages. Hewlett and West have proposed a "parents' bill of rights"—a set of measures that would demonstrate societal support for the honorable, sacrificial, and absolutely critical work of parents. They group their proposals under the following categories: time for children, economic security, a profamily electoral system, a profamily legal structure, a supportive external environment, and honor and dignity.[14]

To pursue this issue further here would take us outside the focus of this chapter, but I concur with the basic claim that public policy has a legitimate role to play in offering broad, *practical* (not just rhetorical) support for strong and healthy marriage and family life.

Entry into Divorce: Considerations and Reform Options

Today, most states approach the regulation of entry into divorce with the same agnostic neutrality that marks state laws related to the entry into marriage. All states require residency of one or both parties to the divorce in the state in which the divorce is being sought. Residency requirements range from six weeks to one year. There are fees and court costs. This could be seen as a modest access regulation strategy, but in general states have not attempted to impose significant burdens here, in keeping with a Supreme Court decision that barred states from setting unaffordable filing fees.

All states specify the permissible legal grounds for divorce. Here one finds two basic but very different patterns: no-fault and fault-based grounds. Since 1985, all states have had no-fault statutes; some have fault-based grounds to go with no-fault approaches; others only have no-fault divorce; some now have "covenant marriages" as well. There is an important history behind the rather strange current structure of our divorce laws.

Through most of our nation's history legal separation or divorce was available only to a husband or wife who could demonstrate that his or her spouse had committed an offense that was serious enough to merit the "relief" of separation or the dissolution of the marriage. The presupposition of the law was that the marriage relationship was a matter of significant public interest that extended well beyond the feelings of either husband or wife. Marriage was viewed as a status that imposes a permanent set of obligations on all who are embedded in the relationships that marriage creates.[15] The law legitimately held people to those obligations, releasing them from these only when one partner's behavior constituted a fundamental offense against the marriage. Clearly, this legal theory was closely tied to the legacy of the Bible and of the Western Christian tradition, with its understanding of the covenant permanence of marriage. But it was also simply realistic about the social significance of marriage as an institution. Most evangelical Christians, at least in theory, still hold to this understanding of the morality of divorce, even if they have given up on ever again seeing it enshrined in the law.

Early in American history the list of offending behaviors, or grounds for divorce, tended to be relatively short and closely tied to a reading of biblical teaching. Thus, for example, the first and premier ground for divorce has always been adultery. Over time those grounds expanded incrementally, with great variations across the fifty states.[16] But what these codes held in common was the view that the dissolution of a marriage was a grave act that should be limited to particular offenses against marriage.

Quietly and with relatively little fanfare, a revolution in divorce law was successfully undertaken in the 1970s. The first to take the plunge was the state of California in 1969. Marking a clean break with the entire history we have been outlining, non-fault-based divorce (popularized under the label "no-fault divorce") became the new benchmark for divorce law. It swept not only the United States but most of Western Europe as well.

The framers of no-fault divorce did not intend to argue that no one is ever at fault when a marriage collapses or that the end of a marriage is not morally significant. They did believe, however, that no one's interests were being served by an adversarial system in which divorcing couples had to go to court to prove to a judge that each other was to blame for a marriage's problems. They believed that the adversarial nature of this structure only aggravated conflicts and was particularly hard on children.

They were also aware that as the demand for divorce began to increase in the 1960s (*before* the laws were changed), current divorce laws were creating an environment of duplicity in the legal process. Couples genuinely and mutually wanting to divorce were having to pretend that one or the other was guilty of some particular marital offense, usually adultery. These "disguised mutual consent" divorces generally involved offering perjured testimony under oath. Further, the demand for divorce was leading some judges to stretch the permitted grounds beyond recognition; for example, "cruelty" as a ground for divorce now became "mental cruelty," which could be recognized whenever one or the other partner appeared miserable.[17]

The reformers' idea was to eliminate all of this by waiving the requirement of showing fault. Much like no-fault auto insurance, which was introduced at the same time and clearly influenced the public perception of this divorce law reform, no-fault divorce would simply remove the legal system from the role of sorting out blame and guilt for a marital "crash." One might say that the legal fiction of a marital offense as cause of every divorce was replaced by the legal fiction of *no* offense as a cause for *any* divorce. The public interest consisted not in keeping troubled marriages together but in enabling their dissolution to be as painless as possible.[18]

Of course, these legal changes were driven not only by legal logic but also by profound cultural shifts occurring at the time. Marriage was becoming an always-up-for-review relationship. Because my "unhappi-ness" or "failure to thrive" or "lack of sexual satisfaction" does not neces-sarily involve fault on my spouse's part, there should be no need to prove that she did anything wrong. I should be free to leave as I continue that search for personal fulfillment that is every American's birthright. Thus the entry into divorce was almost entirely deregulated. This fundamen-tally anti-Christian worldview swept through the nation and the law.

The no-fault vision, if implemented in pure form, would have elimi-nated all fault grounds from legal codes. However, not all states were willing to go this far: A majority has retained both fault and no-fault grounds. Yet the fault grounds are at this point mere vestiges; their pri-mary use appears to be in the postdivorce financial settlement process where state law still permits fault to be considered at all. Our actual divorce laws essentially permit divorce to be initiated by either spouse for any reason at any time in the marriage. Simply by claiming "irrec-oncilable differences," or "marriage breakdown," refusing counseling or mediation, and waiting out the legal process, a spouse in most states can find a way of escape from marital commitments. This is divorce-on-demand, and it should be viewed by all evangelicals as little more appealing than abortion-on-demand.

Today there is some discussion in think tanks and among policy-makers as to whether this thirty-year-old experiment in legal reform should be reconsidered or even abandoned. I believe that it should be modified profoundly, though not abandoned. The argument for some kind of rollback of no-fault divorce can be made in several ways.

Legal Considerations

Milton Regan and others have argued that marriage was once under-stood as a status relationship, but now has become contractual in nature. Yet under no-fault what we have is a flimsy contract. Contract law regulates the entry of parties into a binding legal agreement, speci-fies the means by which such contracts may be ended and metes out punishments to those who violate contractual agreements. But no-fault divorce allows a person to abandon the marriage relationship unilat-erally, without penalty, and without recourse by the offended contract partner. In legal terms, this is a "terminable at will" relationship. The state's continued participation in the supposed regulation and licensing of marriage is revealed as a sham, little more than "notarized dating." As Bryce J. Christensen has written, "No fault divorce put[s] the state . . . in the absurd position of requiring a license for the pronouncing of public vows which the state subsequently regards with indifference."[19]

Moral Considerations

The law is a teacher, even if at times we might prefer not to notice this. If it is a teacher, no-fault divorce teaches all the wrong things. It teaches men and women that marriage can be casually entered and exited. It teaches that contracts can be violated with impunity. By its very name, it teaches that no one is to be "faulted" for offenses against marriage, such as adultery and abandonment. It permits gross injustices against spouses and children without penalty; indeed, by its structure no-fault divorce allies the state with the irresponsible party.[20] It teaches that marriage itself is not of particular social significance. It thus contributes to the weakening of personal character, relational stability, public justice, and social virtue. It further contributes to weakened links between American law and our common moral heritage. These are core concerns for evangelicals.

Economic Considerations

The ease with which anyone can obtain a divorce places the economically dependent spouse (usually the wife) in a very precarious situation. If she is abandoned, the fact that no fault is claimed tends to reduce the value of the property settlement she obtains during the legal process of divorce. Given that 90 percent of divorces leave custody with the mother, she and her children are at risk of impoverishment.[21] This injustice toward women and children violates core biblical values as well.

Despite considerable unease related to no-fault divorce, no state has done away with it, nor does it appear that any state is likely to do so in the near future. Not every antidivorce analyst is convinced that the return to a fault-based system would be constructive.[22]

But is there something short of a rollback of no-fault divorce that we can propose?

I suggest four "speed bumps" for consideration: enhanced waiting periods, a more vital role for mutual consent, stronger counseling and education requirements, and modest judicial discretion in granting divorces.

Waiting Periods

When states require substantial waiting periods from the time a plaintiff files for divorce until a divorce can be legally granted, they communicate a public interest in preventing unnecessary or rash divorces. In Virginia and several other states, marriages in which children are present cannot be legally dissolved without a one-year period of "living separate and apart without cohabitation."[23]

I suggest the possibility that each state should adopt waiting-period require-ments at least this rigorous. Amy Black suggests that these waiting periods should be extended to the two- to five-year range, as is the case in some Western European nations.[24] In thinking about this issue, we need to be realistic about what waiting periods can accomplish, and the chaos that emerges when the next relationship begins during a spouse's court-enforced waiting period (as already happens so frequently now). We must be especially concerned to protect the interests of abused spouses and children. Exceptions can and should be made in these cases. Yet clearly a substantial waiting period is called for under most circumstances.[25] Such legislation is being considered in several states.

Mutual Consent

There is much ferment concerning the entire issue of consent. The legal fiction that a marriage has "broken down" or suffers from "irreconcilable differences," even when both parties do not share that view, is under withering assault. Some argue for the reinstatement of mutual-consent requirements at every stage of the divorce process in every case. This proposal would probably be unworkable and is politically infeasible. However, proposals are surfacing, such as one in Virginia, that would eliminate unilateral no-fault divorce.[26] Other proposals would eliminate no-fault divorce without mutual consent when there are children involved. Various proposals have surfaced that would permit unilateral no-fault but would treat the process differently than where there is mutual consent. William Galston has proposed eliminating unilateral no-fault where there are children, with the alternative of a five-year waiting period.[27] The principle at stake is important: the decision to divorce is of a fundamentally different nature where there is mutual consent and where there is not, and where there are children and where there are not, and the law should almost always side with the nonconsenting partner where it can.

Counseling and Education

A focus of considerable attention in recent divorce law reform efforts has been the strengthening of counseling and education requirements. This is to be heartily endorsed. Some states require a period of counseling before granting a divorce. Others have no such requirements or limit them to the requests of one party or the discretion of a judge. Here I think evangelicals should support a mandatory sixty- to ninety-day period of counseling for every divorcing couple.

Education efforts should be an integral part of any counseling or instruction obtained during the divorce consideration process. Several states have launched recent initiatives requiring divorcing parents to receive some sobering education concerning the effects of divorce on children. Some, including Tennessee, require the couple to write and have approved a child custody and parenting plan. This education or counseling process should also include a prior emphasis on marriage-building practices, such as communication and conflict resolution. The bias should first be toward the resolution of marital conflict, with the goal of preventing unnecessary divorces. Of course, some angry, alienated, or irresponsible ex-spouses will resist compliance with such programs. But to the extent that even a percentage of adults and children are helped, the social good is advanced.

Judicial Discretion

While nearly every state involves judges in the divorce process, generally they have little discretion in their decision making, and those who do have some discretion rarely seem to employ it. They do not normally take the time to undertake a real inquiry into the circumstances facing the couple, but instead the process is generally little more than a summary administrative procedure.[28] Some states permit judges to require counseling, and those judges are heavily involved in postdivorce financial and custody issues. Being a family court judge seems to be deeply dispiriting work. My suggestion here is simply that judges should be given the leeway at least to delay the granting of a divorce where it is fundamentally frivolous or unnecessary; my hope is that more of them will make use of the discretion that they are given. As Carl E. Schneider has written:

> Many laws now make divorce available where there has been an "irretrievable breakdown" of the marriage. In practice, however, this standard is essentially ignored in favor of divorce on demand. Revitalizing that standard might . . . allow courts to, in effect, send some divorce petitions back for reconsideration.[29]

Mary Ann Glendon has pointed out that several European countries include "hardship clauses" in their no-fault divorce laws. For example, a 1976 West German law permitted judges to deny divorces "if dissolution of the marriage would impose severe hardship on the unwilling spouse" or if preventing divorce was "exceptionally necessary" for the well-being of the children.[30] This extremely sensible provision—which apparently was never really used—would be one way of limiting divorce on demand and holding people accountable to the obligations they have taken upon themselves in marriage. Judges should also have the freedom to assess the circumstances of marriage breakdown, especially egregious fault, in determining divorce settlements. States that have stripped such considerations out of their laws should think again.

❀ ❀ ❀

In summary, then, I think all evangelicals should support the following steps in relation to the entry into divorce:[31]

- Retain the possibility of mutual consent, no-fault divorce for couples without children.
- Retain and use fault grounds where appropriate both for the entry into divorce and for the just determination of divorce settlements.

- Require substantial waiting periods prior to divorce—longer where there are children.
- Eliminate unilateral no-fault divorce, at least where there are children present.
- Require counseling and education before granting divorce, in specialized and more extensive form where children are present.
- Enhance judicial discretion to deny divorce, especially in hardship cases.

Systemic Reforms Options

Let us consider two systemic reform options. These attack the divorce problem through an overhaul of the entire marriage and divorce system. We will look first at what has come to be known as "covenant marriage."

Covenant Marriage

The 1997 passage in Louisiana of the Covenant Marriage Law (and similar laws in Arizona and Arkansas) has created considerable public interest. Nowhere has conservative evangelical policy engagement in relation to heterosexual marriage been more extensive. Covenant marriage is best understood as an effort to create *an optional fault-based marriage covenant as a supplement to the current no-fault regime*. It uses the public policy lever of option-creation as an expression of public values related to the importance of marriage.

The covenant marriage idea can be traced back at least as far as a 1990 article by Elizabeth Scott, a law professor at the University of Virginia, who employed the language of "precommitments" to discuss the possibility of a couple's making an advance commitment to marital permanence, or of the state requiring couples to do so.[32] The first legislative proposal related to covenant marriage surfaced in Florida, also in 1990.[33] The influential communitarian Amitai Etzioni wrote an influential *Time* magazine article in 1993 in which he proposed the use of "supervows," premarital contracts committing couples to do more than the law requires to keep their marriages together.[34] Since that time the idea has picked up momentum, so that by now it is probably the leading divorce reform concept in the nation. Bills have not only been passed in Louisiana, Arizona, and Arkansas but are being considered in many other states. Let us look closely here at the pioneering Louisiana law.

As of August 15, 1997, married couples in Louisiana can choose voluntarily to enter into a covenant marriage. The language of the law implicitly recognizes that a covenant marriage contract is a different kind of arrangement than the typical current marriage, and it is to be treated as such by the legal system *at every stage*; this makes it a systemic reform. Note how each aspect of the marriage law system is addressed in the following provisions:

THE ENTRY INTO MARRIAGE

- The couple must execute a formal declaration of intent to enter into a covenant marriage. The declaration in Louisiana reads as follows:

> We do solemnly declare that marriage is a covenant between a man and a woman who agree to live together as husband and wife for so long as they both may live. We have chosen each other carefully and disclosed to one another everything which could adversely affect the decision to enter into this marriage. We have read the Covenant Marriage Act, and we understand that a Covenant Marriage is for life. If we experience marital difficulties, we commit ourselves to take all reasonable efforts to preserve our marriage, including marriage counseling.[35]

- This declaration must accompany an application for a marriage license.
- The marriage certificate also indicates whether this is a covenant marriage; witnesses to the marriage must certify that this is the case.
- Those seeking covenant marriage must be able to certify by a notarized affidavit that they have received premarital counseling; the law specifies in detail the key elements of the content of this counseling, which includes discussion of a pamphlet from

the state attorney general's office concerning the nature of a covenant marriage. The counselor must also offer a notarized attestation of the counseling.

THE CONDUCT OF MARRIAGE

• The declaration of intent to enter a covenant marriage *requires* the couple to seek marital counseling if they experience difficulties.

THE ENTRY INTO DIVORCE

• Divorce or separation in a covenant marriage is intended to be fault-based: Adultery, imprisonment for a felony, desertion, and physical/sexual abuse of child or spouse are listed as fault grounds.
• Otherwise, the couple has to show that they have been living separately without reconciliation for two years, longer than is typical in state divorce laws.

How shall evangelicals evaluate this innovative legislation? Covenant marriage is an attempt to *encourage* rather than mandate a return to pre-1969 divorce law. The mechanism it uses to offer this encouragement is solely the creation of an optional "marriage deluxe" legal structure. No incentives or disincentives, mandates or prohibitions, are employed. That is one reason why the law was passed: It could be presented in the language of choice rather than mandate.

Even so, a close reading of the law reveals its clear intent to encourage a return to older ways of looking at the permanence of marriage. The state wants to encourage couples to believe that marriage is a lifetime commitment. It is prepared to help them do so by structuring its marriage laws to make it more difficult to end a marriage if couples contract to play by those rules from the outset. The net result is the creation of a two-tier marriage system: intentionally permanent marriages, governed by the covenant marriage laws, and other (implicitly impermanent) marriages, governed by no-fault laws. Clearly, Louisiana and other covenant states hope that the number of the former will grow and the latter decline.

Criticism of this approach could come from two directions: that covenant marriage is going too far, or not far enough. Already there are critics who argue that lawmakers have no business enshrining their moral convictions about marital permanence into law. Even the vocabulary, with its clearly biblical overtones, signals the religious and moral convictions that helped motivate this legislation. The fact that the legislation first emerged from the South heightened the suspicions of some. Future Family Research Council president Tony Perkins played a key role in advancing covenant marriage in Louisiana, evidence enough to oppose it, for some.

On the other hand, this law can be seen by serious advocates of divorce reform as not going far enough. Louisiana's law does not abolish or even modify no-fault divorce but simply seeks to supplement it with an optional fault-based alternative. It can be questioned whether a purely optional system communicates public values in a sufficiently vigorous manner. One could at least consider the potential of adding a set of incentives into the mix.

More broadly, it is reasonable to ask whether a two-tier legal system related to marriage is coherent. It is hard to think of any other area of the law in which citizens can choose from two sets of rules. Here lawmakers are attempting to articulate a public valuing of marital permanence but without requiring or even using incentives to encourage anyone to act in a way that accomplishes that goal. It is as if they are saying: "We want you to stay married, but only if *you* want to. If you do, here's a legal option that can help. That's all we'll do for you, but we hope you're interested." That approach may simply be too weak. Yet it appeals to our preference for freedom of choice. Indeed, some are now arguing for a totally deregulated free market in marriage contracts—not just two options, but the freedom to make whatever marriage contract we want to make. In a sense, this is what prenuptial agreements already do.[36]

Returns from Louisiana indicate that requests for covenant marriage have trickled rather than flowed in. It is hard to know whether these numbers will ever increase. The law has encountered a distressing lack of cooperation from court clerks, from the state's media, and even from many key religious leaders and groups in the state. This included the influential Roman Catholic Church in Louisiana, which in a devastating decision chose to remain neutral on the law because it requires counselors to discuss divorce as a legal option.[37] (A clear example of the best being the enemy of the good.) Some thought that what one Internet wag called "the diplomacy of love" would lead courting couples to agree to covenant marriages rather than admit in advance that they wanted the low-octane variety. So far this has not happened.

It may turn out that citizens will prove to be unwilling to voluntarily bind themselves to laws that are stricter than those that apply to their neighbors. One cannot imagine people doing so in any other area of the law. It may well not work here, either, despite the legislature's good intentions. My suggestion is that covenant marriage approaches be strengthened through the intentional use of incentives, and that, despite discouraging responses thus far, this experiment should continue to be attempted wherever feasible. And yet I do not consider this voluntary, optional regime the most important current divorce-reform strategy.

A Child-Focused, Two-Tier Approach

The concept of a two-tier divorce law could take another form: a mandatory system hinging on the presence of children. The presence of children should automatically transform the legal status of marriage and raise the "guard rails" against divorce. I believe that this is the main direction that divorce law reform should take, and that evangelicals should rally around it.[38]

Society has a strong interest in supporting marriages that both endure and are worth enduring, and among the most persuasive supports for this claim is divorce's lasting impact in the lives of children. And it is children whose interests are most frequently the last to be considered in our modern culture of divorce.

What would our family law system look like if those interests were taken seriously?

First, a strong case could be made that because roughly two-thirds of all divorces do involve children, the kinds of "entry into marriage" reforms we have already considered should ultimately be mandated for all couples. When we consider the engaged couple, we should see not only who they are now but the children they will likely bring into the world—and the predictable impact of divorce on those children. Those impacts are becoming painfully clear to the generation of children who have suffered the serial monogamy of their parents.[39]

But let us bracket that proposal and now consider the couple that already has children, either through out-of-wedlock birth or through a prior marriage. A two-tier marriage law system that takes the needs and interests of those children seriously would *mandate* rather than merely encourage a course of premarital testing and counseling and a lengthy waiting period before marriage. The freedom of the couple in this case should give way to the well-being of the children involved and to society's stake in that well-being.

The same basic principle applies when it comes to the entry into divorce. Certainly, where children are involved, states should require lengthy waiting periods of perhaps as much as two years or more (as in Virginia, these waiting periods should be longer where children are present—and of course, abuse situations should always be treated differently). Couples with children who are considering divorce should be required to attend classes related to the impact of divorce on children and all child-related post-divorce issues. The educational process at this pivotal point should operate with a bias toward preserving the marriage and should require reconciliation counseling. Judges should have the discretion to delay or discourage unnecessary or frivolous divorces where children are involved.

Amy Black has argued that mutual consent should be required in divorces involving children, even if it is not required for other divorces.[40] Galston would agree but would leave a five-year waiting period as an escape clause.[41] Although I can see needed exceptions to this approach, I do believe that it is appropriate to return to a modified fault-based system for divorce where children are present. In such a system, the presence of children in the home would raise the state's threshold for permitting divorce to something approaching the older fault-based standards that prevailed in U.S. law until 1969. Child or spouse abuse should always be one of the permitted grounds. But a unilaterally initiated divorce for purpose of personal self-fulfillment or career advancement (or whatever) should not be permitted where children will be affected. Or, if an escape clause ultimately is required, the person seeking it should be required to pay dearly for the privilege, both in terms of a waiting period and financial settlement.

With this final proposal I may have stepped over that line of personal liberty that must be carefully guarded in our political system. I do believe, however, that a mandatory two-tier divorce law system that takes into account the well-being of children is morally justified, fits with evangelical values, takes the common good seriously, and could be politically feasible. Such a proposal would constitute a systemic reform that includes most of the specific incremental proposals outlined above. It is stronger than covenant marriage in that it would be mandatory rather than voluntary and would apply to at least two-thirds of all marriages. Indeed, one might say that it would constitute legal recognition that once children enter the picture, every marriage is, and must be, a "covenant marriage" because bringing children into the world imposes covenantal obligations on parents that they must not be permitted to evade in the quest for personal fulfillment.

❀ ❀ ❀

I want to address the sensitive issue of how or whether the state should offer legal recognition to same-sex relationships. I showed previously when comparing the evangelical left, right, and center that clear divergences exist on this front. The evangelical left is generally open to gay civil unions if not gay marriage itself. The center is clearly opposed to gay marriage but has said relatively little about civil unions. The right is fiercely opposed to gay marriage and only a little less fiercely opposed to civil unions. On this one, the center of gravity has rested with the right, or at least the center-right, leaving the left looking more than a little marginalized. Especially given that the continued *moral* evaluation of homosexual acts as outside of God's will has become something of a litmus test for determining who falls within the evangelical camp, any discussion of what legal recognition to advocate for gay relationships is extremely sensitive within the internal politics of evangelicalism. This makes it especially hard to think about it clearly and from the ground up, rather than with one eye on one's political survival as a recognized evangelical.

I do want to risk the effort to think about this issue clearly and from the ground up. So I want to think in terms of the framework that I have set up in this chapter as I have discussed heterosexual marriage. That means the place to begin is by asking whether the state has a compelling reason to deny gays and lesbians *entry into marriage*—properly understood as including both its rights and its responsibilities, its benefits and its burdens. Should homosexuals as a class/category continue to be excluded from entry into marriage (or a quasimarital equivalent like civil unions)? What social benefits are gained by this exclusion, this limitation on personal freedom? What reasons related to public justice and the common good can be offered?

Heterosexuals are barred from marrying, as we saw above, only in such rare cases as when they want to marry close blood kin, or are mentally incompetent, or are too young. We can readily see why these entry regulation lines are drawn. Is the reason similarly clear for homosexual relationships? And is it a reason that passes muster within the framework of how and why laws are made in this particular nation rather than the internal logic and life of orthodox Christian faith?

I think that evangelical Christians should frankly acknowledge that the fundamental reason we have opposed gay marriage is because we believe that the Bible (God's inspired Word) teaches that heterosexual relationships are normative and that homosexual behavior falls outside of God's plan. This biblically based belief is reinforced by two thousand years of essentially unanimous Christian tradition. This tradition has had a permeating impact on the entire understanding of marriage in Western culture and therefore in Western law. This influence includes but is not limited to the norm of heterosexuality. Western law related to marriage is incomprehensible apart from the impact of Christian thought, as I have already suggested. The gradual fading of Christian influence in Western culture over many long centuries has eroded most aspects of what Western people understand marriage to be: that it is supposed to last for a lifetime, that it is the only legitimate place for sexual intercourse or childbirth, or that marriage is even necessary at all.

One of the last vestiges of the once-pervasive Christian influence on the Western understanding of marriage is the belief that marriage by definition is a relationship between a man (one man) and a woman (one woman). Given the steady erosion of other aspects of the historic Western understanding of marriage, it was predictable that eventually the heterosexuality norm would also be challenged. One could predict a direct correlation between the fading of Christian influence in a nation and the rewriting of its laws related to marriage. This helps explain why European nations have moved toward domestic partnership and gay relationship laws more quickly than has the United States and why within the United States some regions rather than others are moving toward finding ways to offer some legal status to gay relationships.

Evangelical Christians (like traditional Catholics and traditional Eastern Orthodox) are not likely to accept that their historic understanding of the Bible's message about God's plan for sexuality has been wrong for two thousand years. I do not accept it. They are not likely to join revisionist voices in concluding that the Christian faith really can embrace the full moral legitimacy of homosexual acts. Those who seek to lead evangelicals into a revision of their historic understanding of this issue will not find many converts. The evangelical right and center and most of the left will resist. And those who seek to *demand or require* that evangelicals change their thinking, teaching, and internal practices in relation to this issue will evoke spirited opposition across the entirety of the evangelical spectrum, even civil disobedience if it should come to that. It would be a sure prescription for dramatically heightened tensions in the "culture wars." Indeed, this is already occurring.

I have already argued that one distinctive mark of the evangelical right is the tendency to try to defend what remains of the cultural impact/ hegemony of Christian symbols and convictions in American culture, even as that hegemony shows signs of slowly fading. If we argue, as I have, that historic American (Western) marriage laws clearly reflect the impact of Christian theological and moral convictions, the right will probably be happy to concur and happy to try to defend that legacy as long and as vigorously as possible.

But what if we suggest that worldview and lifestyle pluralism is a fact of life in America, it is not going away, and it is at least to some extent protected by the Constitution of the United States? What do we as evangelical Christians do with the brute fact that *whatever we may believe about the morality of homosexual acts and relationships, they do and will exist in the United States?* What does it mean to live in a country sufficiently pluralistic that even divergences as fundamental as this one are irrevocably a part of our national life? What kinds of laws should we advocate to regulate marriage in such a nation? If we are right in drawing a link between making good laws and loving our neighbors, what then does neighbor love require in relation to the homosexual neighbors who seek marriage or a similar status?

Recognizing that reason giving in a pluralistic society requires making publicly accessible arguments, many Christians have sought to offer a variety of "public reasons" for why the ban on legal recognition of gay relationships should continue. I once attended a rather high-powered private strategy session in Washington in which some of the most formidable intellects on the conservative side of the Christian world (both Catholic and Protestant) tried out various public arguments against gay marriage. These included an appeal to natural law (nature clearly teaches that sex is to be between male and female and that children should be raised by their heterosexual biological parents), judicial restraint (judges should not legislate from the bench), national tradition (any redefinition of marriage violates the historical practices of our nation), interstate confusion (developing an array of marriage laws that vary by state will bring chaos), the weakened state of marriage (do nothing that further damages this wounded institution of marriage), and children's well-being (protect children from growing up either in gay/lesbian households or in a society in which marriage is being fundamentally redefined and confusion reigns).

The counterarguments are immediately apparent and already in circulation, to wit: Natural law is itself a theological concept that does not gain universal assent. It is not a judicial restraint issue if legislators actually write and approve revised marriage laws, as some are now doing. National traditions are sometimes quite fallible (e.g., racist segregation law)s. Marriage laws have always varied state by state, sometimes dramatically. Granting gays the rights and responsibilities of marriage will strengthen, not weaken, the institution of marriage. Children in households led by gays and lesbians are much better off if protected by a heightened legal status for the adults who raise them, whereas children in traditionalist households can simply be told by their parents what the family believes about the matter and do not need to be paralyzed by confusion.

It is my view that the various "publicly accessible" arguments that evangelicals (and Catholics and others) array against gay marriage clearly are secondary to the core religious and moral traditions and beliefs that foundationally drive them. These public arguments vary in their cogency, but they appear to be unpersuasive to those who are not already pre-persuaded on the basis of their religious beliefs—rooted in the authority of the Bible (or the Christian tradition) and the nature of its teaching on this matter. If this is the case, then it is unlikely that the anti-gay marriage stance will prevail in public policy on the basis of accessible public reasons. It will prevail, where it does, on the basis of the strength of the citizenry's commitment to traditional Christian beliefs about the Bible and about sexuality. In states in which a critical mass remains anchored to such beliefs, legislators will never vote to approve gay marriage or probably even civil unions. In states in which this is not the case, legislators may well do so. This is not a terribly satisfying outcome for anybody. But it is where we are.

A 1997 Government Accounting Office study commissioned after passage of the 1996 Defense of Marriage Act found over one thousand laws applicable only to married people, most of these offering benefits unavailable to the unmarried. By now, five states offer some or all of these benefits to those qualifying under new civil unions or gay marriage laws. The chart on pages 172–73 outlines some of the most important of these benefits.

If as evangelicals we grant, however reluctantly, that homosexual relationships exist and will continue to exist, and if we grant that homosexual people have the same kinds of economic and relational vulnerabilities and needs that heterosexuals have (if not more), it is hard to see what compelling Christian moral principles are served by insisting on the denial of such benefits as medical decision-making rights, access to health insurance, inheritance rights, and retirement benefits. And if we take seriously all that was said previously about the need for marriage and divorce laws that are especially geared toward the protection of children, it is hard to see why we would not want some provision to be made for the sad but inevitable business of seeing to the care of children whose homosexual or bisexual parents/guardians dissolve their relation-ships—just like heterosexuals do.

Are civil unions the answer? Some have thought that perhaps laws that offer such core legal protections and benefits, but do not also confer the official status of marriage, might be a workable grand compromise. Cultural or religious traditionalists could be asked to give ground from the right, offering humane legal benefits but not the religiomoral status of marriage. Gay rights activists could be asked to give ground from the left, gaining the benefits so central to their cause but compromising on the status of marriage in deference to tradition and to the sensibilities of tens of millions of their fellow Americans. Several states have already made this jump, including New England as an entire region. Other states appear poised to do so.

But as of the time of this writing, the possibility of such a grand compromise still seems doubtful. News from the gay community indi-cates relatively little enthusiasm for civil unions, with a rather small percentage registering so far and some complaining about the limits actually conferred by the benefits and the confusion surrounding their implementation. Others continue to yearn for the full social recognition that only marriage symbolizes. This has evoked the cry from religious conservatives that, just as they had feared, any compromise on gay civil unions will end up being simply a temporary stopping point on the way to gay marriage. Such developments will undoubtedly harden conserva-tive evangelical opposition to gay civil unions and weaken any support among centrists.

Some suggest that the state should get entirely out of the marriage business. Marriage, it is argued, is a private relationship and no busi-ness of the state. But this is not so, which is especially clear in relation to those two-thirds of marriages involving children. Children are the fundamental reason why adult sexual relationships must be a matter of state concern. Laws related to marriage should in many ways hinge on the well-being of children, as I said earlier. One could possibly reframe marriage and family law by crafting provisions around the presence of children at the inception of the relationship or the intent to conceive or adopt children during the course of the relationship. The well-being of children would be the bottom line, rather than sexual orientation, about

Marriage vesus Civil Unions: Camparison of Legal Benefits

Rights and Benefits	Marriage	Civil Unions	No Marital Status Available
Probability of Rights	Automatically recognized in all fifty states.	Recognition not guaranteed outside the state that grants it.	Some of the documents named must be carried at all times to ensure they are enforced.
Medical Decisions/ Emergencies	A spouse or family member may make decisions for an incompetent or disabled person unless contrary written instructions exist and can generally visit their partner in the hospital.	Partner's right to visitation and medical decision making may not be recognized out of state.	A healthcare proxy is required to convey decision-making authority.
Gift and Property Transfer Tax	May make unlimited transfers and gifts to each other without paying taxes.	Large gifts and transfers are subject to federal tax.	Must pay federal tax and state tax in many states for large gifts and transfers.
Inheritance	Automatic right to inherit without a will; inheritance not taxed at the state or federal level.	Not taxed at the state level; fully taxed at the federal level; not automatic outside granting state	No automatic inheritance; must be designated in will and is fully taxable; without a will, relationship is invisible.
Income Tax	Can file taxes jointly, which works to the advantage of couples when one earns much more than the other but creates penalty when incomes are similar.	Can file only state returns jointly; federal returns must be filed as single.	Must file individually.

Social Security and Veteran Death Benefits	Married people receive Social Security and veteran veteran-benefit payments upon the death of a spouse.	None.	None.
Retirement Savings	Married people receive payment from retirement savings upon the death of a spouse and can roll over savings for continued tax deferment.	Benefits are immediately taxed, if retirement retirement-savings plan even allows non-spouse to be named as beneficiary.	Benefits are immediately taxed, if retirement retirement-savings plan even allows non-spouse to be named as beneficiary.
Divorce	Divorce provides legal structure for couples to dissolve their marriages and divide property equitably.	No such system can be guaranteed for the dissolution of civil unions outside of the state where the union is granted.	Relationship contract dictating property division in advance may be enforced upon dissolution of relationship.
Spousal Support	Criminal penalties are imposed on spouses who abandon a child or a spouse.	Outside granting state, partners may have no legal obligation to support their partners.	Unmarried partners have no legal obligation to support their partners.
Immigration Benefits	U.S. citizens and legal permanent residents can sponsor their a spouse and other family members for immigration.	None.	None.

* Adapted from www.glad.org/rights/Marriage_v_CV_chart.pdf, accessed November 15, 2007.

which the state would remain agnostic for civil liberties reasons, while citizens and churches would of course be free to believe what they want to believe about who *ought* to marry. This is one possible way forward.

I am not sure that we have yet seen anywhere in our nation a way of crafting family law that can untangle the Gordian knot we have been considering. Maybe it will just come down to dispiriting and exhausting mortal combat in the political arena. But maybe, just maybe, our federalist system will work in such a way as to surface new possibilities as the states experiment with legislation. It is my hope that legislative creativity and skill will come up with a solution that respects the basic human rights and takes care of the basic human needs of all Americans, addresses the particular vulnerabilities of America's children, and strengthens rather than weakens the fraying ties that bind our religiously and morally diverse nation. And for evangelicals, it is my hope that a centrist position can emerge that does not compromise our moral convictions about God's design for sexuality but moves from right to center by ending gay bashing, respecting gay civil rights, demonstrating genuine Christian charity toward homosexuals, reducing the significance of the homosexuality issue within the overall evangelical family agenda, and looking for ways to make the well-being of children in every kind of household the centerpiece of family policy.

Chapter 7

CREATION CARE AND THE CLIMATE CHANGE DEBATE

In October 2006 I engaged in a lengthy face-to-face debate with E. Calvin Beisner of Knox Theological Seminary on the issue of climate change. I knew enough about Beisner's ideology, theology, and handling of data to know that he was a formidable adversary and also a cunning one. While the mainstream debate about human-induced climate change was already over by the time of our encounter, it is still not quite over in the evangelical community. Triggered by the release of the Evangelical Climate Initiative (ECI) in February 2006 (see appendix 4), which I led in drafting, a counterattack was waged by a group called the Interfaith Stewardship Alliance, led by Beisner. Our 2006 debate at Union University was an argument about the claims of the ECI statement. It was also a memorable encounter at the border of the evangelical right and center.

I have been involved in evangelical environmentalism since 1993, when Ron Sider's Evangelicals for Social Action (ESA) launched the Evangelical Environmental Network (EEN). At the time, evangelical environmentalism (or creation care) was clearly confined to the left wing of evangelicalism. It was not a significant enough issue within the evangelical community to attract that much attention (positive or negative) from the right or the inchoate center. Broad concerns about various environmental challenges, such as species loss or the ozone hole, failed to galvanize evangelicals in any serious way. The idea that an evangelical pastor might preach a sermon about the environment seemed almost laughably remote. And those interested in creation care had to constantly guard their flanks against the charge that environmental concern was a front for pantheism or New Age mysticism.

The climate issue has changed all of that. No single environmental concern has attracted such sustained international or (now) evangelical attention. The magisterial process undertaken by the Intergovernmental Panel on Climate Change over the past twenty years or so has finally proven impossible to ignore—though all but a small number of evangelicals did ignore it until just a few years ago. Now climate change is among the most heavily reported stories, and in my view one of the gravest human challenges, of the twenty-first century.

The decision of Rich Cizik of the National Association of Evangelicals (NAE) to take up the climate change issue was one of two major developments that have moved creation care from the evangelical left to the center. The other was the skillful work of EEN's Jim Ball to engage a widening circle of evangelical leaders in addressing climate change along with other issues. These events occurred in tandem with the explosion of national media attention to the climate change phenomenon. By now, creation care, and especially the overarching issue of climate, has become a predominant concern for both the evangelical left and center. Just about all of the left and center leaders and groups that have been profiled in this book thus far are "on board" on creation care and climate. Many signed the ECI statement. But none of the evangelical right leaders are similarly on board, and few enough of leaders in what might be called the center right. (An exception would be Timothy George, dean of Beeson Divinity School in Alabama). Thus it is fair to say that few contemporary moral/policy issues offer a more trenchant demarcation of the left/center versus right boundary line in American evangelical Christianity. As with the torture issue but unlike the homosexuality issue, here the left and center stand united over against the right. And the right appears deeply uncomfortable with this fact.

And so the right has developed a kind of offensive defense. Often in tandem with conservative think tanks and politicians, auxiliary groups have formed on the evangelical right to address environmental issues or defuse them. The most conspicuous of these at the time of this writing is the "Cornwall Alliance for the Stewardship of Creation," formerly known as the Interfaith Stewardship Alliance. In its new incarnation, this organization continues to be led by Cal Beisner, a long-time libertarian conservative Christian writer on energy and environmental issues. Beisner had been laboring in the trenches of the conservative evangelical world for decades, but like other evangelicals (such as Jim Wallis), he has risen to national renown recently as the media has turned its gaze in the direction of evangelicalism. Beisner's niche has become his role as *the* anti-EEN, anti-ECI spokesman. It is almost as if the evangelical right has subcontracted its environmental portfolio to Beisner, who has not been hesitant to take it up. This may be because men like James Dobson and the late Jerry Falwell have felt that they lack the scientific competence to take up these complex issues for themselves. But one also wonders whether the right is subtly seeking a kind of "plausible deniability" for its anti-creation care (especially anti-climate change) stance; if and when it collapses, they can blame Beisner—whose quotes they now use even as they rarely add their names to his declarations and official statements.

I must admit that I have found myself somewhat baffled by my encounters with the evangelical climate change skeptics of the right. I was raised by an energy/environment policy wonk who worked within the mainstream world of policy analysis at the Congressional Research Service. My father's job was to provide balanced, nonpartisan policy research for congressional staff and members. I learned at his feet such basic values as trust in the peer review process as it exists in mainstream science and the need for legislators to lead in making rational policy and lifestyle responses to clearly established scientific findings. I also learned about the power of self-interestedness, especially economic self-interest, as it affects policy advocacy and decision making. So I can understand why, say, ExxonMobil would not be too interested in embracing climate change science if it leads to costly congressionally mandated changes in their business practices. It may be, as some have suggested, that this is really all the explanation needed for evangelical right foot dragging on climate change: that it is purely a matter of internal alliances within the Republican bloc.

But my own encounters with Beisner and his ilk lead me to the conclusion that there are forces indigenous to at least a large sector of evangelical Christianity that contribute to a kind of revanchist, die-hard climate change skepticism. I am convinced that these forces are fundamentally theological, not economic or political, though these latter factors do play a major part. Beisner, at least, expresses considerable distrust of mainstream science, trusts the free market implicitly and distrusts government regulation entirely, adheres to an archaic version of a dominionist theology of creation, and holds fast to a hyper-Calvinist theology related to God's sovereignty (over against human responsibility) for what happens in human affairs. If I had to summarize all of the major ingredients that make up the climate change skeptic recipe, they might look like this:

- Begin with a longstanding disdain for the ("leftist") environmental movement.
- Add deep distrust of mainstream science, its leaders and academies, traceable to the still unresolved debate over Darwin and evolution.
- Blend in a similar mistrust of the mainstream mass media; if they are hyping an issue, it should be treated with skepticism.
- Throw in loyalty to a (Republican) president or party, which tends to be skeptical of environmental worries or commitments.
- Combine with libertarian, free market economics and distrust of government and its interventions with the market.
- Add a dash of general human reluctance to accept the hard-to-comprehend, unprecedented news that human beings are actually changing the climate.
- Mix in the belief that God ordains all that happens on this planet, and therefore all is in his hands and we need fear nothing.
- Add the conviction that the Bible gives human beings free rein to manage the creation as we see fit.
- Season with the belief that human beings are too frail, small, and insignificant to change something as big as the planetary climate.

Whatever the actual sources of the skeptics' view, the net result is that they are sowing sufficient doubt in the American evangelical mind (or reflecting the doubt that is already there) to block political movement to address climate change. Picture all of the red states on the famous electoral map, heavily Southern and Midwestern, most filled with evangelical Christians, most represented by evangelical friendly congressmen and senators. Thus far these have not been hospitable locales for action on climate, either at the state or federal level. The 2008 elections may break the power of this foot-dragging bloc. Already, though, it has slowed climate legislation by a decade or more. Those of us who are convinced that climate change is a major problem, and who work in red state evangelical America, are in the fight of our lives on this one. We are trying to change the hearts and minds of our religious/political communities from the inside.

I have sought to summarize the sources of climate change skepticism. In the rest of this chapter I would like to make my best case for climate change action. I will structure my comments to track the terms of the debate that I had with Beisner, a debate that still exists in the evangelical community today.

❊ ❊ ❊

Proposition 1: Anthropogenic (human-caused) climate change is responsible for most global warming over the past thirty years and projected to occur over the remainder of the century.

The climate is warming and in general is changing rapidly.[1] The evidence is being seen across the board: a rise in temperatures, an increase in the duration and intensity and possibly the frequency of extreme weather events, dramatic changes in the Arctic on both sea and land, obvious impacts on agriculture, species loss, change in animal habitats and ecosystems, and already considerable economic and human costs.

Currently you still find some claiming that global warming is a hoax. But note that this is not what Beisner and his group are now saying. Their statement says that: "We do not contest" that global warming is real. This is definitely a change from the earlier position of such skeptics. *And it is a key part of the first of the four major claims of the ECI statement.*

Even Cornwall agrees that global warming is happening. Perhaps if together we say that loud enough, we can cut the ground out from under the Michael Crichton fans and others like Senator Inhofe (R-OK) who say there is no global warming at all. Nor is the current scientific debate about whether human beings are primarily responsible for it (even though Cornwall still wants to debate this). Instead, the issues are how serious the impacts of climate change will be, and the best approaches for addressing it.

WHY THE CLIMATE IS CHANGING

The science of this issue begins with understanding the planetary energy exchange. Scientists have long known about the natural greenhouse effect, the way water vapor, carbon dioxide, and other gases present in the atmosphere absorb some of the thermal radiation leaving the surface, acting as a partial blanket for this radiation and causing the surface temperature to be *warm enough* to be livable for human beings and other creatures. This is God's gift to us and also sets Earth apart from any other known planet. This is the "firmament," an extraordinary gift indeed that makes our life possible.

Since the Industrial Revolution, human beings have actually been carrying out an unintentional atmospheric experiment by pumping carbon dioxide (as well as other gases) into the atmosphere in massive quantities and also by significantly reducing the forestation levels on the planet. The trapping of these gases and loss of the main way of neutralizing them is accelerating the greenhouse effect so that we are now beginning to overwarm the planet.

A handful of scientists who knew about the greenhouse effect and the mix of gases that constituted it began projecting as early as the late nineteenth century the possibility that radical increases in carbon dioxide would lead to rises in the global average temperature. A Swedish chemist predicted *in 1896* that doubling the concentration of CO_2 would increase the global average temperature by 5 to 6 °C (9 to 10 °F). This is not too far away from current mainstream projections; we are on the way to fulfilling his predictions.[2]

Beginning in the late 1950s scientists began taking routine measurements of CO_2 in the atmosphere. Beginning in the 1980s satellites came into use. Water temperature is measured all over the world. Ice-core drilling and testing are able to give us great data on the climate history of the planet. It has been exciting to learn about the extent of human ingenuity in studying climate. For a nonscientist like me, it has been quite impressive.

As of 2007, carbon dioxide concentrations in the atmosphere had risen to 380 parts per million (ppm) from a steady, pre-Industrial Revolution level of 280 ppm—a number that before that had held steady for 425,000 years. That is an increase of 36 percent. This is unprecedented and falls well outside the range of natural variability.

About 95 percent of fossil fuel burning (gas for our cars, coal for our power plants, heating oil for our homes, jet fuel for our planes) occurs in the wealthier Northern Hemisphere. So it should not surprise us that there is somewhat more CO_2 here than in the Southern Hemisphere, though it also circulates freely around the entire globe. And it should be noted that over the years, the CO_2 numbers have grown in parallel with fossil fuel emissions, providing further compelling evidence that the atmospheric increase in CO_2 levels results primarily from these emissions.

Carbon dioxide accounts for about 70 percent of greenhouse gases (GHGs). Such CO_2 concentrations are rising steadily. Right now, 7,000 million tons (gigatons) of CO_2 are pumped into the atmosphere each year, where they trap heat for decades, perhaps as many as two hundred years. The current pretty cautious estimate is that if we do not change course. we will reach at least 560 ppm by 2100, double the pre–Industrial Revolution figure.[3] Meanwhile, carbon gets stored in the oceans and on land, not just in the atmosphere, where it waits for later release—kind of a ticking time bomb. Another way to say this is that we are today precommitted to global warming based on what we have already stored up in air, sea, and land. We will be dealing with this climate change problem for centuries, not decades.

Deforestation around the world reduces the ability of nature to capture and store carbon dioxide through what a layperson might call the tree respiration process, which functions as a "sink" for carbon dioxide. It is a precious sink indeed. Trees breathe in carbon dioxide and emit oxygen. Deforestation is thus a considerable problem in its own right and needs to be addressed in all treatments of climate change (and its problems go well beyond climate change).

There are other relevant greenhouse gases (GHGs) such as methane (24 percent) and nitrous oxide (6 percent), together accounting for about 30 percent of GHGs. Many of these are in agriculture and present different, and difficult, mitigation challenges. Their importance is increasingly clear: methane, for example, is much more potent as a GHG than carbon dioxide.[4] Strategies need to be devised to address all of the major types of GHGs.

What all of this amounts to is a gradual, documentable alteration of the carbon exchange cycle and thus of the planetary climate system as a whole.

Developed countries contain 22 percent of the world's population and account for 63 percent of the GHG emissions. The United States emits 5.5 metric tons of carbon (mtc) per person, way above the rest of the world—compared to the level of 0.5 mtc per person in the developing world, and an average in the developed nations of 3 mtc per person. The United States, with 5 percent of the world's population, is responsible for 25 percent of GHG emissions. This disproportionate contribution to the GHG problem, and thus to the global warming problem, combined with our so far balky unwillingness to do much about it, creates a deep problem for U.S. relations with the rest of the world. It is obvious that unless we are willing to take steps to address this problem, developing countries like China and India will be even more unwilling to do so.

There is an obvious *correlation* between human alteration of the land (deforestation) and release of GHGs, with rising global temperatures and other phenomena. The most sophisticated climate modeling done in the world led to the projection that such human climate alterations would produce such global warming. The evidence of our senses and of the most sensitive measuring instruments shows that the changes are already happening, actually ahead of most projections.

Together, all of this leads to the conclusion that not only is the climate changing, but that human behavior is primarily responsible for this change. Representing the conclusions of the Intergovernmental Panel on Climate Change (IPCC), Sir John Houghton (one of its leaders) concluded in 2001 that it is very likely (greater than 90 percent probability) that at least 75 percent of the warming over the past fifty years has been due to human activities.[5] This assertion was again supported in the 2007 IPCC report. Few climate scientists would state the matter any more cautiously than this.

Christians meanwhile should not be surprised that human beings would have the ability to alter the atmosphere through their actions. We have dominion over the planet (which should be exercised as careful stewardship), and it is unsurprising, especially given our growing technological capacity, that we could affect the climate. Our greater technological power requires of us greater responsibility. It is also unsurprising to any student of human nature that we could unwittingly foul our own nest. Murphy's Law (whatever can go wrong, will go wrong), human sinfulness, and our inability to fully anticipate the consequences of our own actions: these are constant factors in human life. And yet evangelical Christians often seem invested in theological convictions that require a disbelief in the human capacity to affect the natural world in any serious way.

The Christian concept both of God's creative goodness and of our stewardship responsibility should make us deeply uneasy about any evidence that we are messing up something as foundational and complex as the planetary energy exchange and the carbon cycle. Theologically, we would want to assert that God set this amazing system up as his gift to make life habitable here for us and other creatures, and it is frightening to notice that we are changing what God has set up. It is hard to believe that such a fundamental change in the conditions in which all planetary life exists could be good or even insignificant. Certainly it is part of our stewardship responsibility to address this problem.

Proposition 2: Human-induced global warming is likely to have significant consequences for humanity and the rest of the biosphere if not mitigated.

This point is a matter of greater uncertainty than the previous one. The discussion in the mainstream scientific literature seems to range from the idea that the consequences of global warming will be significant but survivable to the more frightening claim that we are facing a planetary emergency within the lifetime of our children. The idea that the consequences will be insignificant is fading rapidly.

There are indeed some sources of uncertainty:

- About how the oceans will react in absorbing/releasing heat and carbon dioxide; this involves the highly complex science of ocean circulation.
- About the role of different types of aerosols, about cloud function, and about glacier melt dynamics.
- About the potential for unpredictability in the global weather system, especially as it faces new atmospheric conditions created by gradual but inexorable climate change.
- About the potential for abrupt shifts in the global climate if we reach a tipping point, and the likely nature of such an abrupt shift.
- And of course there is always uncertainty about how human beings will respond. Thus various scenarios are proposed by climate scientists, and computer modeling goes from there.

Still, we know much about what is already happening. We are already committed to global warming through GHGs already in "stock," and already in the pipeline. So the list of already observable phenomena can be projected to intensify over the next half-century or more.

We have seen a rise in average global temperature of 1.4°F over the twentieth century, most of it in the last thirty years or so. We can anticipate a considerable increase in temperatures over the course of the twenty-first century, the extent of it depending greatly on what actions we decide to take to reduce GHGs. We are already within 1°C of passing the maximum temperature of the last million years. A consensus seems to be developing that we really, really do not want to raise the temperature by 2°C, or the consequences could be quite dire. The temperature trend line is clearly and rapidly rising, extending well beyond the range of natural variability related to such factors as volcanoes or changes in the Earth's tilt or rotation.

There has also been a decrease in the daily surface temperature *range* from 1950 to 2000, with nighttime minimum temperatures increasing at twice the rate of daytime maximums. The "low of the day" is higher than it used to be. It never really cools, lending to that feeling of living in a greenhouse that we are increasingly having at night. (This was certainly true in the south this summer, where it was often 80°F at 10 p.m.)

There has been an obvious increase in the number of extremely hot days. Consider the European heat wave of 2003 that killed thirty thousand people in cities entirely unprepared for that kind of weather. In the summer of 2005 more than two hundred cities in the western United States broke all-time records for high temperatures and for consecutive days at 100°F or more. Anyone who has lived awhile and traveled in Northern Hemisphere cities can see it. You used to take a sweater to visit London in August. Not anymore.

Scientists are also noticing an increase in heavy precipitation events at mid- and high-northern latitudes. Warming ocean water is increasing the *duration and intensity* and possibly the number of major weather events like hurricanes, typhoons, and cyclones over the last thirty years. Hurricane Katrina may stand as a warning of what is to come. In 2004 for the first time ever, a hurricane hit Brazil from the south Atlantic. These vicious storms then also lead to an increase in flooding in many parts of the world.

There is increased summer drying and the associated incidence of drought and desertification in vulnerable areas of the world. The most badly affected are Africa and the western coast of South America. The Middle East is also affected. Water shortages are not only life threatening but can also be politically fraught, with significant implications for domestic and international conflicts.

The Arctic is ocean surrounded by land. Sea ice there tends to be only ten feet thick on average. Rapidly increasing temperatures there are melting the ice quickly, at a rate of 2.7 percent a decade.[6] News stories and visitors witness the breaking up of Arctic ice in ways that are dramatically changing navigability there. Nearby land is warming, affecting the trees, some of which are keeling over, and human settlements long built on the tundra. Now this thawing land is also releasing some very potent stored carbon and stored methane.

The loss of white snow and ice cover also affects the impact of sunlight. Instead of being reflected back to space, it stays here because there is less to reflect it back. This is called the albedo effect, which will likely contribute to an intensified global warming feedback loop.

Antarctica is the coldest place on the planet. Temperatures in the air and ocean began rising there in the 1970s. Overall the sea ice is decreasing in parts of Antarctica, while land ice is thinning. NASA estimates that Antarctic ice melt is contributing thirty-one billion tons of water to the ocean per year. Every couple of years parts of the Antarctic ice shelf are breaking up. A dramatic example was the Larsen B ice shelf in 2002: 150 miles long and 30 miles wide, bigger than Luxembourg or Rhode Island, it broke up in thirty-five days. Sea-level rise can be expected to accelerate as this ice falls or melts into the sea. The big fear here is that if the West Antarctic ice shelf melts or slips into the sea, it will raise sea level dramatically. In Greenland, the same kind of process appears to be happening. There has been a dramatic acceleration of melting since 1992. Greenland's ice cap is shrinking every year.

Related to this is an overall decrease of the duration of ice cover of rivers and lakes by about two weeks in mid-latitudes and high latitudes of the Northern Hemisphere. There has been a 10 percent decrease in snow cover since satellite pictures became available in the 1960s. This is obvious from numerous pictures and is confirmed by those who live in the affected regions; skiing and tourism are already affected around the world.

There has been a widespread retreat of nonpolar glaciers during the twentieth century in South America, Alaska, Europe, and Asia. This is obvious from pictures and visible to inhabitants and visitors. Globally, 85 percent of the world's glaciers are shrinking. Glaciers store 70 percent of the world's fresh water. Their melting or disappearance could have a dramatic effect on the world's supply of water.

The oceans reveal a massive bleaching and loss of coral reefs as a result of global warming and other factors. Coral reefs constitute an important part of the food chain and also serve as shelter for numerous species of fish. This may be an advance sign of what will happen due to developing changes in the acidity of ocean water. Other signs include growing dead zones in the ocean and huge, unprecedented algae blooms.

In terms of agriculture, the growing season has lengthened by one to four days per decade during the last forty years in the Northern Hemisphere, especially in high latitudes. This may be helpful to us, but there also has been a loss of soil moisture that could become severe if trends continue. Loss of soil moisture not only affects agriculture but leaves the soil more dry and vulnerable to wildfires, which have increased decade by decade, with a dramatic jump in the 1990s both in the Americas and around the world. Many areas of the United States, such as in the southwest, are noticing changes in weather patterns and negative impacts on agriculture. Leaders of a number of states are deeply concerned about drought and water issues.

Other signs of warming in the Northern Hemisphere include earlier plant flowering, bird arrival, breeding seasons, and insect emergence. Basically, climate change is disrupting millions of ecological relationships among species.

Animals are attempting to adapt via habitat change. Those species that need colder weather are heading toward the poles, both north and south. But not all species will be able to adapt, leading to species endangerment and heightened extinction rates. The rate of extinction is already one thousand times higher than the normal background rate. One study has shown that two-thirds of 677 species had adapted to climate change by bringing forward the dates on their calendar (breeding, migration, hibernation); and that of these, four-fifths had moved northward or to higher ground.

One early indicator is the polar bear population. A study in North America suggests that the population is 15 percent thinner than thirty years ago, and has dropped by 17 percent in the Hudson Bay in the past ten years. Polar bears are now being considered for inclusion on the endangered species list by the American Fish and Wildlife Service.

All of these changes are costing money and will cost more. There has been a dramatic rise in global losses (by an order of magnitude) as a result of weather-related events. This is certainly being taken seriously by insurers who are adjusting to the new realities by raising rates except for where regulation prevents them from doing so. In the last thirty years, insurers have seen a fifteenfold increase in loss payoffs related to extreme weather events. Rising rates are already following; some will simply stop coverage of vulnerable areas, such as along the Gulf Coast. Clem Booth of the Allianz group has said, "To me as an insurance person, climate change is an absolute reality."[7] As these prices get passed on to the consumer, people are going to have to start moving away from the coasts in much of the world. This is already a major political issue in Florida.

Investors are also taking climate change seriously and building it into their investment decisions. The Investor Network on Climate Risk reflects this development. This group, which meets annually, manages assets totaling nearly $3 trillion. News reports suggest that they are looking hard at the impact of climate change on their investments, and of their investments on climate change.[8] These are hardly naive tree huggers.

Worries about climate change are especially intense in relation to Africa. In sub-Saharan Africa over 90 percent of agriculture is rain fed.[9] About 300 million Africans currently live in a water-scarce environment, and by 2025 an increasing population could boost this to 600 million.[10] Approximately 70 percent of African employment is based on agriculture, and agriculture creates over 60 percent of the profits from international trade.[11] More than half of the population lives on food grown locally. African food production overall has been declining over the last several decades, while the rest of the world has seen an increase.[12] In some African countries, yields from rain-fed agriculture could be reduced by up to 50 percent by 2020.[13] The poor in sub-Saharan Africa spend 60 to 80 percent of their income on food. These facts make it clear that any disruption in Africa's ability to grow rain-fed crops will have serious consequences, especially for the poor. This is exactly what climate change will do. Rain-fed agriculture requires predictable rainfall in moderate amounts over time. Floods and droughts devastate crops, and climate change will increase floods and droughts. Across Africa, global warming is projected to reduce rainfall in water-scarce environments by 5 percent in some areas and up to 20 percent in others.[14] In addition, climate change will impact agriculture by shifting the times seasons begin and end as well as by increasing agricultural pests. But drought will not only impact crops. Inland fisheries and livestock will also be severely impacted in some areas. *In sum, an additional 56 to 72 million poor people in Africa could be at risk of hunger and malnutrition in this century due to global warming.*[15]

Worries over rising sea levels are also especially significant in Africa, as in Asia. Consider Africa: Over 25 percent of Africans live within one hundred kilometers of a seacoast. Sea level rise could significantly increase the number of Africans impacted by coastal flooding, with a worst case being 70 million in this century. Inland flash flooding on account of heavy rains is also projected to increase in intensity and occurrences. Such inland flooding has devastating consequences. For example, the 1997–1998 floods in Kenya resulted in $1 billion in damage,[16] and the floods in Mozambique in 2000 resulted in two million people being displaced, with 350,000 jobs lost impacting the livelihoods of up to 1.5 million people.[17]

A related concern is the already evident increase in the number of people exposed to waterborne diseases, such as cholera and malaria. As weather warms, disease vectors, like algae, mosquitoes, and ticks, start to show up in new areas and cover a wider range, therefore infecting more people. Thirty new diseases have emerged over the last thirty years, and older diseases are showing up in new areas. An example is the West Nile virus. Disease-carrying pests are being seen at altitudes never before reached, such as mosquitoes at 7200 feet in the Andes. Global warming will cause increased incidences of malaria, dengue fever, yellow fever, encephalitis, and respiratory diseases, and increased impact as people are affected by diseases new to their region.

The possibility of abrupt climate change is the main scenario that may take us from "significant" to "catastrophic" global impacts. Abrupt climate change occurs "when the climate system is forced to cross some threshold, triggering a transition to a new state at a rate determined by the climate system itself and faster than the cause. . . . The system does not return to its original state."[18] Some quite mainstream climate scientists are now warning us about this, saying that unless we begin changing our ways dramatically, we will be precommitted to a course that will trigger abrupt climate change. One scenario involves a combination of a shutdown of the Gulf Stream ocean circulation system, quick melting of the ice sheets in Greenland and West Antarctica, the release of massive amounts of methane from the tundra in the Arctic region, all looping together with what is already happening in a devastating feedback effect. I think that it is the height of foolishness to ignore such fears and the evidence upon which they are based.

Human civilization for the last ten thousand years (all of recorded history) has been built on a relatively stable climate pattern, with steady levels of GHGs, survivable natural variability in temperatures, and a way of redistributing heat that has been reliable. It has been a global climate system of amazing complexity and effectiveness that turns our hearts to worship God. We are currently tampering with this climate pattern, and therefore we risk creating an unprecedented climate system with possibly devastating effects. Wouldn't it be something if we boil or drown ourselves and the creatures that dwell here with us, all because we ignored the warning signs that our own very sophisticated technology made available to us, and with plenty of lead time? The first time, God sent the flood. This time, we would do it ourselves.

I stand by ECI's claim that "Christian moral convictions demand our response to the climate change problem." The issue is too real, the consequences already beginning to be apparent, and the downside risk too profound, to ignore this problem. And as a Christian, I find it morally impossible to support taking unnecessary chances with the planet's very future. I wouldn't do it with my own children. I cannot do it with everyone's children.

Proposition 3—Mandatory reductions in carbon dioxide emissions would mitigate human-induced global warming sufficiently to make its consequences noncatastrophic at a cost that would be preferable to the costs of adaptation.

ECI's claim is that governments, businesses, churches, and individuals all have a role to play in addressing climate change. The skeptics seem most frightened of some kind of runaway government regulatory scheme that destroys the economy. This seems to flow from a mixture of healthy concern for the economy and captivity to a libertarian ideology that loathes all government intervention in the economy. It also reflects a close ideological proximity to the most recalcitrant strand of corporate America.

We instead argued in ECI for a mix of public and private actions. The choice between mitigation (directly attacking the level of carbon emissions, and so on) and adaptation (dealing with the inevitable consequences of climate change) is a false one. It is clear that we will have to do both. This is a global challenge both in the sense that it is relevant to the entire world and also that all sectors of society will need to be motivated to respond. A massive literature and public policy response is already underway. It is not helped by those who are still busy denying the problem or its seriousness. If we grant both, we can talk together about what to do.

Some key realistic climate policy principles would be the following:

1. *Christian moral imperatives must be kept in mind throughout.* These include faithful care of creation, love of neighbor (all of them), intergenerational moral responsibility, a preferential option for the poor, respect for democratic processes, respect for truth, basic human equality, and the sacredness of every human life.

2. *Research and development is critical.* We do not today have the technologies to solve the problems at acceptable costs, but hopefully we can eventually identify and develop them. We need social support for very significant research and development, as well as price signals to spur the best minds to get to work on the problem.

3. *International cooperation and coordination are imperative.* This problem cannot be solved by a region, state, or nation, though each can pioneer possible approaches. It is the ultimate international problem. It tests whether there is or can be a world community. But meanwhile, every nation that takes a positive step forward does the right thing. The United States should lead by example.

   A further thought about the difficulty of finding international solutions is this: Though we need an international system for addressing this problem, the distribution of costs and benefits, now and in the future, makes national economic interests diverge radically. We need all countries to impose similar price-based emissions controls or to participate in a cap-and-trade system, with allowance for the special needs of developing countries. It is not clear how or whether such a global system could be developed and enforced, and there are also questions about which aspects of the economy and GHGs can really be captured. It would be much easier to regulate fossil fuels than emissions related to agriculture; forestation and soil issues pose their own challenges. Probably we should work first on the largest problems (coal and forests) and the largest polluters.

International efforts to address climate change are not new, nor are they radical. Efforts began with the 1992 UN Convention on Climate Change, which was signed by all of the world's countries. The agreed goal was stabilization of GHG concentrations in the atmosphere at a level that would prevent dangerous anthropogenic interference with the climate system.

The next step in the process was the 1997 Kyoto Protocol, which set a cap on GHG emissions from thirty-eight developed nations to below 1990 levels sometime between 2008 and 2012. It has been officially accepted by 160 countries but was famously rejected by the United States and Australia. (Drought in Australia is now radically affecting Australian attitudes toward this issue.) Kyoto includes a cap-and-trade mechanism between signatory countries and other ways to get "credits" for a nation's work on carbon emissions. Skeptics argue that even if fully implemented, Kyoto would likely have only a small impact on temperature increases, but the real point of any cap-and-trade system is that it sends robust market signals that will change investment decisions. At some point economies of scale and learning curves will have the economy moving faster than what governments have mandated.

4. *We need policies that both sustain the world economy and address the environmental problems that our GHG-emitting economy produces.* I agree with Beisner that we do not want to crush developing economies. But this problem should not be set up as jobs versus the environment. No, as many commentators have said, global warming itself will significantly affect the global economy. It is hard to predict how much, but the Stern Review on the Economics of Climate Change, a comprehensive study produced in November 2006, now predicts a 5 percent negative impact on the global economy if temperatures continue to rise.

5. *This is a long-term problem still requiring immediate attention.* It will take us a century or more to put in place the values and practices required to sustain a world economy in the face of climate-related environmental constraints.

We cannot wait forever while risks grow and damages store up and we possibly create the conditions for an abrupt climate change that devastates the entire global community. Even if we are looking at the very long term, we have to act now because we cannot change the energy system overnight. So we need to work even now on projects involving long lead times or with long lifetimes. What kind of power plants will we build now, what cars will we drive now, how will we build our buildings now? Some of these decisions have forty- to fifty-year time horizons. So one way to think about it is to take reasonable and prudent steps now while continuing further research and assessment of what the climate itself is telling us.

6. *Uncertainty at many levels must be factored in.* There is indeed considerable uncertainty when assessing potential risks from climate change and the costs of averting it, as well as potential benefits to be gained by limiting emissions today.

There are also considerable uncertainties about future trends in emissions, including technological developments that may affect emission levels as well as such factors as population growth, government policies, market developments, and so on.

Uncertainty is often an argument for going slow or doing nothing. But uncertainty cuts both ways. Skeptics say the possible consequences are uncertain and may not be that bad. But mainstream climate scientists are predicting a range of certain definite consequences, and their uncertainty estimates range to include far greater damages as well as lesser ones. These greater damage estimates also must be factored into cost-benefit analyses. A comparison: A terrorist attack may be very unlikely, but the level of awfulness of such an attack must be taken seriously when you analyze what you are willing to pay to prevent one.

7. *The United States cannot (or at least will not) sign on to programs that would do more harm to the U.S. economy than to the economies of other countries.* It is just politically impossible. This is why the Kyoto process failed here. It is a fact about national politics: nations will act in their self-interest. They at least need to see fairness in the distribution of benefits and burdens. Part of that process, however, is careful assessment of the best science of climate change as it continues to develop.

8. *There should be programs with short fuses, mid-term fuses, and long-term fuses.* We do what we can immediately and work out other plans as need develops, technology makes possible, political will can be generated, and so on. We cannot solve this problem within any of our planning horizons; we can only work on it. But this we must do.

9. *One of God's variables affecting climate is human intelligence.* That got us into this fix; it will help us cope (adapt) and reverse (mitigate) this problem too, provided we harness it to this end. We will need both adaptation and mitigation strategies. Both are already under development. I agree with the Cornwall organization that we want to create the conditions for maximum human creativity to go to work on this problem, rather than adopting strategies that undercut such creativity.

10. *Basic human motivations should be the basis for programs.* We want to employ market mechanisms as far as possible rather than command and control, stewardship rather than "subdue the earth." We need to identify and nurture the best motivational mix available.

One basic motivational problem is already apparent: costs will be incurred now for damages to be prevented (mainly) later. This is a hard sell indeed due to human selfishness and short-term thinking. Unless you can use market capitalism as an ally to build benefits into the system now (including profits) and not just benefits over the horizon, policy change will likely falter. But if policymakers find a way to appeal to national self-interest, humanitarian goodwill, and planetary stewardship, the combination just might bring the support needed to make real change happen.

In sum, I am arguing for a mix of research and development, adaptation strategies, and mitigation approaches. I think it is only this mix that is an adequate response to the climate change problem. All sectors of society have parts to play. That includes families, businesses, universities, and governments.

❈ ❈ ❈

The ECI statement made four primary claims. Consider them as this chapter concludes:

1. *Human-induced climate change is real.* My opponents have now granted that it is real. The overwhelming majority of the world's credentialed specialists on this issue agree that it is largely human-induced—related fundamentally to our emissions of GHGs.

2. *The consequences of climate change will be significant and will hit the poor the hardest.* I believe that the long list of consequences already being experienced and the projections of future consequences from current trends makes it hard to deny except through *the will to disbelieve* that the consequences will be significant. Whether they will be catastrophic is somewhat more uncertain. But I do not believe in playing dice with my grandchildren's future.

   Whether the consequences will be worse for the poor may not matter to everyone, though it should. I think they will be quite bad enough for all of us. But both because of the geographical locations and livelihoods of many of the poor, and because they simply have fewer resources for adapting or responding to the likely problems, I think that on this issue—like most others—the poor will be the ones hardest hit.

3. *Christian moral convictions demand our response to the climate change problem.* We must care about climate change because we love God the Creator and Jesus our Lord. This is God's

world. This love should not take the form of passive indifference, but instead active service.

We must care about climate change because we are called
to love our neighbors, especially the least of these.

We must care about climate change because we are called
to exercise stewardship over the earth and its creatures—not
a kind of dominionism where we can do whatever we want
with the planet. To be the image of God is to reflect the kind of
dominion God would exercise.

We dare not allow any alien ideology or idolatrous loyalty,
such as an ideological commitment to libertarianism or laissez-faire capitalism, to override our primary loyalty to Jesus
Christ and the moral responsibilities that flow from our commitment to him.

4. *The need to act now is urgent. Governments, businesses, churches,
and individuals all have roles to play.* There are many kinds of
actions that thoughtful people are already taking to address
this problem. These are not woolly folks but chief executive
officers, insurance executives, and investment bankers. Many
churches are involved. Many individuals are making their
own investment and energy decisions accordingly.

But Americans are the least engaged of any major country, and
too few evangelicals have been paying much attention. Exceptions, of
course, include the hundred plus who signed the ECI, which includes
Rick Warren, Bill Hybels (Willow Creek), Joel Hunter, Bob Andringa
(retired president of the CCCU), Timothy George (dean of Beeson
Divinity School), Duane Litfin (president of Wheaton College),
Gordon MacDonald (author, pastor, World Relief board chair), David
Neff (*Christianity Today* editor), and Richard Stearns (president of World
Vision). This was a significant list whose very significance evoked
the fierce counterattack represented by Beisner and other sources of
criticism.

Evangelicals represent 25 percent of the American population; as we
go, so goes the nation. But on this issue we have not yet engaged very

deeply. And so neither has our nation. Are we not supposed to offer moral leadership in this society?

The position articulated by our adversaries is quite wrong on the science related to climate change, reflecting a rear-guard action with fewer and fewer adherents. Soon enough this position too will crumble under the weight of contrary evidence, as did their earlier claim that climate change is a hoax. It is quite likely wrong about the level of seriousness of the consequences of climate change. It misreads the nature of our Christian moral obligations. And it is so wedded to the public policy positions articulated by a few in the corporate world, as well as its own libertarian ideology, that it cannot consider the value of the right mix of government policies and personal choices to address this problem.

A basic principle of life is that when you are digging yourself a hole, stop digging or at least slow down your pace while you figure out how to get out of the hole. But first people have to be convinced that they are digging the hole; then they need to be convinced that they really do not want to be in that hole; and finally they need to see that the price required to get out of the hole is a price worth paying.

We do not need to panic as if God's creation had no resiliency—and human ingenuity no possibilities. Indeed, we will need all of that resiliency and every bit of that ingenuity to get out of this hole. We will need the best that our politicians, researchers, business people, religious thinkers, and moral leaders can offer us. And while we trust God, we dare not presume on God or blame him for the consequences of our own bad choices. If we ignore the merciful signs he is now sending us from every corner of creation, telling us to exercise our creation stewardship obligations *now* before it is too late, we human beings alone will bear the responsibility. And judgment will begin with the household of God. But we can do better. Let's start now.

Chapter 8

EVANGELICALS AND WAR

I noted earlier that the evangelical left cannot seem to find any U.S. war it can support and that this tendency toward a functional or actual pacifism leaves the left radically out of step with the rest of the evangelical world. The evangelical right, although not generally focusing on the moral issues associated with war, tends toward an instinctive support for U.S. war fighting, rooted in its uncritical patriotism, close ties with the military, and (in times of Republican rule) support for their political party of choice. Review of evangelical right Web sites from 2005–2007 demonstrated that this tendency to support the president, the troops, and the country (and therefore the war in Iraq and the "war on terror") reigned almost universally, though with a bit of an isolationist strand apparent in groups such as Phyllis Schlafly's Eagle Forum (EF). With this exception, probably no group of Americans can be counted on to offer more steadfast support for American military engagement than the evangelical right community.

While most evangelicals do not appear to think seriously about the ethics of war, evangelical elites who are not pacifists turn almost universally to just-war theory as the foundation for their approach to war. Evangelical right leaders employ just-war theory in a manner that almost always leads them to justify wars that American presidents want to fight. (Sometimes they also employ it to support torture, but that is another chapter.) My view is that for the evangelical left just-war theory is not its native language because pacifism or a basic Jesus-centered rejection of war tends to come more naturally. However, when the left does employ just-war-theory language, it does so in such a way as to lead to the rejection of the moral legitimacy of most if not all U.S. wars. This is a puzzle that needs to be pieced together: How can the same theory have such radically different outcomes? Does this discredit the theory altogether?

The emergence of Glen Stassen's just-peacemaking theory adds a new wrinkle. Just-peacemaking theory has been met with enthusiasm on the left and has slowly spread to the evangelical center. This theory, as indicated previously, focuses on concrete measures that can and sometimes do prevent wars from occurring. It parallels just-war theory in offering a list of criteria (in this case, ten practices) that can and must be undertaken by nations and by citizens to prevent war.[1] Stassen treats just-peacemaking theory not as a formal alternative to either pacifism or just-war theory but instead as a complement to both. Pacifists can use it to move toward a more activist peacemaking stance rather than simply a war-rejecting one. Just warriors can employ it, among other things, as an accountability yardstick for the "last resort" criterion of just-war theory. No nation can say it has gone to war as a last resort unless it has attempted the practices of just peacemaking, such as taking independent initiatives and acknowledging its own responsibility for the tensions between two nations. My sense is that the evangelical right seems no closer to embracing just-peacemaking theory—despite Stassen's two decades of effort on this front—than it is to embracing pacifism. I think that this is a mistake, one that flows partly from their dismissal of the theory as a product of the evangelical left. But it does mean that in much of the evangelical world, just-war theory remains the only game in town.

Where does this leave the evangelical center? I think it leaves us with the opportunity to reclaim a refined version of just-war theory while also employing the legitimate insights of just peacemaking. As it stands, the right's uncritical embrace of just about every U.S. war has not been answered by a cogent alternative from the center, which does not share the left's pacifism but has not articulated an alternative. This has left the moderate center of the evangelical world without the resources to sift through the war-making proposals and claims of our government. Thus we have tended to say little directly on the general issue of war's morality or a particular war's morality (such as Iraq). This will not do, because the propaganda operations of any national government are sufficiently powerful that they must be met by a coherent framework for critically evaluating them. Otherwise, citizens, Christian or otherwise, will have no ability to sift, evaluate, and, if necessary, resist the claims of government.

During the runup to the Iraq War in 2002, I reflected in print on what was becoming a characteristic split among the many Christians (not just evangelicals) who claim to be adherents of just-war theory.[2] As I just suggested, politically conservative just-war people seemed to operate from an application of just-war criteria leading to a tendency to support most wars; politically liberal thinkers seemed to operate from a different application of the same criteria, leading them to oppose most wars. I called the conservative version "hard" just-war theory, mainly because it was the position taken by those I would consider hard-liners, and the liberal approach "soft" just-war theory, because it tended to be the dovish stance. I now believe that these positions need relabeling for clarity "Soft" just-war theory is actually "strict" in that it tests government claims about the need for war with great stringency. "Hard" just-war theory is better labeled "permissive" because it tends to open the door to war more easily. This framework received a fair amount of attention and use, and I think that this analysis remains correct. It has a particular poignancy in light of the Iraq quagmire. In light of all that has happened since 2003, it seems fitting to revisit the basic approach of this essay and suggest that strict just-war theory provides a way forward for the American evangelical center.

❀ ❀ ❀

In a June 1, 2002, commencement speech at West Point, President Bush offered an expansive statement suggesting a U.S. military doctrine of preemptive action against rogue states and terrorist groups. Though Iraq was not mentioned by name, we can now see that the speech was part of an effort to lay a foundation for military action against that nation. When the president moved ahead with such plans in 2003, American Christians were once again faced with the decision whether to support military action or not.

When that day came, Christian theologians, ethicists, church leaders, and others broke out the just-war theory and put it to work—like they always do. In the all-encompassing shadow of September 11th and the Iraq War, it is easy to forget that in the 1990s alone just-war theory was applied to U.S. military engagements (or lack thereof) in Iraq, Bosnia, Somalia, Kosovo, Haiti, and Rwanda. And the tradition extends back well into U.S.—and of course Western—history. It is not too simple to say that our nation is constantly fighting wars and that as we do, we are constantly assessing those wars according to some version of just-war theory. Evangelicals are now an important part of this process.

But a chorus of dissatisfaction with just-war theory has been gaining strength. It is not just that pacifists and others dissent from the tradition on principle, but that the tradition itself is, in just-war theorist James Turner Johnson's phrase, "broken."[3] I would substitute the word "riven." Today, and for some time, there has been an apparently irreconcilable ideological split among American Christians concerning the application of just-war criteria to U.S. military engagements, a split so profound that the usefulness of the tradition itself has been called into radical question.

The most pessimistic reading of this evidence would be that the just-war theory has decayed into nothing more than an ornament that can be used at will by partisans to decorate their political loyalties and convictions via the illusion of supposedly "objective" confirmation. The implication of this thesis would be that references to just-war theory should simply be ignored, and the theory itself abandoned.

My actual proposal here is a bit less radical. My thesis is that in contemporary American Christian usage, there exist two just-war theories, or at least two strikingly divergent patterns in interpretation of this ancient tradition of Christian reflection, rooted in a variety of theoretical differences but most fundamentally in an ideological split over the role of the United States in the world.

Recognizing this bifurcation in just-war theory can at a minimum enable us to predict and understand in advance the differences in moral reasoning that will emerge the next time evangelical Christians confront the decision of whether or not to support a U.S. military action. More profoundly, exploring the roots of these differences has the potential to move evangelical thinking both about war and about the United States in a more constructive direction.

I want to call these strict and permissive just-war theory. This indicates that both approaches belong to the same family but are significantly different not just in their conclusions but in their intellectual substructure.

In the technical just-war literature, the different positions are sometimes called "presumption against war" just-war theory (for strict just-war theory) and "presumption for justice" just-war theory (for permissive just-war theory), though these terms create their own problems. Perhaps others will suggest better labels.

To illustrate my thesis, I will compare a collectively-authored Catholic document with an individually written evangelical Protestant text, separated by two decades in their composition. This will help to demonstrate that the distinction I am noticing is neither merely contemporary nor confined to evangelicals. For strict just-war theory, I will work with *The Challenge of Peace*, a document offered at the height of the second phase of the Cold War (1983) by the United States Conference of Catholic Bishops (USCCB). The document's driving force is generally agreed to have been Father Bryan Hehir, formerly of Georgetown University and the staff of USCCB. For permissive just-war theory, I will quote Keith Pavlischek, a conservative Reformed Protestant who serves as a fellow at the Center for Public Justice in Washington and writes frequently on just-war theory. Pavlischek, a lieutenant colonel (retired) in the Marine Corps Reserves, served extensively in Iraq.

Other writers could easily have been selected. Those familiar with the landscape on this issue will be able to see strict just-war theory in the denominational documents emerging from the (nonpacifist) mainline churches during the Cold War and today, and the work of most Protestant ethicists claiming just-war identification, such as James Childress and Ralph Potter in the 1970s and centrist evangelicals Stephen Mott and

Richard Mouw more recently. Permissive just-war theory can likewise be seen in Catholic voices such as George Weigel, long associated with the Ethics and Public Policy Center in Washington, Protestants such as the late Paul Ramsey of Princeton and political theorist Johnson of Rutgers, and at a more popular level the application of just-war theory among most leading conservative evangelical popularizers, such as Charles Colson, founder of Prison Fellowship.

A note of personal disclosure before proceeding: As an ethicist-in-training, I cut my teeth on what I am now calling strict just-war theory, but what I thought at the time *simply was* just-war theory. As I have said, I later worked at Ron Sider's Evangelicals for Social Action, a strict just-war/pacifist organization. There I met and worked with Keith Pavlischek and watched him struggle against the strict just-war theory (and sometimes pacifism) of an organization whose perspective on war issues he never shared. The struggle within just-war theory that I articulate here is in a real sense a struggle within my own soul, rooted in my own personal pilgrimage, though not, I believe, unique to me.

STRICT JUST-WAR THEORY

Strict just-war theory is characterized by a strongly articulated horror of war, a strong presumption for peace and against violence and war; a tendency to be skeptical of government claims about the need for military buildups and military action; an inclination to use just-war theory as a tool for citizen discernment and prophetic critique; a pattern of trusting the efficacy of international treaties and multilateral approaches (over against U.S. unilateralism) and the information and perspective offered by global peace and human rights groups and the international press (over against those offered by the U.S. government and American media outlets); a quite stringent application of just-war criteria, both in entry into war and conduct of war; and a claim of common ground with Christian pacifists despite obvious differences.

The Challenge of Peace, for example, begins its treatment of just-war theory with a discussion of the "nature of peace."[4] Peace is described as a reality that humans must construct out of such ingredients as truth, justice, freedom, and love; yet it is also a divine gift. Peace, for the bishops, is clearly normative. It is God's will for humanity, our origin and our destiny, and our task in the time given us on this planet.

Quoting earlier Catholic documents, especially statements crafted during Vatican II, *The Challenge of Peace* moves on to a stark condemnation of the savagery and horror of war, especially modern war and an envisioned nuclear war. The bishops cite approvingly a Vatican II declaration in favor of the outlawing of war "by international consent," recognizing that this would require the strengthening of international law and public authority well beyond its current realities.

The right of governments to defend themselves is granted by the bishops only within the context of this lack of adequate international governance. Given this (to them) lamentable reality, however, and in the context of a strong presumption against war, the bishops do grant governments a right and obligation to defend peace against aggression. Although individuals may renounce the right to self-defense, governments may not do so without violating their mandate.

After granting this point, however, the bishops come around again to emphasize the importance of nonviolent means of national defense and conflict resolution as most in keeping with "the call of Jesus." The horrors of war, especially war involving weapons of mass destruction, are again emphasized.

The presumption that binds all Christians, according to the bishops, is that "the possibility of taking even one human life is something we should consider in fear and trembling." Just-war "teaching" is actually an effort to prevent war. Only if "extraordinarily strong reasons" exist "for overriding the presumption in favor of peace and against war" may war be considered. Even then, just-war theory's primary function is to "seek to restrict and reduce [war's] horrors."

The classic *jus ad bellum* (just entry into war) criteria are then reviewed and expounded: just cause, competent authority, right intention, comparative justice, last resort, probability of success, and proportionality. The discussion of competent authority notes bitter divisions in American life over whether many U.S. military actions have met this test given the lack of formal declarations of war by Congress in recent decades. The bishops' reflection on comparative justice emphasizes limiting both the ferocity of war and any kind of "absolute justice" moral absolutism on our part; it also notes the role of propaganda and the "ease with which nations and individuals either assume or delude themselves into believing that God or right is clearly on their side."[5]

The treatment of last resort notes and laments the difficulty of applying this requirement given the lack of "sufficient internationally recognized authority" to mediate disputes, and calls for support for the United Nations—quoting Pope Paul VI to the effect that the UN is the "last hope for peace" on earth.[6] Discussion of proportionality emphasizes the grave costs of war, not just in blood and treasure but in its spiritual dimension, and notes that proportionality must be considered at all stages of a war—footnoting the fact that this same body of bishops publicly rejected the Vietnam War in 1971 as a result of its failure to meet this test.

Further discussion of the *jus in bello* (just conduct of war) criteria of proportionality and discrimination (noncombatant immunity) includes a striking condemnation of the horrors of technologically advanced weapons of war, such as nuclear, biological, and chemical weapons, claiming that the nature of war in the modern era is fundamentally changed. Modern war, especially any war involving a nuclear-armed superpower, is especially dangerous and resolutely to be avoided. The section on just-war theory closes with a warm affirmation of the value of the pacifist witness within the Catholic Church, claiming that it shares with just-war theory "a common presumption against the use of force as a means of settling disputes."[7]

My familiarity with the literature of just-war theory, both Catholic and Protestant, leads me to the conclusion that the essential cluster of themes and emphases found in *The Challenge of Peace* is likewise found in strict just-war theory of all types. Indeed, this document itself played a significant role in shaping what I think should now be called strict just-war theory, a fact much lamented among its adversaries, who believe that *Challenge* played a key role in essentially hijacking classic just-war theory.

PERMISSIVE JUST-WAR THEORY

Permissive just-war theory is characterized by a strongly articulated horror of injustice and disorder; an assumption that war is a tragic but essentially inevitable aspect of human affairs in a fallen world and that protecting national security through war is a necessary task of government; a tendency to trust the U.S. government and its claims of a need for military action when it makes such claims and to employ just-war theory as a tool to aid policymakers and military personnel in their decisions; an inclination to distrust the efficacy of international treaties as a means of national security and to downplay the value of international/ transnational actors, agencies, and perspectives; a less stringent or differently oriented application of some just-war criteria; and no sense of common ground with Christian pacifists who oppose all governmental use of lethal force.

In an October 2001 paper titled "Just War Theory and Terrorism: Applying the Ancient Doctrine to the Current Conundrum," Pavlischek laments what he calls the "irresponsib[le]", "blame America first" perspective of many religious leaders and others after 9/11.[8] In response, he calls for rigorous retrieval of "classic" just-war theory. While Pavlischek's essay was not intended as a comprehensive theoretical treatment of just-war theory, it is possible to find within its pages and that of other writings by Pavlischek the elements of permissive just-war theory as I am defining it.

Pavlischek claims that the foundational presumption of just-war theory is the government's mandate to pursue justice (including freedom), order, and peace. Government is ordained by God to prevent the victimization of the innocent, the violation of public order, and the disruption of peace. It is granted a monopoly on coercive, even lethal, force in order to accomplish this mandate. In a fallen world, such force will be required both in domestic and international relations. This use of force is to be restrained and law governed, to be sure, but it is a necessity—not an evil but a good and proper exercise of "God's governance in a fallen world." Thus, classic just-war theory, according to Pavlischek, "do[es] not begin with a presumption against force or violence, but rather with a presumption for justice" and recognition that until history ends governments will need to use force to deter, punish, and rectify injustice.[9]

This is not intended as a "realist" or Machiavellian embrace of a stance implying that no moral considerations apply to governmental conduct. To the contrary, governments must be held to stringent moral criteria related to their mandate to pursue justice and secure order and peace. Just-war theory is a critical part of that work. Yet in a tendency generally apparent in permissive just-war theory, at no point in Pavlischek's essay does he indicate a concern about the overall trustworthiness of the U.S. government (or any other) in its application of just-war criteria or its general use of force.

In a related essay, Pavlischek (and coauthor Jim Skillen of the Center for Public Justice) acknowledge that governments do "often exhibit structures and policies and practices of injustice."[10] But that essay goes on to claim that all who hold divinely mandated authority (parents, pastors, elders, etc.) do sometimes misuse their authority because we are all sinners. Thus the fact that governments cannot always be trusted with their authority has no impact whatsoever on whether Christians should recognize that war-making is a part of the mandate of government in a fallen world, just as the fact that parents sometimes exhibit unloving actions toward their children has no impact on whether Christians should generally support the divinely mandated exercise of parental authority.

Unlike The Challenge of Peace, Pavlischek's permissive just-war theory reflects no yearning for the establishment of an international governing authority that can ensure justice, peace, and order in a manner transcending the actions of individual states. The normative "political community" or "competent authority" for Pavlischek is the mature, competent, relatively just individual nation-state relating with other nation-states. The Challenge of Peace recognized that for now nation-states are the highest form of political community but emphasized their limited ability to resolve conflicts peaceably and thus turned considerable attention to the UN and other international actors. Indeed, Vatican II–era Catholic documents clearly call for the formation of some kind of world government. Pavlischek, like Johnson, argues that international organizations like the UN lack the cohesion, sovereignty, and military chain of command necessary to be effective in international statecraft.

In working through the just-war criteria, Pavlischek offers some strikingly different interpretations than those offered by the bishops in The Challenge of Peace. Under just cause, for example, he follows Thomas

Aquinas in including retributive justice; that is, punishment for evil; the bishops raised questions as to whether this had ever been a legitimate cause for war and rejected it as a just cause for modern war. Pavlischek disagrees. This debate was played out many times in the days after September 11th and made an appearance as well in the discussion of going to war with Iraq.

In Pavlischek's discussion of just-war theory, he quotes Augustine, Aquinas, Luther, and Calvin extensively to the effect that God places coercive power in the hands of political authorities to use for the common good as they see fit both domestically and in international affairs. Whereas *The Challenge of Peace* offered an extensive discussion of conscientious objection to the unjust application of government power, Pavlischek does not address the point in the essays I have reviewed, though he does support selective conscientious objection on just-war grounds (a right that has never been recognized by the U.S. government). Even so, government leaders, duly authorized by God to exercise public authority, are the focus of his analysis. Just-war theory is especially useful for statecraft and military planning by such authorities, Pavlischek argues. (Indeed, just-war theory continues to receive vigorous attention in international law and military training, and in the scholarly apparatus that serves these venues.) The role of just-war theory as a tool for conscientious individual or ecclesial reflection is also noted but has somewhat lower priority.

Finally, Pavlischek has no use for pacifism and is especially concerned about what he considers a "crypto-pacifist" corruption of just-war theory. Where the bishops linked just war and pacifism as "distinct but interdependent methods of evaluating warfare,"[11] Pavlischek argues that pacifists are profoundly unbiblical when they claim that governments should not threaten and use force or when they argue that "the use of force is evil, perhaps a necessary evil, but still an evil."[12] Indeed, the bulk of his paper claims that pacifism and corrupted versions of just-war theory have corroded the sturdy recognition of the need for lethal force on the part of governments that once grounded just-war theory and that this threatens to weaken our national resolve to fight terrorism today as it needs to be fought.

Where Do We Go from Here?

Complex questions of Christian ethics, international relations, and political theory lie at the heart of the dispute between strict and permissive versions of just-war theory. Some of these questions are: What is the mandate of government, and how shall the various goods it pursues be ranked in importance? Has the nature of modern war necessitated a revision in classic just-war theory? Whose information is to be trusted as our nation prepares for war? What does an appropriate national loyalty look like in this country at this time? What is the political and moral value of international treaties, opinions, and agencies? To whom is just-war theory properly addressed—citizens or policymakers? Should war fighting and criminal justice be treated as essentially parallel tasks undertaken by the left and right hand of government and inevitable in a fallen world? Still, amidst these many questions, I want to focus on three others by way of conclusion:

Which approach to just-war theory is more in keeping with the thought of its historic proponents, such as Augustine, Aquinas, Luther, and Calvin? This is the question of intellectual genealogy. Pavlischek, Weigel, and Johnson all view their version of just-war theory as the classic tradition and treat strict just war as an unfortunate corruption. Yet the strict just-war theory of the Catholic bishops and others certainly lays claim to the same intellectual inheritance. After rereading the classic Christian voices, it is clear to me (despite my personal preferences) that permissive just-war theory clearly prevails. Bryan Hehir has admitted as much.[13]

Close review of the twentieth-century development of just-war theory, at least the Catholic side, reveals that its turn to a horrified rejection of war and sharp constricting of just-war criteria was clearly an evolution of the historic tradition in response to the carnage of the era. World War I, World War II, the Holocaust, the atomic bombings of Hiroshima and Nagasaki, the arms race and the Cold War all scalded international Christian consciousness to an extraordinary degree. Many leaders, both Catholic and Protestant, became convinced that the world was rushing to a mutual assured incineration. The fact that historically Christian nations had led the way in both world wars and then in pointing nuclear weapons at each other clearly contributed to this alteration of the tradition. Historic pacifism converged with a chastened just-war approach to yield strict just-war theory.

Those revising the tradition probably should have been more honest in saying they were doing so. Time and circumstance *sometimes* "render ancient good uncouth." The intellectual tradition of the just-war theory does not carry any intrinsic authority. In my view it has been a valuable tool for Christian reflection, but from an evangelical Protestant perspective, at least, it is not authoritative in any confessional sense. Seeing this enables us to understand the classic theory for what it is and to see the limits imposed by its composition in various premodern contexts. In particular, its crafting and refinement occurred in nondemocratic, indeed quasitheocratic contexts in which far less destructive military technology was available. If the theory needs to be democratized and updated to account for modern technology, so be it. Genealogy does not settle the argument, though it is important to get our history right.

Which approach to just-war theory is more likely to bear the fruit of justice, peace, and order today? That is, which is more likely to enable Christian citizens and policymakers to help advance God's will on this planet under contemporary conditions? This is undoubtedly a pragmatic test, but given that just-war theory is not revealed in scripture, it is not inappropriate to ask the question. Just-war theory in this sense has always constituted the use of reason applied to the materials of scripture in the context of contemporary realities. How we construe just-war theory must bear good fruit or that construal must be altered.

In this case, I find that permissive just-war theory can make American Christians too likely to relinquish their critical faculties and support marginal or unjust wars and in general to be unreflective about our nation's activities in the world. I think this was especially apparent during the runup to the Iraq War in 2002–2003. On the other hand, strict just-war theory, with its stringency and sometimes agonizing rigor, can weaken our moral clarity on those occasions when we must have sufficient resolve to fight truly just wars. Which is the greater problem today? In my view, a struggle against groups that would fly jetliners into buildings and seek the means to bring nuclear weapons to our homeland requires the steely resolve that permissive just-war theory contributes. And yet, if this occurs at the expense of other, nonmilitary forms of response to global terrorism or costs us the ability to think critically about our own nation, we will go badly astray. In light of the debacle of the Iraq War, it is clear to me which is the more serious problem today.

Which approach to just-war theory is more likely to help American Christian citizens (especially evangelicals) and policymakers to discern their particular responsibilities? The gravest flaw of all recent discussions of just-war theory in this nation has been their ahistorical and uncontextual quality. When *we Americans* talk about war and its injustice, we are not Swedes, Costa Ricans, or Malaysians—we are Americans, citizens of the most powerful nation on earth, with the largest military—the single nation in the world today most likely to threaten and use military force, which makes us either the world's most redemptive or most dangerous citizen, depending on one's perspective on the uses of American power. Which version of just-war theory best helps us to remember both the opportunities and the dangers of our extraordinary international power? Which helps us to have an *appropriately* critical stance toward the claims of our own government?

It is no coincidence that the intellectual origins of *American* strict just-war theory can be traced to the Catholic bishops' turn against the Vietnam War, against the backdrop of the Vatican's anti-Cold War internationalism of the early 1960s. In a very real sense, the American Christian debate about just-war theory is nothing other than a debate about America, a debate little changed since, say, 1968. This also helps to account for the passions this debate arouses. In the end, competing perceptions of the moral virtue of our own nation lie at the heart of the division between strict and permissive just-war theory.

What is America, after all? Are we the leading international force for "human dignity, the rule of law, limits on the power of the state . . . private property, free speech, equal justice, and religious tolerance," as the president put it in his 2002 West Point address?[14] Or are we instead, to pull together the claims of so many critics, the global empire, the Rome of the modern world—bullying less powerful nations, throwing our military weight around in many parts of the world, parsimonious in our generosity while pursuing economic excess, demonstrating indifference to how our actions negatively affect other nations, and consuming far more of the world's resources than any nation deserves?

What if we are *both*? What if the split in just-war theory, in part at least, reflects the inability of American Christians to cope with the tensions between our cherished ideals and our power-distorted selfishness, both of which are facts about who we are as a nation? What would it mean to think Christianly about the foreign policy of a nation like that?

I believe that strict just-war theory is the way forward for American evangelicals. Because this means a more stringent application of all just-war criteria, including last resort, strict just-war theory stands in natural complementarity with just-peacemaking theory. It fits with the center's growing interest in a human-rights-oriented internationalism and its growing wariness about offering an uncritical embrace of the claims and pretensions of our beloved country. Strict just-war theory says: in a sinful and violent and unjust world, there are times when it is necessary for our nation to fight. But every time is not such a time, and there is something alarming about how many times our troops have been mobilized in the last generation. To say no to a particular war is not to say no to God, country, or the troops. It may be to say yes to all three, properly understood. It would be nice to be able to see this ahead of time and resist while there is still time, rather than only in retrospect. A Christian community without the capacity to say no to the state on war is an entirely domesticated community in which Jesus no longer functions as Lord.

It is my fond hope that the evangelical center now has the sophistication to manage a strict just-war-theory approach to our nation's wars, while making respectful space for a pacifist witness and employing the insights of just peacemaking in considering every situation of actual or prospective armed conflict.

Conclusion

A WAY AHEAD FOR EVANGELICALS AND AMERICAN CULTURE

If those who talk about American public life walk away from this book convinced that there is such a thing as an evangelical center, related to but distinct from the evangelical right and left, an important part of the purpose of this book will have been accomplished. It is time to get this right.

Evangelicals have been the focus of considerable media attention in recent years. But often the descriptions offered of our community have been far from adequate. There are still some commentators who equate all evangelicals with the late Jerry Falwell and with Pat Robertson, leaving many of us cringing in horror. This is less often the case with U.S. writers, but one still sees it from European observers. The fresh emergence of Jim Wallis has helped push most mainstream journalists and scholars of evangelicalism beyond this monolithic picture of evangelicals to develop a right-left dichotomy. This is better and more accurate but still does not quite grasp the full picture. I have tried to show in this book that a community of evangelical centrists exists that must be named for what it is and must be taken seriously in terms of its distinctive vision. I have sought to populate that center with a wide range of thinkers, activists, pastors, and organizations that must be considered whenever evangelicals are discussed. There really can be no excuse any longer for either a unipolar or bipolar depiction of American evangelical public engagement. Like most political spectrums known to humanity, this population of as many as 75 million ranges in its social and political views across an entire right-center-left spectrum.

There is no single authoritative reckoning of how many evangelical Christians fall into which particular niche on this landscape. One reason for this is because most pollsters have not recognized the existence of an evangelical center and so have not tested for it. Probably the best resource on this issue is "The Twelve Tribes of American Politics," by the peerless scholar of evangelicalism named John Green, with Steven Waldman of Beliefnet.[1] Though this study is now three years old, its value lies in breaking down the voting behavior of what they count as twelve major religious "tribes" in the United States. In terms of their percentages of the voting age population as of 2004, these run as follows:

Religious Right:	12.6%
Heartland Culture Warriors:	11.4%
Moderate Evangelicals:	10.8%
White-Bread Protestants:	8.0%
Convertible Catholics:	8.1%
Religious Left:	12.6%
Spiritual but Not Religious:	5.3%
Seculars:	10.7%
Latinos:	7.3%
Jews:	1.9%
Muslims and Other Faiths:	2.7%
Black Protestants:	9.6%

This categorization does not make for a perfect match with the typology I have presented here. However, one can approximate the groups in the following way:

> Evangelical Right = Religious Right (12.6%)
> Evangelical Center = Moderate Evangelicals (10.8%)
> Evangelical Left = Religious Left (12.6%) minus the mainline
>   and Catholic Left

Now consider the nonwhite groups we have discussed in this book as well:

> Latinos (33% evangelical): Conservative (28%), Moderate (45%), Liberal (27%)
>
> Black Protestants: Conservative (27%), Moderate (48%), Liberal (25%)

Not attempting to offer the kind of number crunching that people like Green do so well, it suffices here to say that the evangelical community clearly has its own right, center, and left and that (surprisingly enough) the right and the center may be roughly equal in numerical strength, with the left not that far behind. In terms of parachurch organizations and public profile, the evangelical right far exceeds either the center or the left. But this may be to oversimplify matters because it is really only recently that fellowship-threatening ideological cleavages have surfaced within the evangelical world. It is still not uncommon for politically moderate evangelicals to send money to Focus on the Family because they like what James Dobson writes about child rearing, or for conservative evangelicals to support World Vision (WV) or the International Justice Mission (IJM) because they believe in the causes pursued by these centrist organizations.

It is increasingly clear that when it comes to public engagement—advocacy related to the pressing issues of the day as they are debated in Washington—evangelicals now offer three distinct sets of voices—right, left, and center—which can be symbolized in the persons of Dobson, Wallis, and Cizik, with a cast of characters around each one of these men and distinctive contributions made by nonwhite evangelical leaders and groups. They represent not just blocs within the evangelical world but broader moral visions that reflect the views of millions of their fellow evangelicals, and other American citizens. Sometimes these three evangelical blocs find common ground, and evangelicals enter Washington with a roar commensurate to their numbers. But often, sadly but perhaps inevitably, they do not find such common ground and end up competing with one another for the evangelical heart and mind, as well as for impact in Washington—leaving them deeply frustrated with one another.

It is my hope that this right-left-center trichotomy proves helpful in analyzing many confusing and vexatious questions related to evangelical life, and perhaps even beyond. I have tried to show how it might work out when thinking about specific issues such as torture, marriage, creation care, and war. A similar analysis could be offered related to other key issues, such as economics, abortion, and race. Appendixes 1 and 2 offer the full text of the leading centrist evangelical policy manifesto—"For the Health of the Nation"—along with my analysis of that document, which addresses these three issues and several others which have not received much attention here. My book, *Kingdom Ethics*, co-authored with Glen Stassen, would also help those interested in seeing an evangelical centrist approach to a number of issues.

Another value of this paradigm can probably be found in analyzing denominational groups and not just issue areas. Consider the denomination of my background, the Southern Baptist Convention (SBC). Most close observers of American religious life know that a "conservative resurgence" in the SBC beginning in 1979 led to a swing to the right among the leadership of this 16-million-member denomination. This then contributed to unease and eventually an exodus among other "southern Baptists" who no longer wanted to be known as "Southern Baptists." So the Southland now consists both of Southern Baptists and southern Baptists who align with other bodies such as the Cooperative Baptist Fellowship (CBF), the Alliance of Baptists, or rebel state conventions, such as in Texas and Virginia, which are southern and Baptist but not Southern Baptist.

Having lived through these changes over the last thirty years, I am quite persuaded that views related to politics and public engagement are fundamental to these developments within Baptist life in the South. To employ the trichotomy: The official SBC, as embodied in its institutional leadership, is strongly aligned with the evangelical right. This does not mean that all members of still officially Southern Baptist congregations are similarly aligned; though certainly many are, a spectrum of opinions on public/social issues exists in official Southern Baptist churches as it does everywhere else in the evangelical world. (Still, the official embrace of the evangelical right explains much, including why centrists often feel marginalized.) The moderate or CBF schools and churches reflect pretty well the approach of the evangelical center or the evangelical left. The Alliance of Baptists seems to fit with either the evangelical left or has crossed out of evangelicalism theologically and fits better with the mainline left. One might venture a guess that even though the South remains the firmest base of support for the evangelical right, a massive denomination, such as the SBC, that implicitly requires embrace of the evangelical right agenda for those seeking to be in good standing with that denomination, is likely to pay a large price in dollars and people for doing so. Indeed, one might say that it has already begun to pay such a price.

I have been asked whether American Catholicism can be analyzed according to the same paradigm. To some extent the answer is yes. According to Green and Waldman, conservative Catholics fit within the "Heartland Culture Warriors" group that overall represents 11.4 percent of the voting-age population as of 2004, while there is also a moderate Catholic group ("Convertible Catholics," 8.1 percent of the voting age population), and a Catholic left, representing some percentage of the overall "religious left" that came in at 12.6 percent of the population. My travels in the ecumenical world lead me to the conclusion that the ideological splits that divide these Catholic groups are at least as intense as anything we are experiencing within evangelicalism. One difference between our two communities is the unique role that a conservative Vatican leadership plays here. American Catholics often seem to define themselves and other Catholics in terms of whether they are loyal or not loyal to the pope and the official teaching tradition of the Catholic Church.

This ideological fracturing within Catholicism is unfortunate. Those of us on the evangelical side of the fence often draw on the profound resources of the magisterial Roman Catholic social-teaching tradition. Many of us wish for a similarly sturdy and well-reasoned teaching tradition of our own. The value of that Catholic teaching tradition, among other things, is the way (we evangelicals think) it enables the Church to avoid swaying to and fro with every ideological breeze. The instinct to withdraw from public engagement when frustrated is met with a determined tradition of public engagement. The instinct to get too cozy with politicians is met with tradition-determined boundaries on that kind of activity. The tendency toward a narrow agenda, or to be pulled left or right, is met with the holistic, genuinely consistent pro-life ethic of the tradition, especially as incarnated and articulated by Pope John Paul II, a hero to many of us.

I do not think that evangelicals can just borrow the Catholic tradition lock, stock, and barrel. I fear that this has in fact occurred among many evangelicals, especially on the right. It is not a surprise that many end up crossing the Tiber and converting to Catholicism—as occurred recently and most shockingly with the president of the Evangelical Theological Society, Frank Beckwith of Baylor. Like Beckwith, I myself grew up Catholic and appreciate the tradition immensely, especially the moral tradition, but I have come to see that there are significant differences in approach between Protestant and Roman Catholic ethics that should not be underestimated or effaced. I would like to borrow the theological sturdiness of the tradition; the careful group-deliberation process for major documents; the richness of the sacramental vision of life; the sophistication in parsing the facts, values, and interests involved in major social policy issues; the hundred years of reflection on modern economic, social, and political life; the hard lessons of Christendom; and the transition to post-Christendom. But we evangelicals need to develop our own social teaching tradition that more aptly reflects our particular theological, ecclesial, and moral commitments. Perhaps that is what "For the Health of the Nation" represents—a start on that kind of tradition.

It will take more than public declarations of that type, though, no matter how well-constructed they are. Our community needs more mature scholarship and an ethos of serious intellectual engagement. Mark Noll pointed out this problem some years ago in *The Scandal of the Evangelical Mind*.[2] If we are to have over one hundred liberal arts colleges and universities, let them produce not just pious hearts but rigorous intellects. We need to graduate more and better economists, diplomats, lawyers, philosophers, political theorists, hard scientists, ethicists, and judges. *Our* best and brightest graduates—not just conservative Catholics or sophisticated liberals—need to make their way onto the Supreme Court. We have to carry our own intellectual weight in this country, or our contribution to public life will never be taken as seriously as it should be. We may be recognized, we may be mobilized, we may even be feared, but we will not be respected. Our public activism needs to be built on a foundation of scholarship and a growing base of hands-on experience in public service. We have to grow up—past conspiracy theories, demagoguery, single-issue voting, partisan seductions, mudslinging, and God-and-country conflations and confusions. We have to get past one-sided voting guides, political handicapping in the name of Christ, endorsements or quasiendorsements from the pulpit, and transparent "moral advocacy" equaling political consulting.

All of this will require much more serious theological, ethical, and political philosophical reflection that goes to the core of how Christians engage public life. We need to think more deeply about the meaning and goal of human history, the nature of the human person and human community, the purpose of government, the structure of U.S. constitutionalism, the implications of various kinds of pluralism, and the overriding moral imperatives, such as the sacredness of life, that ought to govern our treatment of people. We definitely need to come to terms with both the practical and theoretical problem posed by the Christendom issue as it exists in this peculiar American setting—a half-pagan, half-Christian nation, with vestiges of Christian influence felt everywhere but the overall impact of the Christian moral vision in decline.

And we need to rethink what it means to be the church and to be a part of churches; what our mission is, what part of that mission involves civic engagement, and how that engagement is to be carried out in the name of Jesus Christ.

In the end, of course, what matters for Christians is not that we be right, left, or center but that we be faithful to our Lord. No evangelical Christian would or should go to the wall to defend centrist (or rightist or leftist) evangelicalism. Heaven forbid. These categories are provisional and in many ways unsatisfactory. No, we seek to follow Jesus, who was not and could never be confined within our ideological categories or political loyalties. He is our Lord, and in the end his is the only vote that matters.

Appendix 1

"FOR THE HEALTH OF THE NATION"

An Evangelical Call to Civic Responsibility (2004)

PREAMBLE

Evangelical Christians in America face a historic opportunity. We make up fully one quarter of all voters in the most powerful nation in history. Never before has God given American evangelicals such an awesome opportunity to shape public policy in ways that could contribute to the well-being of the entire world. Disengagement is not an option.

We must seek God's face for biblical faithfulness and abundant wisdom to rise to this unique challenge.

The special circumstances of this historic moment underline both the opportunity and the challenge.

- Although we have the privilege to help shape the actions of the world's lone superpower, only half of all evangelical Christians bother to vote.
- The presence and role of religion in public life is attacked more fiercely now than ever, making the bias of aggressive secularism the last acceptable prejudice in America.
- Since the atrocities of September 11, 2001, the spiritual and religious dimensions of global conflict have been sharpened.
- Secular media outlets have long acknowledged evangelical involvement in prolife and family issues, but are taking belated notice of evangelicals' global involvement in activities such as disaster relief, refugee resettlement, and the fights against AIDS/HIV, human rights abuses, slavery, sexual trafficking, and prison rape.

- Some key American political leaders now conceive of their roles in moral terms. And they see themselves as stewards of the blessings of representative democracy, religious freedom, and human rights in a world where many nations are endangered by the forces of authoritarianism or radical secularism.

Evangelicals may not always agree about policy, but we realize that we have many callings and commitments in common: commitments to the protection and well-being of families and children, of the poor, the sick, the disabled, and the unborn, of the persecuted and oppressed, and of the rest of the created order. While these issues do not exhaust the concerns of good government, they provide the platform for evangelicals to engage in common action.

Despite our common commitments and this moment of opportunity, American evangelicals continue to be ambivalent about civic engagement.

In 1947, Carl F. H. Henry pricked our uneasy consciences and spurred us toward responsible social and political engagement. In the years since, the National Association of Evangelicals has routinely engaged our political leaders through its Office of Governmental Affairs and worked to educate member churches on current issues. In recent decades, a variety of evangelical political voices have emerged. Yet evangelicals have failed to engage with the breadth, depth, and consistency to which we are called.

Scholars and leaders have inspired us by drawing attention to historical exemplars of evangelical public responsibility from Wilberforce and the Booths in England to Edwards, Backus, Garnet, Finney, and Palmer in America. Our spiritual ancestors did not always agree on the specifics of governance and the best roads to social reform. Yet their passion and sacrifice inspire us to creative engagement, even when we cannot fully agree on policy prescriptions.

Against this historical background and in view of these common commitments, we offer the following principled framework for evangelical public engagement.

THE BASIS FOR CHRISTIAN CIVIC ENGAGEMENT

We engage in public life because God created our first parents in his image and gave them dominion over the earth (Gen. 1:27-28). The responsibilities that emerge from that mandate are many, and in a modern society those responsibilities rightly flow to many different institutions, including governments, families, churches, schools, businesses, and labor unions. Just governance is part of our calling in creation.

We also engage in public life because Jesus is Lord over every area of life. Through him all things were created (Col. 1:16-17), and by him all things will be brought to fullness (Rom. 8:19-21). To restrict our stewardship to the private sphere would be to deny an important part of his dominion and to functionally abandon it to the Evil One. To restrict our political concerns to matters that touch only on the private and the domestic spheres is to deny the all-encompassing Lordship of Jesus (Rev. 19:16).

Following in the tradition of the Hebrew prophets, Jesus announced the arrival of God's kingdom (God's "reign" or "rule") (Matt. 4:17; Mark 1:15). This kingdom would be marked by justice, peace, forgiveness, restoration, and healing for all. Jesus' followers have come to understand the time between his first and second comings as a period of "already, but not yet," in which we experience many of the blessings of God's reign and see initial signs of restoration, while we continue to suffer many of the results of the Fall. We know that we must wait for God to bring about the fullness of the kingdom at Christ's return. But in this interim, the Lord calls the church to speak prophetically to society and work for the renewal and reform of its structures. The Lord also calls the church to practice the righteous deeds of the kingdom and point to the kingdom by the wholeness and integrity of the church's common life. This example will require us to demonstrate God's love for all, by crossing racial, ethnic, economic, and national boundaries. It will also often involve following Jesus' example by suffering and living sacrificially for others.

As Christian citizens, we believe it is our calling to help government live up to its divine mandate to render justice (Rom. 13:1-7; 1 Pet. 2:13-17). From the teachings of the Bible and our experience of salvation, we Christians bring a unique vision to our participation in the political order and a conviction that changed people and transformed communities are possible. In the power of the Holy Spirit, we are compelled outward in service to God and neighbor.

Jesus calls us as his followers to love our neighbors as ourselves. Our goal in civic engagement is to bless our neighbors by making good laws. Because we have been called to do justice to our neighbors, we foster a free press, participate in open debate, vote, and hold public office. When Christians do justice, it speaks loudly about God. And it can show those who are not believers how the Christian vision can contribute to the common good and help alleviate the ills of society.

The Method of Christian Civic Engagement

Every political judgment requires both a normative vision and factual analysis. The more carefully and precisely we Christians think about the complex details of both, the more clearly we will be able to explain our views to others and understand—and perhaps overcome—disagreements with others.

Every normative vision has some understanding of persons, creation, history, justice, life, family, and peace. As Christians committed to the full authority of Scripture, our normative vision must flow from the Bible and from the moral order that God has embedded in his creation.

Evangelical Christians seek in every area of life to submit to the authority of Scripture (2 Tim. 3:16-17; Rom. 15:4; 1 Cor. 10:11). Nevertheless, many contemporary political decisions—whether about environmental science, HIV/AIDS, or international trade—deal with complex sociological or technological issues not discussed explicitly in the Bible. As Christians engaged in public policy, we must do detailed social, economic, historical, jurisprudential, and political analysis if we are to understand our society and wisely apply our normative vision to political questions. Only if we deepen our Christian vision and also study our contemporary world can we engage in politics faithfully and wisely.

From the Bible, experience, and social analysis, we learn that social problems arise and can be substantially corrected by both personal decisions and structural changes. On the one hand, personal sinful choices contribute significantly to destructive social problems (Prov. 6:9-11), and personal conversion through faith in Christ can transform broken persons into wholesome, productive citizens. On the other hand, unjust systems also help create social problems (Amos 5:10-15; Isa. 10:1-2) and wise structural change (for example legislation to strengthen marriage or increase economic opportunity for all) can improve society. Thus Christian civic engagement must seek to transform both individuals and institutions. While individuals transformed by the gospel change surrounding society, social institutions also shape individuals. While good laws encourage good behavior, bad laws and systems foster destructive action. Lasting social change requires both personal conversion and institutional renewal and reform. The Bible makes it clear that God cares a great deal about the well-being of marriage, the family, the sanctity of human life, justice for the poor, care for creation, peace, freedom, and racial justice. While individual persons and organizations are at times called by God to concentrate on one or two issues, faithful evangelical civic engagement must champion a biblically balanced agenda.

HUMILITY AND CIVILITY

As sinners who are thankful for God's grace, we know that we do not always live up to our civic responsibility. Christians must approach political engagement with humility and with earnest prayer for divine guidance and wisdom. Because power structures are often entrenched, perfect solutions are unobtainable. Because cultural changes produce problems that are often not amenable to legislative solutions, we must not expect political activity to achieve more than it can. Because social systems are complex and our knowledge is incomplete, we cannot predict all the effects of laws, policies, and regulations. As a result, we must match our high ideals with careful social analysis and critical reflection on our experience in order to avoid supporting policies that produce unintended and unfortunate consequences.

We will differ with other Christians and with non-Christians over the best policies. Thus we must practice humility and cooperation to achieve modest and attainable goals for the good of society. We must take care to employ the language of civility and to avoid denigrating those with whom we disagree. Because political work requires persuasion and cooperation with those who do not share our Christian commitment, we must offer a reasoned and easy-to-grasp defense of our goals.

When we as Christians engage in political activity, we must maintain our integrity and keep our biblical values intact. While we may frequently settle for "half-a-loaf," we must never compromise principle by engaging in unethical behavior or endorsing or fostering sin. As we rightly engage in supporting legislation, candidates and political parties, we must be clear that biblical faith is vastly larger and richer than every limited, inevitably imperfect political agenda and that commitment to the Lordship of Christ and his one body far transcends all political commitments.

THE STRUCTURES OF PUBLIC LIFE

In the beginning, God called human beings to govern and to care for the creation. Faithfulness to this call has taken different forms as human beings have lived in family groups, in tribes and clans, in kingdoms and empires, and now in modern nation-states in an increasingly interconnected global community. Today we live in a complex society in which few people are directly involved in governing and in which complicated problems do not readily yield straightforward solutions.

God has ordered human society with various institutions and set in place forms of government to maintain public order, to restrain human evil, and to promote the common good. God has called all people to share responsibility for creating a healthy society.

Human beings work out their different ways of obeying God's call as spouses, parents, workers, and participants in the wide variety of human networks. Some, however, are called to particular roles of governance. We must support and pray for all those who shoulder the burdens of government (1 Tim. 2:1-2).

REPRESENTATIVE DEMOCRACY

We thank God for the blessings of representative democracy, which allow all citizens to participate in government by electing their representatives, helping to set the priorities for government, and by sharing publicly the insights derived from their experience. We are grateful that we live in a society in which citizens can hold government responsible for fulfilling its responsibilities to God and abiding by the norms of justice.

We support the democratic process in part because people continue to be sufficiently blessed by God's common grace that they can seek not only their own betterment, but also the welfare of others. We also support democracy because we know that since the Fall, people often abuse power for selfish purposes. As Lord Acton noted, power tends to corrupt and absolute power corrupts absolutely. Thus we thank God for a constitutional system that decentralizes power through the separation of powers, fair elections, limited terms of office, and division among national, state, and local authorities.

As Christians we confess that our primary allegiance is to Christ, his kingdom, and Christ's worldwide body of believers, not to any nation. God has blessed America with bounty and with strength, but unless these blessings are used for the good of all, they will turn to our destruction. As Christian citizens of the United States, we must keep our eyes open to the potentially self-destructive tendencies of our society and our government. We must also balance our natural affection for our country with a love for people of all nations and an active desire to see them prosper. We invite Christians outside the United States to aid us in broadening our perspectives on American life and action.

JUST GOVERNMENT AND FUNDAMENTAL LIBERTY

God is the source of all true law and genuine liberty. He both legitimates and limits the state's authority. Thus, while we owe Caesar his due (Matt. 22:15-22; Mark 12:13-17; Luke 20:20-26), we regard only Jesus as Lord. As King of kings, Jesus' authority extends over Caesar. As followers of Jesus, we obey government authorities when they act in accord with God's justice and his laws (Titus 3:1). But we also resist government when it exercises its power in an unjust manner (Acts 5:27-32) or tries to dominate other institutions in society. A good government preserves the God-ordained responsibilities of society's other institutions, such as churches, other faith-centered organizations, schools, families, labor unions, and businesses.

PRINCIPLES OF CHRISTIAN POLITICAL ENGAGEMENT

1. WE WORK TO PROTECT RELIGIOUS FREEDOM AND LIBERTY OF CONSCIENCE

God has ordained the two coexisting institutions of church and state as distinct and independent of each other with each having its own areas of responsibility (Rom. 13:1-7; Mark 12:13-17; Eph. 4:15-16, 5:23-32). We affirm the principles of religious freedom and liberty of conscience, which are both historically and logically at the foundation of the American experiment. They are properly called the First Freedom and are now vested in the First Amendment. The First Amendment's guarantees of freedom of speech, association, and religion provide the political space in which we can carry out our differing responsibilities. Because human beings are responsible to God, these guarantees are crucial to the exercise of their God-given freedom. As God allows the wheat and tares to grow together until the harvest, and as God sends the rain on the just and on the unjust, so those who obey and those who disobey God coexist in society and share in its blessings (Matt. 5:45, 13:24-30). This "gospel pluralism" is foundational to the religious liberty of all.

Participating in the public square does not require people to put aside their beliefs or suspend the practice of their religion. All persons should have equal access to public forums, regardless of the religious content or viewpoint of their speech. Likewise, judicial standards should protect and respect not only religiously compelled practices, but also religiously motivated behavior.

The First Amendment's Establishment Clause is directed only at government and restrains its power. Thus, for example, the clause was never intended to shield individuals from exposure to the religious views of nongovernmental speakers. Exemptions from regulations or tax burdens do not violate the Establishment Clause, for government does not establish religion by leaving it alone. When government assists nongovernmental organizations as part of an evenhanded educational, social service, or health-care program, religious organizations receiving such aid do not become "state actors" with constitutional duties. Courts should respect church autonomy in matters relating to doctrine, polity, the application of its governing documents, church discipline, clergy and staff employment practices, and other matters within the province of the church (Acts 18:12-17).

Religion is not just an individual matter, but also refers to rich communal traditions of ultimate belief and practice. We resist the definition of religion becoming either radically individualized or flattened out to mean anything that passes for a serious conviction. Thus, while the First Amendment protects religiously informed conscience, it does not protect all matters of sincere concern.

2. WE WORK TO NURTURE FAMILY LIFE AND PROTECT CHILDREN

From Genesis onward, the Bible tells us that the family is central to God's vision for human society. God has revealed himself to us in the language of family, adopting us as his children (Rom. 8:23, Gal. 4:5) and teaching us by the Holy Spirit to call him *Abba Father* (Rom. 8:15, Gal. 4:6). Marriage, which is a lifetime relationship between one man and one woman, is the predominant biblical icon of God's relationship with his people (Isa. 54:5; Jer. 3:20, 31:32; Ezek. 16:32; Eph. 5:23, 31-32). In turn, family life reveals something to us about God, as human families mirror, however faintly, the inner life of the Trinity.

The mutuality and service of family life contrast strongly with the hypermodern emphasis on individual freedom and rights. Marriage, sexuality, and family life are fundamental to society. Whether we are married or single, it is in the family that we learn mutual responsibility, we learn to live in an ordered society with complementary and distinct roles, we learn to submit and to obey, we learn to love and to trust, we learn both justice and mercy, and we learn to deny ourselves for the well-being of others. Thus the family is at the heart of the organic functioning of society.

Government does not have the primary responsibility for guaranteeing wholesome family life. That is the job of families themselves and of other institutions, especially churches. But governments should understand that people are more than autonomous individuals; they live in families and many are married. While providing individuals with ways to remedy or escape abusive relationships, governments should promote laws and policies that strengthen the well-being of families.

Many social evils—such as alcohol, drug, gambling, or credit-card abuse, pornography, sexual libertinism, spousal or child sexual abuse, easy divorce, abortion on demand—represent the abandonment of responsibility or the violation of trust by family members, and they seriously impair the ability of family members to function in society. These evils must be viewed not only as matters of individual sin and dysfunction, but also as violations of family integrity. Because the family is so important to society, violations of its integrity threaten public order. Similarly, employment, labor, housing, health care, and educational policies concern not only individuals but seriously affect families. In order to strengthen the family, we must promote biblical moral principles, responsible personal choices, and good public policies on marriage and divorce law, shelter, food, health care, education, and a family wage (Jas. 5:1-6).

Good family life is so important to healthy human functioning that we oppose government efforts to trespass on its territory: whether by encroaching on parental responsibilities to educate their children, by treating other kinds of households as the family's social and legal equivalent, or by creating economic disincentives to marriage. We commit ourselves to work for laws that protect and foster family life, and against government attempts to interfere with the integrity of the family. We also oppose innovations such as same-sex "marriage." We will work for measures that strengthen the economic viability of marriages and families, especially among the poor. We likewise commit ourselves to work within the church and society to strengthen marriages, to reduce the rate of divorce, and to prepare young adults for healthy family life.

3. WE WORK TO PROTECT THE SANCTITY OF HUMAN LIFE AND TO SAFEGUARD ITS NATURE

Because God created human beings in his image, all people share in the divine dignity. And because the Bible reveals God's calling and care of persons before they are born, the preborn share in this dignity (Ps. 139:13).

We believe that abortion, euthanasia, and unethical human experimentation violate the God-given dignity of human beings. As these practices gain social approval and become legitimized in law, they undermine the legal and cultural protections that our society has provided for vulnerable persons. Human dignity is indivisible. A threat to the aged, to the very young, to the unborn, to those with disabilities, or to those with genetic diseases is a threat to all.

The book of Genesis portrays human attempts to transcend creaturely humility before God as rebellion against God. Christians must witness in the political sphere to the limits of our creatureliness and warn against the dangers of dissatisfaction with human limits. As many others in the West, we have had such faith in science and its doctrine of progress that we are unprepared for the choices biotechnology now brings us. We urge evangelicals with specialized scientific knowledge to help Christians and policymakers to think through these issues. As technologies related to cloning and creating inheritable genetic modifications are being refined, society is less able to create a consensus on what is good and what limits we should place on human modification. The uniqueness of human nature is at stake.

Where the negative implications of biotechnology are unknown, government ought to err on the side of caution. Christians must welcome and support medical research that uses stem cells from adult donors and other ethical avenues of research. But we must work toward complete bans on human cloning and embryonic stem-cell research, as well as for laws against discrimination based on genetic information.

4. WE SEEK JUSTICE AND COMPASSION FOR THE POOR AND VULNERABLE

Jesus summed up God's law by commanding us to love God with all that we are and to love our neighbors as ourselves (Matt. 22:35-40). By deed and parable, he taught us that anyone in need is our neighbor (Luke 10:29-37). Because all people are created in the image of God, we owe one another help in time of need.

God identifies with the poor (Ps. 146:5-9) and says that those who "are kind to the poor lend to the Lord" (Prov. 19:17), while those who oppress the poor "show contempt for their Maker" (Prov. 14:31). Jesus said that those who do not care for the needy and the imprisoned will depart eternally from the living God (Matt. 25:31-46). The vulnerable may include not only the poor, but women, children, the aged, persons with disabilities, immigrants, refugees, minorities, the persecuted, and prisoners. God measures societies by how they treat the people at the bottom.

God's prophets call his people to create just and righteous societies (Isa. 10:1-4, 58:3-12; Jer. 5:26-29, 22:13-19; Amos 2:6-7, 4:1-3, 5:10-15). The prophetic teaching insists on both a fair legal system (which does not favor either the rich or the poor) and a fair economic system (which does not tolerate perpetual poverty). Though the Bible does not call for economic equality, it condemns gross disparities in opportunity and outcome that cause suffering and perpetuate poverty, and it calls us to work toward equality of opportunity. God wants every person and family to have access to productive resources so that if they act responsibly, they can care for their economic needs and be dignified members of their community. Christians reach out to help others in various ways: through personal charity, effective faith-based ministries, and other nongovernmental associations, and by advocating for effective government programs and structural changes.

Economic justice includes both the mitigation of suffering and also the restoration of wholeness. Wholeness includes full participation in the life of the community. Health care, nutrition, and education are important ingredients in helping people transcend the stigma and agony of poverty and reenter community. Since healthy family systems are important for nurturing healthy individuals and overcoming poverty, public policy should encourage marriage and sexual abstinence outside marriage, while discouraging early onset of sexual activity, out-of-wedlock births, and easy divorce. Government should also hold fathers and mothers responsible for the maintenance of their families, enforcing where necessary the collection of child-support payments.

Restoring people to wholeness means that governmental social welfare must aim to provide opportunity and restore people to self-sufficiency. While basic standards of support must be put in place to provide for those who cannot care for their families and themselves, incentives and training in marketable skills must be part of any well-rounded program. We urge Christians who work in the political realm to shape wise laws pertaining to the creation of wealth, wages, education, taxation, immigration, health care, and social welfare that will protect those trapped in poverty and empower the poor to improve their circumstances.

We further believe that care for the vulnerable should extend beyond our national borders. American foreign policy and trade policies often have an impact on the poor. We should try to persuade our leaders to change patterns of trade that harm the poor and to make the reduction of global poverty a central concern of American foreign policy. We must support policies that encourage honesty in government, correct unfair socioeconomic structures, generously support effective programs that empower the poor, and foster economic development and prosperity.

Christians should also encourage continued government support of international aid agencies, including those that are faith based.

Especially in the developing world, extreme poverty, lack of health care, the spread of HIV/AIDS, inadequate nutrition, unjust and unstable economies, slavery and sexual trafficking, the use of rape as a tool of terror and oppression, civil war, and government cronyism and graft create the conditions in which large populations become vulnerable. We support Christian agencies and American foreign policy that effectively correct these political problems and promote just, democratic structures.

5. WE WORK TO PROTECT HUMAN RIGHTS

Because God created human beings in his image, we are endowed with rights and responsibilities. In order to carry out these responsibilities, human beings need the freedom to form associations, formulate and express beliefs, and act on conscientiously held commitments.

As recipients of God's gift of embodied life, people need food, nurture, shelter, and care. In order to fulfill their God-given tasks, all people have a right to private property. God's design for human existence also implies a right to marry, enjoy family life, and raise and educate children. While it is not the primary role of government to provide everything that humans need for their well-being, governments are obligated to ensure that people are not unjustly deprived of them and to strengthen families, schools, businesses, hospitals, social-service organizations, and other institutions so they can contribute to human welfare. At the same time, government must fulfill its responsibilities to provide for the general welfare and promote the common good.

Governments should be constitutionally obligated to protect basic human rights. Documents like the UN's Universal Declaration of Human Rights are attempts to articulate the kind of treatment that every person deserves from the government under which they live. Insofar as a person has a human right, that person should be able to appeal to an executive, legislative, or judicial authority to enforce or adjudicate that right. We believe that American foreign policy should reward those countries that respect human rights and should not reward (and prudently employ certain sanctions against) those countries that abuse or deny such rights. We urge the United States to increase its commitments to developing democracy and civil society in former colonial lands, Muslim nations, and countries emerging from Communism.

Because the Creator gave human beings liberty, we believe that religious liberty, including the right to change one's religion, is a foundational right that must be respected by governments (Article 18, Universal Declaration of Human Rights). Freedom of expression and freedom of assembly are closely related to religious liberty, and people must be free to express their vision for a just social order without fear of torture or other reprisal.

We also oppose the expansion of "rights talk" to encompass so-called rights such as "same-sex marriage" or "the right to die." Inappropriately expanded rights language has begun to function as a trump card in American discourse that unfairly shuts down needed discussion.

America has a tragic history of mistreating Native Americans, the cruel practice of slavery, and the subsequent segregation and exploitation of the descendants of slaves. While the United States has achieved legal and social equality in principle, the legacy of racism still makes many African Americans, Hispanics, and other ethnic minorities particularly vulnerable to a variety of social ills. Our churches have a special responsibility to model good race relations (Rom. 10:12). To correct the lingering effects of our racist history, Christians should support well-conceived efforts that foster dignity and responsibility.

6. WE SEEK PEACE AND WORK TO RESTRAIN VIOLENCE

Jesus and the prophets looked forward to the time when God's reign would bring about just and peaceful societies in which people would enjoy the fruits of their labor without interference from foreign oppressors or unjust rulers. But from the beginning, Christians have recognized that God did not call them to bring in God's kingdom by force. While all Christians have agreed that governments should protect and restore just and peaceful social orders, we have long differed on when governments may use force and whether we may participate in government-authorized force to defend our homelands, rescue others from attack, or liberate other people from oppression.

The peaceful settling of disputes is a gift of common grace. We urge governments to pursue thoroughly nonviolent paths to peace before resorting to military force. We believe that if governments are going to use military force, they must use it in the service of peace and not merely in their national interest. Military force must be guided by the classical just-war principles, which are designed to restrain violence by establishing the right conditions for and right conduct in fighting a war. In an age of nuclear and biological terrorism, such principles are more important than ever. We urge followers of Jesus to engage in practical peacemaking locally, nationally, and internationally. As followers of Jesus, we should, in our civic capacity, work to reduce conflict by promoting international understanding and engaging in nonviolent conflict resolution.

7. WE LABOR TO PROTECT GOD'S CREATION

As we embrace our responsibility to care for God's earth, we reaffirm the important truth that we worship only the Creator and not the creation. God gave the care of his earth and its species to our first parents. That responsibility has passed into our hands. We affirm that God-given dominion is a sacred responsibility to steward the earth and not a license to abuse the creation of which we are a part. We are not the owners of creation, but its stewards, summoned by God to "watch over and care for it" (Gen. 2:15). This implies the principle of sustainability: our uses of the Earth must be designed to conserve and renew the Earth rather than to deplete or destroy it.

The Bible teaches us that God is not only redeeming his people, but is also restoring the whole creation (Rom. 8:18-23). Just as we show our love for the Savior by reaching out to the lost, we believe that we show our love for the Creator by caring for his creation. Because clean air, pure water, and adequate resources are crucial to public health and civic order, government has an obligation to protect its citizens from the effects of environmental degradation. This involves the urgent need to relieve human suffering caused by bad environmental practice. Because natural systems are extremely complex, human actions can have unexpected side effects. We must therefore approach our stewardship of creation with humility and caution.

Human beings have responsibility for creation in a variety of ways. We urge Christians to shape their personal lives in creation-friendly ways: practicing effective recycling, conserving resources, and experiencing the joy of contact with nature. We urge government to encourage fuel efficiency, reduce pollution, encourage sustainable use of natural resources, and provide for the proper care of wildlife and their natural habitats.

OUR COMMITMENT

We commit ourselves to support Christians who engage in political and social action in a manner consistent with biblical teachings. We call on Christian leaders in public office or with expertise in public policy and political life to help us deepen our perspective on public policy and political life so that we might better fulfill our civic responsibility.

We call on all Christians to become informed and then to vote, as well as to regularly communicate biblical values to their government representatives. We urge all Christians to take their civic responsibility seriously even when they are not full-time political activists so that they might more adequately call those in government to their task. We also encourage our children to consider vocations in public service.

We call churches and transdenominational agencies to cultivate an understanding of civic responsibility and public justice among their members. Seminaries and Christian colleges have a special responsibility to imbue future leaders with a sense of civic responsibility. We call all Christians to a renewed political engagement that aims to protect the vulnerable and poor, to guard the sanctity of human life, to further racial reconciliation and justice, to renew the family, to care for creation, and to promote justice, freedom, and peace for all.

Above all, we commit ourselves to regular prayer for those who govern, that God may prosper their efforts to nurture life, justice, freedom, and peace.

Appendix 2

AN ANALYSIS OF "FOR THE HEALTH OF THE NATION"

"For the Health of the Nation: An Evangelical Call to Civic Responsibility" was the result of a three-year process of reflection that began at the National Association of Evangelicals (NAE) convention in Dallas in March 2001 and was officially called "Toward an Evangelical Framework for Public Engagement." Jointly led by the centrist Ron Sider and the late Diane Knippers of the conservative Institute for Religion and Democracy, a seventeen-person steering committee eventually decided both to enlist evangelical scholars in writing a collection of essays on evangelical public ethics and to form an eight-person drafting committee (Sider and Knippers, plus Rich Cizik, JoAnne Lyon, Paul Marshall, David Neff, James Skillen, and Eldin Villafañe) to write a shorter declaration that could reflect the themes of these essays and be read and distributed widely.

I served on the steering committee and drafted a book chapter but did not serve on the drafting committee of "For the Health of the Nation," so my evaluation of the statement is not an evaluation of my own work. I can guess, but not be sure, about the "inside baseball" that went on in drafting the statement. I will offer some of those educated guesses in this analysis.

Over several meetings and more than three years this process moved ahead, eventually producing both the declaration and the book. The declaration was completed first and was approved by the board of directors of the NAE in October 2004, just before the elections of that year. The essays were completed and published in book form the next year.

"For the Health of the Nation" is important at many levels. In its substance, it is the most careful, thorough, and balanced corporate statement of evangelical public witness that has yet been offered. It contains a mix of beliefs that I think characterizes all evangelicals in the United States, together with particular convictions of what I have called the emerging evangelical center. The declaration is also important in the internal politics of evangelical life because it marked the emergence of the NAE itself as a major player in evangelical public ethics. It would be hard to find too many news stories about the NAE's policy positions prior to this declaration; now the NAE is in the news all the time. We can now see that the NAE's involvement in sponsoring the preparation of this statement and in approving it at the board level represents the birth of an evangelical center with the institutional clout to stand up for itself over against either the evangelical left or especially the evangelical right. And yet the breadth of evangelical ideologies represented by the drafters and signers of the document reveals the (occasional?) potential of evangelicals to speak with one voice rather than in three competing voices. Representatives of the evangelical right, left, and center, many of whom have been identified in this book already, helped write the statement and offered their support to it.

Those looking for deeper evidence of the convictions of the evangelical center really should read the full-length companion volume to "For the Health of the Nation." It is called *Toward an Evangelical Public Policy: Political Strategies for the Health of the Nation.*[1] The book contains a mix of essays from within and outside evangelicalism, all in various ways reflecting on the history, principles, and moral commitments of evangelical public witness. The contributors range from what I would characterize as the evangelical center-left to the evangelical right, from Glen Stassen and Sider to Cizik to Glenn Stanton and Tom Minnery of Focus on the Family. One can only lament the breakdown of this broad evangelical consortium in the intervening three years over such issues as climate change and torture. I hope and pray for its reconstruction in years to come. That is one purpose for my own book.

In this appendix, I will offer a close reading of "For the Health of the Nation," indicating what I think are the key moves in the statement, its strengths, its weaknesses, and the probable dynamics that went on behind the scenes. This analysis should be read in conjunction with the statement itself, found in appendix 1.

PREAMBLE

There is no evidence that evangelicals have suddenly jumped in numbers in proportion to the rest of the U.S. population. So why does the document say that "Never before has God given American evangelicals such an awesome opportunity to shape public policy"? Presumably that opportunity was always there. It might be more accurate to say that evangelicals have now awakened to their policy shaping power—no more "slumbering giant" for us, we now see that we are the most powerful religious force in American life. The mainline has been sidelined. It is our day. We better get it right. This awareness is indeed new.

This section of the document also clearly rules out evangelical political disengagement, ambivalence, or apathy. In chapter 1, I discussed the traditions, people, and ideas that still lead evangelicals toward political withdrawal from time to time. This document clearly rejects such withdrawal. It strikes a right-leaning note when it attacks the kind of aggressive secularism that would force religious beliefs and believers out of the public square. Disdain for this secular disdain of religious belief is a deep force within evangelicalism, especially its conservative wing. The text responds to 9/11 by implying that we need *better* religious engagement with culture, not religious disengagement from culture. The document also highlights the broader evangelical moral agenda that I have described as characteristic of the evangelical center. It lists this global involvement as a fact that must be noticed and respected, perhaps to gain a platform for the respectful public hearing of evangelical convictions about global issues. (From the beginning, it suggests that evangelical interest in public policy is global rather than merely focused on American well-being.)

It seems to me that the reference to "some key American leaders [who] now conceive of their roles in moral terms" is primarily about President Bush, who at the time often spoke in a religiomoral vein about global democratization and human rights. I think that this reference suggests that one goal of the statement is to help shape the moral vision and policies of the president and perhaps other political leaders who claim some form of evangelical identity.

Evangelicalism, as I indicated in chapter 1, has a semicoherent and not-quite-consensual understanding of itself as a distinctive religious tradition or movement rather than as just a set of theological beliefs or religious experiences or even denominations. The references to Carl F. H. Henry, and then to Wilberforce, Booth, Edwards, Backus, and others reflect an effort to connect to an evangelical heritage in both Great Britain and the United States. Henry was one of the key founders of post–World War II evangelicalism. William Wilberforce was a committed evangelical parliamentarian who led the fight to end the slave trade; he is honored across the evangelical spectrum. Charles Finney was an abolitionist revivalist of the mid-nineteenth century. Phoebe Palmer was an advocate of Christian holiness, an urban missionary, and an activist for women's ministry (her name probably came from the evangelical left representatives on the committee, reflecting their commitment to gender inclusivity). These are among the stalwarts of blessed evangelical memory. By naming them, the document wants to "inspire us to creative engagement" with our own culture and its problems and needs. It is an effective rhetorical strategy and represents an effort to deepen a sense of evangelical peoplehood.

Every document has a purpose. The particular purpose of this one is signaled when the authors say "In recent decades, a variety of evangelical political voices have emerged. Yet evangelicals have failed to engage with the breadth, depth, and consistency to which we are called." The problem of "breadth" is about an agenda that is too narrow. The problem of "depth" refers to evangelical activism, probably of both left and right, that is not rooted in any kind of coherent theological, ethical, or political vision. The problem of "consistency" has to do with our tendency to engage fiercely and then withdraw sullenly when we do not get what we want.

THE BASIS FOR CHRISTIAN CIVIC ENGAGEMENT

The burden of this section is to demonstrate first to the evangelical world and then to the culture why Christians can and should undertake civic engagement. (Notice that the paradigm is "civic engagement," not politics or even policy. It is a broader and perhaps less polarizing framework.) The intraevangelical goal here is to delegitimize evangelical civic disengagement. The cultural goal here is to stake a claim to the legitimacy of Christian engagement in the public sphere against our secularist despisers.

Methodologically, the argument follows classic evangelical patterns by being rooted almost entirely in scripture. Different strands of scripture are woven together. These different strands actually correspond with different strands of evangelical tradition as well—many represented around the committee table. This feels like a committee product here.

For example, the opening reference to Genesis 1 and the language of "dominion" and "mandate" correspond with the so-called "cultural mandate" as it is explicated in the Reformed tradition. This observation is confirmed by the "principled pluralism" perspective that is offered related to the multiple institutions with various responsibilities that all participate in the just governance of God's created order. This is Kuyperian language and undoubtedly reflects the presence of Jim Skillen on the drafting committee.

The document then makes a turn to the lordship of Christ over all of life. The rhetorical importance of this move here is at the breadth dimension. The authors want evangelicals to avoid any private/public, personal/social morality dichotomies. In just two sentences they offer a Christ-centered theology that brings together creation and eschatology to say that there is nothing that happens from the beginning of time to the end, or from one end of creation to the other, that does not fall under the lordship of Christ. The reference to the "Evil One" suggests that at least some evangelicals (especially Pentecostals, in my experience) are willing to continue to talk about a personal Satan who seeks to destroy and harm God's good world and its inhabitants.

The kingdom of God theology reflected in mine and Stassen's *Kingdom Ethics* and influential in a growing way within evangelicalism is evident in the next paragraph. The kingdom is defined holistically rather than merely spiritually, and the mission of the church is similarly defined. Thus the church bears prophetic witness and works for the "renewal and reform" of society and its structures. A "demonstration ecclesiology" is offered in which the church embodies the kingdom through its common life. But this theme, mentioned as an *alternative* to civic engagement in chapter 1, is here seen as an *aspect* of that engagement.

Romans 13 is referenced in this section. This hugely influential passage of scripture has often been cited, especially in the Lutheran tradition, to reinforce a kind of passive Christian obedience to the mandates of a sword-wielding government, which primarily exists to deter evil and punish wrongdoers. The authors here turn Romans 13 in a more positive direction, taking the stance that this is a mandate to render justice, which means more than punishing evildoers.

The pietist strand of evangelicalism is at work in the reference to "the teachings of the Bible and our experience of salvation," and the "conviction that changed people and transformed communities are possible" in "the power of the Holy Spirit." Evangelical Christianity at its best tends toward a hopefulness (not optimism, but hopefulness) about the prospects for change in human life. But note that the document does not just refer to changed people; it also suggests that *transformed communities* are possible. This is not so familiar a note within evangelical theology and reflects the long, slow years of effort on the part of evangelical scholars, black evangelicals, the evangelical left, and community development activists to get evangelicals to hope for change in, and to invest deeply in, *communities* and not just *individuals*.

The closing paragraph makes a turn toward the classic "double love command" of Matthew 22 to ground civic engagement ultimately in love of God and neighbor. The crucial observation is offered that we bless our neighbors when we make good laws and advance the cause of justice in a free, democratic society. It also advances the evangelistic cause of the church (always an important theme for evangelicals, as one might imagine) as unbelievers see and appreciate the loving actions being done on their behalf by their Christian neighbors. Indeed, I would say that for many of us this is a primary motivation for civic engagement, understood broadly here as the kind of work done by groups ranging from Internaional Justice Mission (IJM) and World Vision (WV) to World Relief to the NAE. "They will know we are Christians by our love." Direct hands-on service coupled with articulate witness to transcendent moral principles seems to mean more to people today than tracts and street-corner preaching.

THE METHOD OF CHRISTIAN CIVIC ENGAGEMENT

This methodological section begins by affirming that Christians must bring more than moral norms into the public arena. They must also be fully informed about the facts and details of the issues under analysis. This has been a major theme of Sider's writing about civic engagement. The statement implicitly points out a weakness of much evangelical public engagement, across the spectrum. We are better at thundering out our biblical citations and moral norms than at integrating these with the data applicable to the case. I would also add that evangelicals often fail to operate out of a coherent social vision or any kind of competence in either the social sciences or the natural sciences. We need more than "facts"; we also need a methodological framework for sifting through those facts. And we lack a deeply developed tradition, such as the Catholic social teaching tradition, for framing and evaluating whatever moral issues arise at any given time.

There is another missing piece here. Besides norms, and besides facts and the theoretical framework with which to interpret them, policy analysis also requires the realistic assessment of *interests* and the roles they play. Policymakers bring their *norms* to bear on the *facts* in front of them, but both are deeply affected by the interests (personal, economic, ideological, political, etc.) that affect their reading of both norms and facts. Evangelicals tend to be politically naive, perhaps because we have been shaped by involvement in our own faith communities to believe the best about people and to believe what people tell us about their ideas and motivations. We are not skilled in evaluating the hidden wellsprings of action and belief, wellsprings that are sometimes hidden to the actors and believers themselves. We think we can "look into the soul" of people and read their "hearts," as President Bush once said he had done with Vladimir Putin. No one has taught us to "follow the money trail" or "follow the power" or "assume professional self-interestedness" or "never trust a politician because all they want is victory." We are not realists, in this sense, but instead tend to be idealists, believing the best about other people as we would want them to believe the best about us. I think we are especially blind to the role of economic self-interest because we operate from a tradition that eschews greed. So, for example, when it turned out that many who were making arguments against the validity of climate change science were actually funded directly or indirectly by ExxonMobil, we were unprepared for that discovery. Or when we discovered that politicians sometimes manipulate evangelicals through symbols rather than actually delivering on their promises, we are likewise shocked. So, yes, the drafters are right here in saying that policy analysis involves both norms and facts, but they did not go far enough to reflect on social theory or on self-interestedness in public life. (Including our own self-interestedness.) We do certainly have the theological resources deep within our tradition—the Augustinian pessimism/realism about human sinfulness—to get this one right.

The statement moves on to repudiate in a decisive way evangelical individualism. That is, in a major breakthrough, the statement says that "social problems arise and can be substantially corrected by both personal decisions and structural changes." It is hard to overstate the significance of the new balance and holism that this move represents after generations in which slogans like "helping changed people change the world" were common in evangelical life. Here the slow, gradual impact of people like Walter Rauschenbusch, Reinhold Niebuhr, and perhaps especially, Martin Luther King Jr., can be felt at last within evangelicalism. People affect structures and structures affect people; social change efforts must be directed at both structures and at individuals. We must address both Wal-Mart as a corporation and the CEO of Wal-Mart. We must address both the city government of Birmingham and the individuals who serve on it. We must change both laws and hearts.

In the next paragraph the statement affirms almost in passing that because the Bible is the final authority for evangelicals, and the Bible affirms God's concern for a wide range of moral issues, evangelicals must likewise have a broad agenda rather than a narrow one. This rather basic affirmation, as we have seen, has been a huge source of controversy on the borderlands between the evangelical right, left, and center.

The closing paragraphs of this section extol the virtues of humility and civility in a quite profound way. Clearly addressing the tone issues I discussed in chapter 2, the document calls for humility about evangelical virtue and about the rightness of our every position. It suggests a need for what philosophers would call epistemological humility about the consequences of various policy choices and solutions. It also calls for what might be labeled teleological humility about what goals we as evangelicals can expect politics to achieve for us. It acknowledges the necessity of accepting "half-a-loaf" solutions when no full loaf is available and working together humbly and cooperatively with others toward our common goals. Meanwhile, toward our adversaries in public life, we are to practice civility and avoid harsh denigration of opponents. We are to avoid sliding into unethical behavior to win the day. We must always remember not to identify our very human and very imperfect policy agendas with biblical faith as a whole. This section closes with the reminder that our commitment to the lordship of Christ and to his one body (the church) "transcends all political commitments." What I see here is a commitment to the moral demands of the Christian faith *in the way we do public engagement*, and not just in the goals that we seek. It is this firm linkage between means and ends that has been broken so often in evangelical public engagement in recent years and that must be recovered if we are to have a credible public witness in years to come.

The Structures of Public Life

This section begins with a sweeping look across the breadth of human history as read through the narrative lens provided by the Genesis creation story. The drafters recognize the vast differences between biblical times and our own time, but do not waver from affirming and applying the basic biblical framework to contemporary public life.

Following the principled pluralism position once again, the document emphasizes the role not just of government but also of "various institutions" to order human society. Thus it is not only the state, but also, for example, the family that contributes to the well-being and good order of human community. This ordering role is further specified in the triad of "maintain[ing] public order, restrain[ing] human evil, and promot[ing] the common good." Undoubtedly this is not accidental, but reflects a conceptual framework in which social order comes first, which is protected by the restraint of evil, and which (if successful) opens the possibility of further efforts to promote the common good. One need only consider the tragedy of contemporary Iraq to understand that basic order and security come first, before government or any other social institution can do more to promote the common good. Notice that in keeping with the non-Anabaptist majority tradition in evangelicalism, government service is affirmed as a special calling under God.

The next section offers a careful and rather thorough exposition of the "blessings of representative democracy," which include citizen participation, representative government, and the accountability of elected leaders to the people and ultimately to God and the principles of justice (which transcend and ground particular laws, though this is not explicitly stated). Specific details of U.S. constitutional democracy are especially affirmed, such as separation of powers, limited terms of office, and the multi-layered federal system. These are good, say the drafters, because they help prevent corruption and abuse of power. Democracy is also affirmed because it draws on the best that is in human nature (*common grace* is the term used, again drawing from the Reformed tradition). This idea that democracy draws on our best while preventing our worst is reminiscent not only of the Founders but also of Niebuhr's famous aphorism: "man's capacity for justice makes democracy possible, but man's inclination to injustice makes democracy necessary."[2] I think it important to notice what ends up being an unequivocal and rather sophisticated embrace of U.S. constitutionalism by this array of evangelicals. This ought to counter the fear that evangelicals as a whole are in the market for a theocracy. I would guess that Stassen made a substantial contribution to the Niebuhrian and prodemocratic strand of this section.

The authors then turn back again in a more ecclesiological direction, affirming that for Christians "our primary allegiance is to Christ, his kingdom, and Christ's worldwide body of believers." One might call this an ecclesial internationalism, and it is a pivotal move dedicated to keeping American evangelicalism more evangelical than American. It was precisely the kind of move that Dietrich Bonhoeffer tried to make in the 1930s over against a German Christianity that was more German (actually, more Nazi) than Christian. It was shocking at the time, and it is stringent in its implications even today, especially among evangelical Christians who tend toward passionate displays of red-white-and-blue patriotism.

And yet the statement does not lean in the direction of any kind of anti-Americanism. There is no critique of American imperialism. A somewhat traditionalist sounding affirmation of God's abundant blessings to our nation is offered, and recognition of our "natural affection for our country," that is, our patriotism, though the word is never used. But these are balanced by warnings about the necessity to use these blessings for the good of all, about the "potentially self-destructive tendencies of our society and our government," about the need to have a "love for people of all nations and an active desire to see them prosper," and by an invitation to Christians outside the United States to help us broaden our perspective of what is happening here. One could sift through these affirmations and warnings to conclude that the statement recognizes the unique economic and political power/blessings of the United States, endorses a sober, honest, self-critical Christian stance toward such a uniquely positioned nation, and promotes efforts to turn the great power and material prosperity of America into an instrument of care for the many billions around the world whose lives are not so secure and prosperous. This is still America as a uniquely God-blessed nation, a nation with a mission, *but in keeping with Jesus' teachings, this is a mission to serve, not to dominate.* And because power corrupts, including corrupting our ability to see ourselves properly, a uniquely powerful nation needs within it a uniquely vigilant Christian community with the capacity and willingness to challenge its government's policies. If only this insight could take root across the evangelical landscape!

In the final paragraph of this section, the document affirms the classic Christian understanding of law and political authority. All "true law," all "genuine liberty," and all legitimate authority flow from God. This same divine source of law, liberty, and authority sets limits on the activities and aspirations of the state. Caesar is owed "his due" but only Christ is Lord. The state does not deserve and must not receive our unconditional obedience, which belongs only to God. We obey the state insofar as it promotes justice and advances its God-given mandate; otherwise, we must be prepared to resist it. Resistance is required not just when particular policies are problematic, but more broadly when the state "tries to dominate other institutions in society," thus outgrowing its limited space in God's sovereign ordering of society. Thus vigilant Christian citizens will be prepared to resist both bad laws and bad regimes, both abortion-on-demand and totalitarianism. This is a much more careful and much more satisfying treatment of the political authority question than has often been offered in an evangelical Christianity sometimes attracted to political authoritarianism. It is interesting, and perhaps not coincidental, that the biblical grounding offered here is not Romans 13, but Matthew 22.

PRINCIPLES OF CHRISTIAN POLITICAL ENGAGEMENT

1. WE WORK TO PROTECT RELIGIOUS FREEDOM AND LIBERTY OF CONSCIENCE

This section clearly reflects the preeminence of a Reformed perspective and the obvious influence of the "principled pluralism" of Skillen and Center for Public Justice.

The statement begins with the classic Reformational articulation of a church-state perspective fundamentally grounded in Romans 13 and reflective of a long heritage of Christian civilization. God rules society by establishing two distinct institutions, church and state. (No mention is made of synagogue and state, or mosque and state, or even church plus synagogue plus mosque plus a dozen other worship centers, and state; this is increasingly the reality in our multifaith American context.) Both church and state serve the well-being of society, but they are and must be independent of each other. Thus totalitarian subjugation of the church is implicitly rejected, as is theocratic control of the state.

The American constitutional framework is affirmed once again, this time with a focus on the value of all of the provisions of the First Amendment, not just the free exercise and establishment clauses. Support for these freedoms is grounded here in the character of God and the responsibilities God has given to each person. All who doubt mainstream evangelical commitment to religious liberty need to take this section seriously. It does represent almost the entirety of evangelicalism, left, center, and all but the fringe of the right.

Having offered a firm affirmation of the First Amendment and religious liberty, the text then moves to defend a substantive neutrality interpretation of that amendment—though the phrase itself is not used. One might say that this perspective seeks to maximize "free exercise" and to quiet worries that such free exercise constitutes de facto establishment of religion. The statement defends specific practices and policies, such as faith-based involvement in public debate, equal access of religious people to public forums without viewpoint discrimination, protection of religiously motivated behavior and beliefs, continued exemptions for religious groups from regulations and tax burdens, and "charitable choice"-type government funding assistance to faith-based organizations on a level playing field with secular organizations. The statement also seeks continued autonomy for religious groups in their internal lives, including the "right to hire" people who conform with church doctrine in their own beliefs and lifestyles. It should be noted that this perspective does represent a near-consensus evangelical opinion over against the strict separationism more common in secularist circles and the nonevangelical religious left. Articulation of this view in this brief document represents the deep concern of the evangelical community that, for example, social approval of homosexuality or abortion-on-demand will soon require the social and legal disapproval and coercion of religious groups that do not concur with majority opinion. Legislators or presidents who seek to coerce religious groups in this way will find themselves met with the fierce opposition of a united evangelical community.

2. We work to nurture family life and protect children

Close reading of this section reminds us that considered against the backdrop of public opinion and practices as a whole, the evangelical center takes a pretty conservative line on family life. Rooted in a high view of biblical authority, the statement treats "the family" (implicitly but clearly understood here under the paradigm of a married man and woman and the children they bring into the world) as a God-designed institution foundational to human well-being and reflective of the relational nature of the triune God.

The inner dynamics of constructive family life are emphasized along with the need of couples, parents, churches, government, and society as a whole to each fulfill their own responsibilities to nurture and protect healthy families. Against the backdrop of mass divorce and serial monogamy, marriage is defined as a lifetime relationship; under pressure to redefine marriage to include same-sex relationships, marriage is defined as heterosexual. (No statement on civil unions or other legal frameworks is offered.) Even though divorce is implicitly accepted as one way "to remedy or escape abusive relationships," the drafters pledge to "work within the church and society to strengthen marriages" and to "reduce the rate of divorce."

The document takes up the family-strengthening prescriptions of both left and right. From the left it emphasizes "employment, labor, housing, health care, and educational policies" and abuse dynamics that affect families. From the right it suggests concerns related to substance abuse, pornography, credit card abuse, marriage and divorce law, and tax policies. It emphasizes the special need to strengthen marriage and family life among the poor, a theme that is taken up again in detail in the section on poverty. This link of the marriage and poverty issue could prove enormously fruitful in years to come in shaping evangelical economic ethics, moving us beyond the unthinking embrace of laissez-faire capitalism toward a more constructive approach in which economic systems and government fiscal and tax policies are viewed through the lens of their impact on poor families. This reflects both left and right sharpening each other within the evangelical community.

The text here does seem to offer an uneasy mix of libertarianism and interventionism when it comes to government's role. The libertarian notes emphasize opposition to government encroachments on the family, such as in childrearing and education. Presumably the authors are concerned about the possibility of government socia welfare agencies intervening unnecessarily in family life; perhaps they are concerned that public schools are sometimes indoctrinating children in values that violate the values of the families that send the children there. On the other hand, the document does suggest a wide range of government interventions to reinforce and strengthen the traditional heterosexual family, ultimately on the grounds of "public order." I think it is legitimate to wonder whether this mix of libertarian and interventionist themes retains full intellectual coherence and certainly whether its cogency depends on biblical worldview commitments about the family that are not universally shared in our pluralistic culture.

3. WE WORK TO PROTECT THE SANCTITY OF HUMAN LIFE AND TO SAFEGUARD ITS NATURE

A brief statement of a sanctity-of-life ethic is offered here to ground opposition to abortion, euthanasia, use of embryonic (but not adult) stem cells, genetic engineering, and human cloning. I am personally disappointed at the thinness of the argumentation in this section as well as the lack of nuance of discussion of exceptional cases, such as in relation to abortion. Persuasive public moral witness on these issues is difficult; it will require more depth than what is offered here. Maybe this was the extent to which consensus could be found.

That is not to say that the general statement of defense for human dignity, especially of human life at its most vulnerable points, is wrongheaded. Quite the contrary. The document probably reflects the influence of Catholic social thought in its conservative and comprehensive rejection of a range of bioethical and biotechnological threats to the sanctity of human life. As well, this section, more than any other, reflects the influence of the growing bioethical research community in evangelical academia and public witness. The conservative positions taken here line up closely with those taken by the Center for Bioethics and Human Dignity, probably the premier evangelical think tank on bioethical issues—and the sponsor of my forthcoming book on the sanctity of life.

Four years since the release of this statement, public opinion on the embryonic stem-cell issue has swung strongly against the position taken in this document. Yet I see no sign that the evangelical right or center is going to abandon the kind of position taken here. The total opposition to the use and destruction of embryos for their stem cells certainly seems extreme in a culture in which in vitro fertilization produces hundreds of thousands of unwanted embryos, and in which not just embryos but fetuses well along in gestation can be aborted—and, for that matter, in a violent culture in which we are constantly at war and 14,000 murders happen every year. Evangelical (and conservative Catholic) opposition has played a key role in preventing federal funding of aggressive embryonic stem-cell research. Probably the passing out of office of President Bush will mean a loosening up of such restrictions. Many will rejoice at that loosening. I for one will not. I think we need a total rethinking of our manipulation, engineering, employment, and destruction of human life, at every stage. This is a cultural issue before it is a legal one, for it goes to the heart of key assumptions and commitments of our society.

4. WE SEEK JUSTICE AND COMPASSION FOR THE POOR AND VULNERABLE

This is the lengthiest, most comprehensive, and perhaps the most surprising section of the document. It is significant in many ways. In one sense it marks the victory (at last) of economic justice advocates like Sider and Wallis in putting poverty on the moral agenda of American evangelicalism. Yet it also reveals the influence of more conservative voices in the way the document suggests that such poverty is to be addressed. It also completely ignores (and thus delegitimizes) some of the populist strands of evangelical thinking on money, such as the "health and wealth gospel" in which God (purportedly) promises wealth to his faithful followers, or the pure libertarian strand in which government is to stay almost entirely out of the affairs of a market economy.

The text begins by laying a biblical basis for concern for the poor—and other vulnerable and marginalized groups, lovingly and thoroughly enumerated in the text. Such concern is grounded in God's character, God's specific commands in scripture, and the general obligation to love our neighbors as ourselves. The document never explicitly takes the Catholic/liberationist "preferential option for the poor" position but it rightly cites scriptural teachings that come awfully close to that very stance.

When talking about the economic and legal structures of society, the text calls for justice, righteousness, and fairness. It does not demand equality of outcome but instead movement toward equality of opportunity so that all willing to work and live responsibly can enjoy a decent and dignified existence. This section reflects the evolution of Ron Sider's economic ethic and employs his language almost to the letter.

In defining what economic justice (or wholeness) looks like, the drafters offer a comprehensive picture that emphasizes "full participation in the life of the community." The text emphasizes health care, nutrition, and education as ways to achieve such participation. Those seeking to understand the heartbeat of the broader evangelical community should notice that there is now a growing evangelical constituency, and a clear hunger from the evangelical center, for significant efforts to address the healthcare crisis in our nation. There is also a recognition that many of the schools that ought to provide access to economic opportunity for all are failing badly. Both education and health care are economic justice issues.

Evangelicals have often clashed over who bears responsibility for addressing poverty. I still hear regularly from those who say that this is the church's responsibility, not the government's job. This statement takes a both/and rather than either/or approach. It calls for Christians to give, serve, and advocate for the poor. It calls on government to develop specific policies that encourage work, prevent poverty, and care for those who cannot care for themselves. (I think that the 1996 welfare reform law, which ended any federal entitlement to government social assistance, dramatically changed the environment for evangelical discussion of the poverty issue.) The document suggests the poverty-related significance of all kinds of policy arenas, such as immigration, taxation, wages, and wealth creation. The emphasis is on wise crafting of government policies that can empower the poor to move out of poverty, not on just getting government out of the way. This is a major advance.

The discussion of global economic issues is less comprehensive but still impressive. While the document does not take the antiglobalization line, it does mention the moral significance of U.S. trade policy. It wants global poverty reduction to be "a central concern of American foreign policy." It takes the "faith-based" line again to support government support of Christian international aid agencies, which, as we have suggested, are abundant in the evangelical world. It closes by listing a large number of atrocious global problems, such as HIV/AIDS, slavery and sex trafficking, corruption, war, and "rape as a tool of terror and oppression," all of which it hopes for Christian agencies and U.S. foreign policy to take on. Here one sees the influence of the IJM vision and other similar agencies. There is realism here about the depth of human misery around the world, but also optimism, about what aggressive actions on behalf of "the least of these" can accomplish. The authors seem to envision the United States as a great force for good in the world if it uses its power to address such desperate situations of human suffering. It sees the American church as a partner in actually delivering such good to the world's poor and suffering, and in motivating the U.S. government to want to do so. The contemporary American evangelical center is becoming deeply internationalist and deeply humanitarian in its vision, which poses a serious challenge to the alternately bellicose and isolationist voices on the right, and to the realists of the foreign policy establishment in academia and government.

5. WE WORK TO PROTECT HUMAN RIGHTS

Notice once again how much "cash value" the concept of the image of God has for evangelical moral witness today. It is used to ground this section's treatment of human rights—and responsibilities, an important rhetorical addition that serves to defang opposition to this treatment of rights from the outset.

The document begins with and also addresses later the "first freedom" associational and convictional rights such as religious liberty that were also addressed previously. This emphasis has been especially important for evangelicals in relation to missionary work in Muslim and Communist lands. A key influence here for evangelicals has been Freedom House, a bipartisan policy group that has been promoting democracy, human rights, and freedom issues since 1941 and has had considerable evangelical support. Paul Marshall, one of the drafters of this statement, serves at the Center for Religious Freedom of Freedom House. Those wanting to understand the emergence of evangelicals as foreign policy internationalists and human rights activists need to attend to the pivotal role of evangelical concern for missionaries and other Christians seeking to practice their faith under situations of sometimes extreme oppression and persecution.

The text then shifts to the language of needs, rather than rights, to talk about how embodied persons (that is, all human beings inhabit bodies, and bodies have needs) need food, shelter, nurture, and care. The authors do not move on to call these "rights," as in the most expansive treatments of rights, but it does call on governments to create, sustain, and protect the social conditions that contribute to these needs being met. It is striking that a right to private property and to marry, rear, and educate children are explicitly enumerated—probably in contradistinction to the collectivist experiments and disasters of the twentieth century. China may well be in mind.

The document alludes to the UN Declaration on Human Rights without quite endorsing it. It does, though, suggest that "governments should be constitutionally obligated to protect basic human rights," and that U.S. foreign policy should build human rights criteria into its relationships with other nations, as we (sometimes) now do. It also calls for our foreign policy to promote democracy and civil society around the world.

Indicating its awareness of the dangers of rights language, the text explicitly rejects a right to same-sex marriage or a right to die. The authors want to defend the legitimacy of rights language within the evangelical community, and this move helps them to set their own boundaries as to what uses of the language will be treated as legitimate. The same issue is dealt with in the human rights/antitorture statement that is reprinted here in chapter 6.

Probably the concluding paragraph on our own "tragic history" in relation to racism and rights strikes others, and not just me, as quite thin. In view of all of the attention to racial justice and racial reconciliation issues in evangelicalism in recent decades, I am quite surprised that the discussion of this set of issues was confined to a single paragraph in a section largely devoted to international issues. Perhaps the lack of racial diversity on the drafting committee (with the single exception of Villafañe) contributed to the weakness of the text at this point. Or perhaps it signals the exhaustion and frustration in relation to these issues that so often bubbles up in various sectors of the evangelical world these days.

6. WE SEEK PEACE AND WORK TO RESTRAIN VIOLENCE

This brief section reflects painful Christian—not just evangelical—disputes over the legitimacy of war and Christian participation in war. It also suggests the growing impact of Stassen of Fuller Seminary (who served on the drafting committee) and his theory of just peacemaking. This theory emphasizes, as the text suggests, the Christian obligation to encourage "practical peacemaking" initiatives such as nonviolent conflict resolution. Among the appealing features of the theory is the way it provides common ground for pacifists and some just-war theorists to be able to say something in common in relation to the issue of war, as happens here.

Theologically, this overall section is framed by two thematic claims that create a presumption against violence on the part of Christians. One is the reference to the prophetic vision of a just peace as an aspect of God's reign. The other is exclusion of violence as an instrument of the advance of that divine reign. If, therefore, war is permissible, it is not for the purpose of advancing Christ's cause or God's kingdom. In this way even a permissible war is desacralized for evangelicals— there can be no holy wars. And any support for government war fighting occurs against the backdrop of the eschatological expectation of an end to killing at the end of history. I think it is fair to say that most everyday evangelicals do not frame their thinking about war in these ways, but they should.

The document in passing suggests three possible legitimations for war. These are "to defend our homelands, rescue others from attack, or liberate other people from oppression." This amounts to at least openness to defensive war, a war to defend allies, and humanitarian war. It seems clear to me that the evangelical center would now be likely to support military action not only to destroy Al Qaeda, or to defend against another homeland attack, but also to prevent genocide. But purely national interest wars—such as wars for economic self-interest, national pride, or territorial gain—are rejected in the statement and probably would be rejected by large numbers of evangelicals.

The just-war theory is invoked at this point in the statement and is defined crucially as "designed to restrain violence by establishing the right conditions for and right conduct in fighting a war." This is a nod in the direction of the strict "presumption against war" approach to just-war theory, more common in both the evangelical and Catholic center and left, as opposed to the permissive "presumption for war to advance justice" approach, which is more common on the right (see chapter 8). The latter approach tends to be much more likely to support particular wars than is the former. Score one for the center and left and for the prevention of foolish and unnecessary wars.

It is interesting that the document mentions neither the war in Afghanistan nor Iraq. Nor does it say anything about the overall "war on terror" or the issue of torture. This may have been because no consensus was possible or because the drafters were reaching for a more timeless rather than time-bound statement. The fact is that evangelicals supported the war in Afghanistan overwhelmingly, the war in Iraq only slightly less so. Only the evangelical left held out in opposition to both. My guess would be that the evangelical center has been chastened by the Iraq war experience sufficiently to be much more careful in the future about evaluating any U.S. president's claims related to the need for a war.

7. WE LABOR TO PROTECT GOD'S CREATION

Just as the poverty plank of "For the Health of the Nation" marked a breakthrough for the evangelical left, this discussion of creation care indicates the embrace of environmental concern by the evangelical center. Undoubtedly that embrace was deeply satisfying to the creation care advocates and activists who worked on these issues for years without much positive evangelical response. As we have already shown, resistance to such a commitment remains fierce on the evangelical right, but I believe that the move made in this document to embrace it was a historic step forward.

The section begins on the kind of careful, even defensive, note that reflects the long history of struggle within the evangelical community on this issue. It affirms that we now do "embrace our responsibility to care for God's earth," but hastens to add that "we worship only the Creator and not the creation." Of course that is true. It is almost embarrassing that it would have to be said. But the association of environmental concern with New Age spirituality, ecofeminist theology, and Eastern religions spooked evangelicals on this issue quite badly in the 1970s and 1980s. Still, the reference feels anachronistic to me; it does not seem to be a worry of younger evangelicals, who understand that taking care of the planet need have nothing to with worshiping Gaia.

The text grounds creation care in the Genesis 1 "dominion" passage. It immediately moves to affirm the common evangelical center/left reconstruction of the dominion concept to mean "stewardship" and "sacred responsibility" to ensure "sustainability" rather than any license to exploit and destroy the earth. What exactly is meant by dominion remains a hot issue as evangelicals argue over environmental issues today.

The only other significant theological suggestion is the idea that part of God's redemptive work includes the restoration of the whole creation. Although this could have been developed much more thoroughly, the implications of this brief note are of great importance. If a restored creation is some part of God's eschatological plan, then Christians should be seeking to contribute to that restoration today, rather than waiting happily for environmental degradation to degenerate the earth into uninhabitability just before Jesus returns to snatch us away from here.

At an ethical level, the text asks Christians to become creation caregivers in their personal lives. A small number of specific areas are mentioned, including recycling and conservation of resources. Meanwhile, the text (amazingly, happily) supports government involvement in environmental protection. Again, given what we have already seen about evangelical right opposition on issues such as climate change, the mention of government efforts to address fuel-efficiency standards, pollution, wildlife, clean water, and so forth, is a huge step forward (or backward, if one is opposed to such government involvement).

Perhaps this was as far as the drafters could go. No mention is made of the climate change issue, which soon enough became a matter of huge controversy in the evangelical world. Most specific environmental issues are not addressed, and the text does not exactly ring with a sense of urgency. Still, in retrospect we can now see that this mainstreaming of evangelical environmentalism laid the foundation for the more aggressive efforts of Cizik (NAE) and others in the intervening four years.

OUR COMMITMENT

This concluding section of "For the Health of the Nation" strikes several significant notes. It indicates that evangelical Christians will stay "in the arena" of civic engagement. The drafters and signers pledge to support Christians who engage in civic life along the lines of the vision offered here and in the right spirit and manner. It calls for publicly engaged Christianity: for Christians to vote, communicate with their democratically elected leaders, and become involved in public service themselves. The text encourages heightened attention to civic responsibility in evangelical churches, agencies, colleges, and seminaries, many of which have neglected the issue entirely. The statement closes with a typically evangelical pledge of regular prayer for those who govern, implicitly reminding them of the norms that ought to determine how they govern—life, justice, freedom, and peace.

"For the Health of the Nation" is not a perfect statement. It has gaps and weaknesses. But it is the best such corporate statement that evangelicals have offered. It is biblical, comprehensive, lucid, and humble. It is politically independent. It reflects both a proper Christian love for and critical distance from these United States. It clearly reflects the vision of the emerging evangelical center.

Appendix 3

"AN EVANGELICAL DECLARATION AGAINST TORTURE"

Protecting Human Rights in an Age of Terror (2007)

1. INTRODUCTION

1.1   The sanctity of human life, a moral status irrevocably bestowed by the Creator upon each person and confirmed in the costly atoning sacrifice of Christ on the cross, is desecrated each day in many ways around the globe. Because we are Christians who are commanded by our Lord Jesus Christ to love God with all of our being and to love our neighbors as ourselves (Mt. 22:36-40), this mistreatment of human persons comes before us as a source of sorrow and a call to action.

1.2   *All* humans who are mistreated or tormented are *somebody's* brothers and sisters, sons and daughters, parents and grandparents. We must think of them as we would our own children or parents. They are, by Jesus' definition, our neighbors (Lk. 10:25-37). They are "the least of these," and so in them and through them we encounter God himself (Mt. 25:31-46). "When human lives are endangered, when human dignity is in jeopardy, national borders and sensitivities become irrelevant," Elie Wiesel declares. "Silence encourages the tormentor, never the tormented."[1]

1.3   However remote to us may be the victim of torture, abuse, or mistreatment, Christians must seek to develop the moral imagination to enter into the suffering of all who are victimized. Having personally witnessed the horrors of the Cambodian genocide of the 1970s, Robert A. Evans writes: "The motivation of basic human rights can never again become a matter of statistics, or theory, or strategy, or legislation, or judicial decision. It will always be, for me, the violation of the dignity of other children of God."[2] Commitment to a transcendent moral vision of human dignity which is rooted in the concrete reality of particular suffering human beings motivates the signers of this statement as well.

1.4   The authors and signatories of this declaration are evangelical Christians and citizens of the United States. As Christians, we long to obey the moral demands of our faith as articulated in the Scriptures. We seek to serve Jesus Christ, who alone is Lord of our lives, of the church, of our nation, and of the world. As citizens, we bring our Christian convictions to bear on the most important matters that arise in the life of our democracy, for the health of our nation and its impact on the lives of people around the world. We know that we may not always succeed in shaping the laws and policies of the United States in the way we believe they should be shaped. But we must, on all occasions, attempt to bear faithful Christian moral witness.

1.5   The immediate occasion for this declaration is the intense debate that has occurred in our country since 2004 over the use of torture and cruel, inhuman, and degrading treatment of those who are detained by our nation and other nations in the "war on terror."[3] In 2005–2006 this debate evolved into a broader discussion of policies related to the legal standards that would be employed in detaining, trying, transferring, or punishing suspected terrorists in what is turning out to be a lengthy struggle against individuals and groups engaged in terrorist plots and acts against our nation.

1.6   This cluster of issues would not have arisen if not for the horrifying and heinous attacks of 9/11, which took nearly 3,000 lives and constituted a mass violation of the very moral standards we witness to in this declaration. The U.S. response to these attacks, including intensified intelligence activities, the invasion of Afghanistan, and later the much-debated invasion of Iraq, has led to the apprehension of thousands of "enemy combatants," terrorists, suspected terrorists, and others. The question we now face is how we protect our society (and other societies) from further terrorist acts within a framework of moral and legal norms. As American Christians, we are above all motivated by a desire that our nation's actions would be consistent with foundational Christian moral norms. We believe that a scrupulous commitment to human rights, among which is the right not to be tortured, is one of these Christian moral convictions.

2. THE SANCTITY OF HUMAN LIFE

"And God said, 'Let us make human beings in our image, in our likeness. . . . So God created human beings in his own image, in the image of God he created them; male and female he created them."
Genesis 1:26a, 27

2.1   We ground our commitment to human rights, including the rights of suspected terrorists, in the core Christian belief that human life is sacred.

Evangelicals join a vast array of other Christian groups and thinkers—Roman Catholics, mainline Protestants, Eastern Orthodox, and others—in a long history of reflection and activism on behalf of this critical yet threatened moral conviction.

2.2   The sanctity of life is the conviction that all human beings, in any and every state of consciousness or self-awareness, of any and every race, color, ethnicity, level of intelligence, religion, language, nationality, gender, character, behavior, physical ability/disability, potential, class, social status, etc., of any and every particular quality of relationship to the viewing subject, are to be perceived as sacred, as persons of equal and immeasurable worth and of inviolable dignity. Therefore they must be treated with the reverence and respect commensurate with this elevated moral status. This begins with a commitment to the preservation of their lives and protection of their basic rights. Understood in all of its fullness, it includes a commitment to the flourishing of every person's life.[4]

2.3   Christian belief in the sanctity of human life is rooted in themes that work their way through the entire biblical canon as well as much of Jewish, Christian, and Western moral thought. Rightly understood, the sanctity of life is a moral norm that both summarizes and transcends all other particular norms in Christian moral thought.

2.4   Scripture reveals that life is sacred. Humans, in particular, are given life by the breath of God (Gen. 2:7) and are made in the image of God (Gen. 1:26-28). The imago Dei serves as a common denominator for all of humanity. Every human being, therefore, deserves respect.

2.5   The sanctity of life is emphasized in legal and covenantal texts in Scripture. Murder is forbidden because human beings are made in the image of God; this theme is evident in the covenants both with Noah and with Moses (Gen. 9:5-6; Ex. 20:13). Everyone has a duty to conserve and respect human life (Gen. 9:5; 4:8-10, 15), and to accept responsibility for the life of their fellow humans (Gen. 4:9; Dt. 21:1-9). Human life is sacred because it is "precious" to God (Ps. 116:15) and must therefore be precious to us as well. The prophets remind Israel of the value of human life, especially life at its most vulnerable (Is. 1:17; Jer. 7:6; Zech. 7:10).

2.6   The incarnation (Jn. 1:1, 14) permanently and decisively elevates the value of human life. It reveals a God who is not dispassionate, but deeply moved by the brokenness of creation.[5] The Incarnation demonstrates the extraordinary value God places upon human life. It also signifies a mysterious bridging of the gap between God and humanity. Henceforth, the human experience in its joys and sorrows is inscribed upon the very Person of God in a new way. Furthermore, the Holy Spirit participates in human pathos with groans and sighs too deep for words. The cries of the tortured are in a very real sense, then, the cries of the Spirit.

2.7   Jesus Christ, God-made-flesh, taught the dignity of human life and practiced it in his treatment of those around him. He reaffirmed the biblical commands which are intended to protect human life. He diagnosed the vicious patterns of sinful behavior that lead us to violate God's commands, and the sickness of the heart and mind that lie behind that sinful behavior. He offered teachings amounting to transforming initiatives to enable us to obey God's will. This is most clearly illustrated in his single largest block of teaching, the Sermon on the Mount (Mt. 5–7).

2.8   In his ministry, Jesus in all contexts treated persons as sacred in God's sight. This was especially apparent in the way he treated the marginalized: women, the sick, the dead, the poor, people of bad reputation, children, and enemies of Israel such as tax collectors, Roman soldiers, and Gentiles in general. He explicitly affirms the worth of human beings in his teaching (Lk. 12:24; Mt. 6:26; 12:11-12). He taught peacemaking rather than violence, and on the cross forgave those who assisted in killing him. He also stood with both the Law and the prophets before him in condemning injustice in its various forms: economic, political, military, and religious (cf. Mt. 23). The justice teachings of Jesus are closely related to a commitment to life's sanctity and serve as a fundamental building block of a Christian commitment to human rights.

2.9   For many centuries, Jesus' teaching about the "least of these" (Mt. 25:31-46) has been especially significant for shaping a Christian moral vision of the sanctity of every human life. Not only does this familiar "sheep and goats" parable emphasize the centrality of practical deeds of service to the least, the last, and the lost, it also teaches us to *see Jesus in* the hungry, the stranger, the naked, the sick, and the imprisoned: "as you did it unto the least of these, you did it unto me" (Mt. 25:40). This dramatic shift of moral vision has profound implications for how we as Christians think about our nation's imprisoned, sometimes hungry, sometimes sick, sometimes naked strangers.

2.10   Ultimately, it is the Cross of Jesus Christ that demonstrates how much God values human life. God-in-flesh dies, at human hands, for human beings who do not love him and are not worthy of his costly sacrifice. "While we were yet sinners, Christ died for us." Radical human equality is emphasized in the reason for this death, the universality of its scope, and the equality of its impact. At the Cross and in the Resurrection, by saying *no* to his Son's cry of dereliction, God says *yes* to all of derelict humanity.

2.11   Considered etymologically, a sacred thing is something that has already been sanctified, dedicated, consecrated, venerated, or hallowed. One might say, then, that our holy God has transferred his holiness onto us and therefore sanctified each person. This confers upon each of us a dignity that our attitudes, attributes, and activities neither deserve nor can nullify.[6]

2.12   In his *Gospel of Life*, Pope John Paul II asserts the sacred value of human life "from its very beginning until its end." He urges a fight against "the culture of death" and a holistic and comprehensive struggle to protect vulnerable humans, sacred in God's sight.

13.13 John Paul II is among those who have made the connection explicit: the concept of human rights is inextricably bound to the belief that human life is sacred and therefore must be held in the highest respect. "Upon the recognition of this right, every human community and the political community itself are founded."[7] Indeed, by focusing on human rights, we direct our attention and energy to those who need it most—those image-bearers whose dignity is being violated.[8] Human rights are not first of all about "my rights," but about the rights of the vulnerable and the violated. And they are about responsibility, indeed obligation, to defend the weak. All people, all societies, and all nations have a responsibility to ensure human rights.

13.14 We believe that a commitment to human rights is strengthened profoundly by the kinds of theological commitments just articulated. They are certainly our convictions. We are very happy to work with persons of other faiths and no faith on behalf of human rights, but as evangelicals our convictions are rooted in God's love and the dignity it gives to all human beings.

3. HUMAN RIGHTS

"Defend the weak and the fatherless; uphold the cause of the poor and the oppressed. Rescue the weak and the needy."

Psalm 82:3-4a

3.1 Human rights *function* to protect the dignity of human life.[9] Because human rights guard what God has made sacred, they cannot be cancelled by any other concern, nor can they be bracketed off as irrelevant in exigent circumstances. This is in contrast to the view that a right can be cancelled or overridden. Human rights are a decisive factor in determining how all persons must be treated in all circumstances.[10] Rights correlate with duties—fundamentally, a duty to protect those whose God-given rights are about to be, or are being, violated.[11] Those who affirm a belief in human rights implicitly accept for themselves a range of moral obligations.[12] Affirmation of human rights and their corresponding duties is an important dimension of Christian belief, and also widely shared by persons of other faiths.

3.2 Human rights place a shield around people, even when (especially when) our hearts cry out for vengeance. It is precisely when we are most inclined to abandon a commitment to human rights that we most need to reaffirm that commitment.[13] The creation of a social order in which such legal and moral norms are honored even in the teeth of popular sentiment is both a high human achievement, and a fragile one.

3.3 Human rights apply to all humans. The rights people have are theirs by virtue of being human, made in God's image. Persons can never be stripped of their humanity, regardless of their actions or of others' actions toward them. In social-contract theory human rights are called *unalienable* rights. Unalienable rights are absolute and completely inviolable; a person cannot legitimately cease to have those rights, whether through waiver, fault, or another's act.[14] This is not biblical vocabulary, but it does seem to us consistent with a biblical understanding of human rights. Consider the way in which even Cain was protected by the divine "mark," and legal provision to protect the rights of killers was made in the Old Testament through the cities of refuge and the processes of judgment required there (Num. 35:9-34).

3.4   Some Christians reject human-rights language because they have witnessed its abuse. They have heard numerous groups claim a right to engage in certain behaviors as expressions of their human rights. Many morally troublesome agendas are punctuated with "rights talk," thereby cheapening those rights that are indeed both unalienable and threatened.[15] But the solution is not to abandon talk of rights. It is instead to clarify the range of legitimate rights claims.

3.5   A variety of approaches can be taken to articulate and organize claims about human rights. An expansive approach argues that there are three dimensions of human rights, and all must be equally valued by any society that respects any of them: the right to certain freedoms, especially including religious liberty, the right to participate in community, and the right to have basic needs met.[16]

3.6   If one takes a more constrained approach to human rights, such as the view which confines human rights to "negative rights," i.e., that which the state may not do to us, the issues under discussion in this declaration still fall well within the boundaries of legitimate human-rights claims.

3.7   Human life is expressed through physicality, and the well-being of persons is tied to their physical existence. Therefore, humans must have the right to security of person. This includes the right not to have one's life taken unjustly (equivalent to the right to life), the right not to have one's body mutilated, and the right not to be abused, maimed, tortured, molested, or starved (sometimes called the right to bodily integrity or the right to remain whole). The right not to be arbitrarily detained (an aspect of due process) and the *writ of habeus corpus* are also based specifically on the concept of bodily rights. In particular, the *writ of habeus corpus* is based on the right not to have the government arbitrarily detain one's body.

4. THE CHRISTIAN HISTORY OF HUMAN RIGHTS

"Thus says the Lord: 'Do justice and righteousness, and deliver from the hand of the oppressor him who has been robbed. And do no wrong or violence to the alien, the fatherless, and the widow, nor shed any blood.'"

Jeremiah 22:3

4.1   Contrary to a common misunderstanding, one that has weakened Christian
support for human rights, human rights are not an Enlightenment notion,
and certainly not to be seen as an Enlightenment *fiction*. Rooted in Scripture,
the concept of human rights was suggested as far back as the 12th century,
and can be traced into the modern period through a variety of routes, all of
them versions of Christianity. Heirs to the English Christian traditions find
especially important the work of Richard Overton, an English Christian
thinker of the 17th century. In 1645, Overton wrote *The Arraignment of Mr.
Persecution*, basing his argument on reason, experience, and Scripture. The
book was penned during a time of great oppression of religious nonconform-
ists in England. Overton proclaimed the equal rights of Jews, Muslims,
atheists, Catholics, Protestants, and all humankind.[17]

4.2   Thus human-rights ideas developed in the English-speaking world during
a movement for religious liberty among "free church" Puritans in England,
and later among religious dissenters in North America like Roger Williams,
and not first among Enlightenment rationalists.[18] The concept of human
rights flourished in the 17th and 18th centuries with documents such as the
American *Declaration of Independence* (1776), the French Assembly's *Declaration
of the Rights of Man and of the Citizen* (1789), and Thomas Paine's *The Rights of
Man* expressing the belief in "natural rights."[19] More secularized versions of
human rights should be seen as derivatives of an earlier, explicitly Christian,
articulation.

4.3   The late 19th century proved an inhospitable environment for belief in "natural rights" worldwide, in both philosophical and political arenas. However,
the totalitarian assault on human dignity in the first half of the 20th century, especially by Nazi Germany, Stalinist Russia, and Imperialist Japan,
led to a reinterpretation of traditional natural-rights talk in the direction
of "human rights."[20] Reacting to the devastation of the Nazi regime, and
responding to the struggle by colonies for independence from their colonial
masters, human rights gained worldwide momentum once again. Shortly
after World War II, the United Nations Declaration of Human Rights was
written, and then signed by the vast majority of nations.[21] The United States
played a key role in drafting and advancing this UN Declaration. Many
deeply committed Christians were involved in this process. Evangelicals
struggled with the secular grounding of the Declaration's norms, but both
then and now embrace its primary principles.

4.4   The Roman Catholic Church and the second Vatican Council (1962–1965)
brought about another development in the maturation of the concept of
human rights. Strongly affirming religious liberty after centuries of teaching otherwise, the Vatican II leaders, as with Overton, articulated strong
concern for world peace and drew the connections between war and the
violation of human rights.[22] A similar emphasis on human rights appears

in many of the documents of the global ecumenical movement, as well as mainline Protestant theologians such as Reinhold Niebuhr. Meanwhile, the social movement of the 1950s and 1960s for African American civil rights provided a powerful articulation of a heartfelt human-rights ethic. It is hard to avoid the conclusion that an emphasis on human rights was very nearly a Christian consensus by the late 20th century.

4.5   Yet talk of human rights evokes opposition as well. We have already noted theological and philosophical objections. But throughout history the primary opposition to a concept of human rights has emerged most intensely from privileged groups (religious, economic, political, ethnic, etc.) determined to maintain their unjust advantages or resist challenges to their mistreatment of those whom they dominated. Meanwhile, support for human rights has helped to spread democracy and in general to break the power of unjust social structures.[23]

4.6   Love for one's neighbor should motivate the believer to act in the interests of those whose rights we are responsible to defend. Commitment to human rights can be seen as a systematic way to look out for the interests of others, and thus as an expression of Christian love. This is now the overwhelming consensus of the Christian community.

5. ETHICAL IMPLICATIONS OF HUMAN RIGHTS

"Father to the fatherless, a defender of widows, is God in his holy dwelling. God sets the lonely in families, he leads out the prisoners with singing."

Psalm 68:5-6

Principles

1.1   It is vital for the future of any good society and for the development of democracy that we, as citizens of the United States and as Christians belonging to the Body of Christ, promote and protect the innate dignity of the human person and therefore honor human rights. In the last century we have witnessed far too many attempts to abolish that divine value in humanity, and to treat human beings in ways far worse than bestial. However, as Pope John Paul II stated, the sanctity of life is a value "which no individual, no majority and no State can ever create, modify or destroy, but must only acknowledge, respect and promote."[24]

5.2   Even when a person has done wrong, poses a threat, or has information necessary to prevent a terrorist attack, he or she is still a human being made in God's image, still a person of immeasurable worth. The crime we abhor, but we must distinguish the error from the person in error. A person might do inhuman acts, but is never inhuman.[25] This distinction is excruciatingly difficult to make, which is all the more reason why we must be vigilant in doing so.

Responsibilities

Individual Responsibility

5.3   As individuals we are responsible for protecting the dignity of others, as the Good Samaritan did when he went out of his way to minister to the victim he found along his path (Lk. 10:25-37). The Lord brings justice, and governments have resources not available to individuals, but that does not release each of us from the obligation to make an urgent and concerted effort to raise every bearer of the image of God to the dignified level at which he or she was intended by the Creator.[26]

5.4   We live in a free society, a representative democracy, and while only a few may be direct perpetrators of human-rights violations or even torture, we all share the responsibility because we are the citizens on whose behalf interrogators and military personnel are working. Whether we commit an offense against humanity, or simply sin by refusing to speak up for someone who is being victimized, as individuals and a society we are accountable for the indignities that are authorized and carried out by our nation.[27] We each have responsibility to exercise our right/obligation to participate in the deliberative processes of our democracy. Those who have greater social or political power have even greater moral responsibility to act.

The Role of the Church

5.5   The churches have a very important responsibility to prepare their members to be faithful disciples of Christ who witness in and to the various contexts in which we find ourselves. Church leaders have a critical role in equipping Christians to think and respond biblically in all major areas of life, including the one we are considering here. One aspect of this discipling process is to help congregants prepare for the exercise of their citizenship responsibilities. Evangelicals alone make up one quarter of all voters in the United States. As evangelicals we are keenly aware of the gravity of our responsibility, and many of us have joined in articulating our own public ethical vision in a document released in 2004, and endorsed by all forty-three members of the Board of the National Association of Evangelicals, "For the Health of the Nation."[28]

The Role of the State

5.6   The government inevitably plays a central role in a nation's treatment of human beings and respect for human life. Unless human rights are embedded in a nation's constitutional documents, in its legislation, and in fair court procedures, and there is governmental respect for international laws that protect human rights, rights claims can become mere abstractions that are not implemented in practice. In light of the sinfulness of humanity there is a need for the protection and restraint of laws.

5.7   Governments should be legally obligated to protect basic human rights. The U.S. government certainly is so obligated.

5.8   It is striking that calls in the 1970s and 1980s for the United States to advance global human rights initially assumed that human rights were an unquestioned part of our own constitutional order. The idea was to spread that vision around the world. Evangelicals have been deeply invested in that project. We have pressed for the rights of religious liberty, especially where religious minorities have been persecuted, for the rights of victims of sex trafficking, and for human rights in countries oppressed by dictatorships. Now we find ourselves having to turn our gaze homeward again, to the eroding human-rights protections of our own practices.

5.9   The goal of a nation that advances human rights for all is one that has been articulated by our current president and members of his administration. President George W. Bush has described the United States as being born from a "simple dream of dignity." The American spirit, he has asserted, is "generous and strong and decent, not because we believe in ourselves, but because we hold beliefs beyond ourselves."[29]

5.10   This dream was not lost after 9/11. On October 31, 2001, Lorne W. Craner, assistant secretary for the Bureau of Democracy, Human Rights, and Labor, stated: "maintaining the focus on human rights and democracy worldwide is an integral part of our response to the attack [on 9/11]. . . . We are proud to bear the mantle of leadership in international human rights in this century." President Bush's speeches are full of belief in the dignity of every human life, regardless of political or national distinctions. "The American flag stands for more than our power and our interests," he has said. "Our founders dedicated this country to the cause of human dignity, the rights of every person, and the possibilities of every life."[30]

5.11   In light of these appealing words, it is clear to us that the terrorist attacks that jolted the nation in 2001 have blurred our national moral vision. National resolve, normally a virtue, can be misdirected, leading to the violation of human rights when it is allowed to overthrow our better selves. As the founding fathers intended, we have checks and balances within our Constitution's framework where Congress and the courts operate to check the presidency and thereby protect human rights. This is how it should be. Meanwhile, the United Nations Human Rights Charter and the great number of other human rights documents to which America has added its name serve as additional boundary setters, so that the government does not act rashly or unjustly.

5.12   The current administration has at times used language that is rich with respect for human rights, even after 9/11. Today this language is less frequently heard, and our actions as a nation do not consistently reflect the values once articulated. Yet there is a structure of national and international principles and laws that can help us to regain our moral footing, and in some ways have already begun to do so.

6. Legal Structures Regarding Human Rights

"A ruler who lacks understanding is a cruel oppressor, but he who hates unjust gain will prolong his days."

Proverbs 28:16

International Law

6.1 The Geneva Conventions, the Convention Against Torture, and many other treaties outlining human rights are in place so each signatory nation is held accountable.[31]

6.2 With a raging "war on terror," American policymakers and interrogators have faced the temptation of looking to torture, and to cruel, inhuman, or degrading treatment of their detainees in Iraq, Afghanistan, Guantánamo, and other U.S. detention centers. Torture has often been a temptation (and far too many times a practice) in other countries facing perceived or actual security threats. Despite these abuses, the ban on torture in the Geneva Convention and of the Convention Against Torture is unambiguous.[32]

6.3 Article 3 of the 3rd Geneva Convention (1949)[33] says:

In the case of armed conflict not of an international character occurring in the territory of one of the High Contracting Parties, each party to the conflict shall be bound to apply, as a minimum, the following provisions:

1. Persons taking no active part in hostilities, including members of armed forces who have laid down their arms and those placed hors de combat by sickness, wounds, detention, or any other cause, shall in all circumstances be treated humanely, without any adverse distinction founded on race, colour, religion or faith, sex, birth or wealth, or any other similar criteria.

   To this end the following acts are and shall remain prohibited at any time and in any place whatsoever with respect to the above-mentioned persons:

   (a) Violence to life and person, in particular, murder of all kinds, mutilation, cruel treatment and torture;

   (b) Taking of hostages;

   (c) Outrages upon personal dignity, in particular, humiliating and degrading treatment;

   (d) The passing of sentences and the carrying out of executions without previous judgment pronounced by a regularly constituted court affording all the judicial guarantees which are recognized as indispensable by civilized peoples.[34]

6.4 Article 2 of the UN Convention Against Torture states: "No exceptional circumstances whatsoever, whether a state of war or a threat or war, internal political instability or any other public emergency, may be invoked as a justification of torture."[35] The UN *International Covenant on Civil and Political Rights* (ICCPR—1966) states in article 7 that "no one shall be subjected to torture or to cruel, inhuman, or degrading treatment or punishment."[36] Article 10 of the ICCPR also establishes a particular right to be treated in a humane and dignified manner for accused or detained persons deprived of their personal liberty. This code of conduct is further clarified in the United Nations High Commission on Human Rights *Civil and Political Rights, Including the Questions of Torture and Detention* (2005). Cruel, inhuman, or degrading treatment (CIDT), although falling short of torture, is still completely prohibited along with all forms of torture. "The overriding factor at the core of the prohibition of CIDT is the concept of [the] powerlessness of the victim."[37]

6.5   International treaties provide *no loopholes* for justifying torture. The ICCPR treaty says that although "in time of public emergency which threatens the life of the nation . . . the State Parties to the present Covenant may take measures derogating from their obligations under the present Covenant to the extent strictly required by the exigencies of the situation, . . . *no derogation from [article] 7 . . . may be made under this provision*."[38] Likewise, the UN Convention Against Torture allows no exceptions for torture whatsoever.[39]

6.6   The United States is a signatory to all of these international treaties and declarations. We have also historically incorporated their principles into military doctrine. However, these practices have come into question during the last five years. We believe that this has been a mistake, and we support a return to full adherence to the straightforward meaning of international conventions against torture.

U.S. Law

6.7   The United States has often sought to position itself as being on the side of the oppressed, including soldiers imprisoned under unjust or cruel circumstances. The Fifth, Eighth, and Fourteenth Amendments prohibit cruel, unusual and inhumane treatment, and Congress has also enacted laws unequivocally banning torture.[40] During the American Revolution, our soldiers were mistreated by the British. Our nation has worked diligently since then to provide legal protection to any person in the custody of the enemy through laws of war.[41] The Geneva Conventions and the Additional Protocols of 1977 are the most recent version of this protection.[42] In 1996 the United States adopted the War Crimes Act, which imposed felony criminal liability on persons that commit "grave breaches" of the Geneva Conventions.[43] It must be remembered that the United States has historically been a *leader* in pressing for such safeguards, not just a reluctant signatory.

6.8   Since human rights first became a prominent issue in the 20th century, the United Nations and the United States have continued to make additions to former agreements, treaties, and statements in order to make them as comprehensive and relevant as possible. This is what a democracy should always be doing. Human rights have always been, and always will be, under attack. However, a democracy works to guard against such violations of human rights through its laws. Its very identity depends upon the confidence that violations of human rights, such as torture, are prohibited.[44]

6.9 Between 9/11 and January 2006, tens of thousands had been detained in U.S. detention centers.[45] The vast majority of these detainees were released without charge. It is important to remember that detention policies pertain to persons, most of whom will end up being charged with no crime and being viewed as no threat to our nation.

6.10 The boundaries of what is legally and morally permissible in war have been crossed in the current "war on terror." The evidence of acts of torture or cruel, inhuman, and degrading treatment against U.S. detainees, especially in Iraq's Abu Ghraib prison, in Afghanistan's Bagram Air Base, in CIA black sites, and at the hands of other nations, has been documented by numerous researchers, including those serving the U.S. government itself. Revelations of these outrages against human dignity led to intense pressure on the federal government to return to its earlier rejection of torture and to clarify its detention and interrogation policies.

6.11 Commendably, the U.S. Army Field Manual, last revised in 1992, has recently undergone more changes in light of recent events. Specific cruel, inhuman, and degrading practices that had taken place at least sporadically from 2002–2006 are now overtly banned. In addition to the general language of the 1992 edition, which prohibited "acts of violence or intimidation, including physical or mental torture, threats [or] insults, . . . as a means of or aid to interrogation,"[46] there is now also more specific wording prohibiting military personnel from engaging in the behavior that put Abu Ghraib in the headlines. Beating prisoners, sexually humiliating them, threatening them with dogs, depriving them of food and water, performing mock executions, shocking them with electricity, burning them, causing other types of pain, and "waterboarding," are all explicitly banned.[47] The Pentagon is to be commended for this strong and positive revision of the Army Field Manual. It should become the policy of every agency of the United States government.[48]

6.12 Tragically, however, despite the military's commendable efforts to remove itself from any involvement with torture, the current administration has decided to retain morally questionable interrogation techniques among the options available to our intelligence agencies. For some time it did so without any form of public disclosure or oversight. In 2006 the administration moved its policies more fully into the light of day, pressing for legislation to authorize what it wanted to do.

6.13 The most recent legislation regarding these issues was signed into law in October 2006.[49] From a human-rights perspective, the Military Commissions

Act includes numerous problematic provisions, such as one in which CIA officials are not required to submit to congressional oversight, and are not held to the same standards as the U.S. military. CIA "black sites" may continue to exist, with interrogation rules established by the president but not specified publicly and now removed from the ability of either Congress or judicial authority to review.[50] This could prove to be a recipe for cruel, inhuman, and degrading treatment of detainees, without the Constitution's checks and balances so crucial for American justice.

6.14 Various procedural issues in the Military Commissions Act are also troubling. The new law does not allow terrorism suspects to challenge their detention or treatment through traditional *habeas corpus* petitions.[51] It permits prosecutors, under certain conditions, to use evidence collected through hearsay or through coercion to seek criminal convictions.[52] The legislation also rejects any right to a speedy trial,[53] and it empowers U.S. officials to detain indefinitely anyone it determines to have "purposefully and materially" supported anti-U.S. hostilities.[54] These provisions are deeply lamentable, in part because of their substance, and in part because they create the conditions in which further prisoner abuse is made more likely. They violate basic principles of due process that have been developed in Western judicial systems, including our own, for centuries. Anti-U.S. "hostilities" is a vague term that a future administration can use against anyone perceived as its enemy.[55] We see this as fraught with danger to basic human rights.

7. Conclusion: Human Rights in an Age of Terror

"And the LORD said, 'What have you done? The voice of your brother's blood is crying to me from the ground.'"

Genesis 4:10

7.1 The terrorist attacks of 9/11 and the attacks that followed blatantly violated human rights in the most outrageous manner imaginable. We declare without hesitation that the terrorist attacks in New York, Washington, London, Madrid, Bali, Casablanca, Amman, and other locations around the globe were heinous assaults on human life. We condemn these worldwide terrorist activities and the radical ideologues that foment them.

7.2 It is certainly the responsibility of a nation's government to protect its people from such callous and cruel disregard of human life.[56] Our military and intelligence forces have worked diligently to prevent further attacks. But such efforts must not include measures that violate our own core values.

7.3 Our current circumstances and national-security concerns do not present us with distinctively new temptations regarding the violation of human rights in relation to interrogation policies, torture, and the legal rights of detainees. Our nation's founders anticipated security threats in the 18th century; indeed, one could argue that they faced a far more threatening security environment than any that we have experienced since their age. Deterring evil ends without resorting to evil means are tasks in tension, but any democracy must face dealing with this tension.

7.4   A significant challenge presented to us as we focus on deterring terrorism is not that terrorism is unprecedented, but that as it spreads and intensifies, terrorism is deeply frightening to people and unsettling to our way of life. The principle that we must "discharge duties to those who have violated their duties to us" seems even more difficult to bear.[57] It also makes it all the more necessary to be vigilant about guarding those moral boundaries.

5.5   Torture is but one of many violations of human rights. Sadly there are more. Even forty years ago, Vatican II was able to list the following such violations:

> The varieties of crime are numerous: all offenses against life itself, such as murder, genocide, abortion, euthanasia and willful suicide; all violations of the integrity of the human person, such as mutilation, physical and mental torture, undue psychological pressures, all offenses against human dignity, such as subhuman living conditions, arbitrary imprisonment, deportation, slavery, prostitution, the selling of women and children, degrading working conditions where men are treated as mere tools for profit rather than free and responsible persons: all these and the like are criminal: they poison civilization; and they debase the perpetrators more than the victims and militate against the honor of the creator.[58]

7.6   Slavery, human and sexual trafficking, genocide, prison rape, abortion, euthanasia, unethical human experimentation—these are some of the other human rights violations listed by the National Association of Evangelicals in its "For the Health of the Nation" statement of 2004.[59] As evangelicals, we are deeply concerned about all violations of human rights. We want to lead the way in honoring and defending human rights wherever they are threatened.

7.7   We gratefully acknowledge our brothers and sisters in other Christian traditions for their thoughtful and Spirit-led work in the area of human rights. In recent times, evangelicals have joined with others to articulate an increasingly vigorous human rights ethic. The Board of the National Association of Evangelicals, representing over 30 million evangelical Christians, in 2004 unanimously approved a statement of social responsibility, which declared that "because God created human beings in his image, we are endowed with rights and responsibilities. . . . Governments should be constitutionally obligated to protect basic human rights." Among those rights articulated in this statement is the right to live "without fear of torture."[60] Little did the NAE know how relevant that particular provision would soon become.

7.8   As evangelicals, we are first obligated to be faithful to Christ and his teaching. We are to be kingdom people, disciples who think biblically about all things. In this particular situation, discipleship requires a clear word from us to our nation and its leaders. We must continue to discuss the moral problems associated with our treatment of detainees both in recent years and still today. Indeed, all citizens in a democracy must step up to the challenge we now face. The enormous burden of defending the human rights of United States citizens while also respecting those of the (suspected and actual) enemy is not one to be carried by our president alone.[61] As fellow Christians, fellow citizens, and fellow human beings, we let our leaders down by remaining silent.

7.9   When torture is employed by a state, that act communicates to the world and to one's own people that human lives are not sacred, that they are not reflections of the Creator, that they are expendable, exploitable, and disposable, and that their intrinsic value can be overridden by utilitarian arguments that trump that value.[62] These are claims that no one who confesses Christ as Lord can accept.

7.10   The most widely publicized acts of torture by the United States came on the heels of the 9/11 attack. As our nation mobilized, the eyes of the Muslim world were on the United States and how a Western civilization—in their eyes a Christian civilization—would respond to such barbarism. In this setting, that our actions were not bound by principles of human rights that we in the West profess was rightly seen by Muslims as hypocrisy and thus all the more damaging.

7.11   Human rights must be protected for all humankind. A commitment to life's sacredness and to human rights is a seamless garment. It cannot be torn anywhere without compromising its integrity everywhere.

7.12   Therefore:

    (a)   We renounce the use of torture and cruel, inhuman, and degrading treatment by any branch of our government (or any other government)—even in the current circumstance of a war between the United States and various radical terrorist groups.

    (b)   We call for the extension of basic human rights and procedural protections to all persons held in United States custody now or in the future, wherever and by whomever they are held.

    (c)   We call for every agency of the U.S. government to join with the U.S. military and to state publicly its commitment to the terms of the Geneva Conventions related to the treatment of prisoners, especially Common Article 3.

    (d)   We call for the legislative or judicial reversal of those executive and legislative provisions that violate the moral and legal standards articulated in this declaration.

7.13 We make these renunciations and calls for action as Christians and as U.S. citizens. Undoubtedly there are occasions where the demands of Christian discipleship and American citizenship conflict. This is not one of them. Returning to the absolute commitment to human rights outlined here is right in terms of Christian convictions and right in terms of the interests of our nation. We commend these moral commitments to our fellow believers, and our fellow citizens, for such a time as this.

SELECTED SIGNATORIES
of "An Evangelical Declaration Against Torture: Protecting Human Rights in an Age of Terror"

Leith Anderson, President, National Association of Evangelicals; **Robert C. Andringa**, Ph.D., President Emeritus, Council for Christian Colleges & Universities; **The Rev. Dr. Randall Balmer**, Professor of American Religious History, Barnard College, Columbia University; **W. Todd Bassett**, Executive Director, NAE; **Shane Bertou**, President, Ardent Faith Community; **Paul Bramer**, Professor of Christian Formation, North Park Theological Seminary; **David C. Brown**, Chairman of the Board, Evangelical Child and Family Agency; **Malcolm Brubaker**, Professor of Bible, Valley Forge Christian College; **David B. Capes**, Chair, Department of Christianity, Houston Baptist University; **Dr. G. William Carlson**, Professor of History and Political Science, Bethel University; **Jeff Carr**, Chief Operating Officer, Sojourners/Call to Renewal; **Joe Carson**, President, Affiliation of Christian Engineers; **Rich Cizik**, Vice President for Governmental Affairs, NAE; **Joseph L. Cumming**, Director, Reconciliation Program, Yale Center for Faith and Culture; **Dr. Alan S. Cureton**, President, Northwestern College and Radio; **Paul de Vries**, Ph.D., President, New York Divinity School; **Henry Earle**, Director, The Temple Initiative, Cleveland County Health Education; **Steven Edmonds**, Chaplain/Director of Pastoral Care, BMH–North Mississippi; **Harvey A. Elder**, M.D., Professor of Medicine, Loma Linda University School of Medicine; **Kimberly Ervin Alexander**, Asst. Professor of Historical Theology, Church of God Theological Seminary; **Carl H. Esbeck**, R. B. Price Professorship and Isabelle Wade and Paul C. Lyda Professor of Law, University of Missouri–Columbia; **Becky Garrison**, Senior Contributing Editor, The *Wittenburg Door*, New York; **Christopher Gehrz**, Assistant Professor of History, Bethel University; **Aaron Graham**, Senior Pastor, Quincy Street Missional Church, Boston, MA; **Diane Grant**, Spiritual Director, Evangelical Covenant Church, Concord, CA; **David Gushee** (principal drafter), Graves Professor of Moral Philosophy, Union University; **Chuck Gutenson**, Associate Professor of Philosophical Theology, Asbury Theological Seminary; **Jim Hancock**, Author, *The Justice Mission*; **Jerry S. Herbert**, Director, American Studies Program/Council for Christian Colleges & Universities; **Roberta Hestenes**, Minister-at-large, World Vision; **Kenneth W. Hicks**, Bishop, retired, United Methodist Church; **Rev. John C. Holmes**, Ed.D., Director of Government Affairs, Association of Christian Schools International; **Ken Hunn**, Executive Director, The Brethren Church; **George Hunsinger**,

McCord Professor of Theology, Princeton Theological Seminary; **Joel Hunter**, Senior Pastor, Northland, A Church Distributed, Longwood, Florida; **Daniel Hutt**, Pastor, Palo Alto Christian Reformed Church; **Cheryl Bridges Johns**, Professor of Discipleship and Christian Formation, Church of God Theological Seminary; **Brad J. Kallenberg**, Associate Professor of Theology, University of Dayton; **Brian Kaylor**, Communications Specialist, Baptist General Convention of Missouri; **Rev. Brian Kluth**, Senior Pastor, First Evangelical Free Church of Colorado Springs and Founder of www.MAXIMUMgenerosity.org; **Sammy T. Mah**, President/CEO, World Relief; **Ron Mahurin**, Vice President of Professional Development and Research, Council for Christian Colleges & Universities; **Jason Martin**, Pastor, Hickory Grove Baptist Church (SBC), Trenton, TN; **Chuck Marvin**, Executive Director for the NAE Chaplains Commission and Ecclesiastical Chaplain Endorser, NAE; **Steve McGlamery**, Associate Pastor, First Baptist Church, Hawkinsville, GA; **Brian McLaren**, Founder, Cedar Ridge Community Church, Spencerville, MD; **Rev. Dr. Raymond Moreland**, Maryland Bible Society; **Stephen Charles Mott**, Retired, Southern New England Annual Conference, United Methodist Church; **David Neff**, Editor, *Christianity Today*; **Carey C. Newman**, Ph.D., Director, Baylor University Press; **Brian F. O'Connell**, President, REACT Services, Mill Creek, WA; **Richard V. Pierard**, Stephen Phillips Professor of History, Gordon College; **Christine Pohl**, Professor, Asbury Theological Seminary; **Dr. Claude O. Pressnell Jr.**, President, Tennessee Independent Colleges and Universities Association; **Wyndy Corbin Reuschling**, Associate Professor of Ethics and Theology, Ashland Theological Seminary; **Rev. Samuel Rodriguez Jr.**, President, National Hispanic Christian Leadership Conference; **Fleming Rutledge**, Priest, Episcopal Diocese of New York; **Will Samson**, Director, The Faith and Society Project; **Mark Sargent**, Provost, Gordon College; **Kevin Saxton**, Associate Pastor, Brewster Baptist Church, Brewster, MA; **Rev. Dr. Douglas Scalise**, Senior Pastor, Brewster Baptist Church, Brewster, MA; **Rev. Ken Sehested**, Circle of Mercy Congregation; **Ron Sider**, Professor of Theology and Culture and Director of the Sider Center on Ministry and Public Policy, Palmer Theological Seminary; Founder, Evangelicals for Social Action; **Glen Stassen**, Lewis B. Smedes Professor of Christian Ethics, Fuller Theological Seminary; **Clyde D. Taylor**, U.S. Ambassador, retired; **Knox Thames**, Columbia Baptist Church, Falls Church, VA; **Reverend Thomas E. Trask**, General Superintendent, General Council of the Assemblies of God; **Miroslav Volf**, Henry B. Wright Professor of Theology; Director, Yale Center for Faith and Culture, Yale Divinity School; **Berten A. Waggoner**, National Director, Vineyard Churches USA; **Richard E. Waldrop**, Associate Professor of World Mission and Evangelism, Church of God Theological Seminary; **Jim Wallis**, President, Sojourners/Call to Renewal; **Michael L. Westmoreland-White**, Ph.D., Theological Consultant, Every Church a Peace Church; **Nicholas Wolterstorff**, Noah Porter Professor of Philosophical Theology, Yale University.

Appendix 4

HOW TO READ "AN EVANGELICAL DECLARATION AGAINST TORTURE"

The release of our statement, "An Evangelical Declaration Against Torture: Protecting Human Rights in an Age of Terror," garnered considerable attention in mid-March 2007. However, surprisingly little of that attention went to themes that I think constitute the real significance of the document. I am grateful to the editors for a few pages to offer my own take, as lead drafter, on the meaning of this declaration.

How should one read "An Evangelical Declaration Against Torture"?

First, read it as an expression of a sanctity-of-life ethic.

Our goal as drafters was to write an intellectually substantive, biblically rooted, theologically rich, definitively Christian treatment of U.S. detainee policy and practice in the war on terror. We sought to move beyond the kinds of brief declarations and slogans that often circulate on torture and other controversial moral issues, and instead tried to offer a serious analysis of a crucial set of moral concerns.

It was important to ground our stance in moral convictions that evangelical Christians (ought to) find nonnegotiable. This was one reason why, as principal drafter, I grounded the declaration on the concept of the sanctity of every human life, a move that was never seriously questioned during the drafting process. One can hardly imagine a moral commitment that evangelicals (supposedly) take more seriously than this one. I personally believe that, rightly understood, the sanctity of life remains among the most powerful moral norms known to the church or to the human family. It is both clearly biblical and yet appealing to many outside of biblical faith. I am working on a book that revisits the sanctity of life concept in detail (Eerdmans, 2009). Here the declaration shows some early fruit of that work as it outlines key dimensions of a theologically rooted belief in life's sanctity and employs these as a beginning point for its treatment of torture.

Second, read it as a concretizing of a Christian human rights ethic that deals with a real area of moral vulnerability for our nation right now.

The sanctity of life becomes the grounding for a treatment of human rights in the declaration. Our treatment of human rights in section 2 of this document was vetted carefully by the drafting committee for its theological, ethical, and legal dimensions. I think it marks a significant step forward in the public articulation among evangelicals of a human-rights ethic.

We argue that respect for human rights is fragile, and that it must include special vigilance on behalf of those whose rights are threatened. In this case, who would more likely qualify as vulnerable than a suspected terrorist moldering without charges and without public oversight in detention somewhere by a nation that still faces nightmares about 9/11?

We argue that even a fairly constrained understanding of human rights includes the right to security of person, which includes the right not to be tortured. We also make the critically important move of arguing that human rights cannot be cancelled, forfeited, or overridden. Most evangelicals—right, center, and left— say that they care about human rights. This is a concrete test of that affirmation. We know we really care about human rights when we care about the rights of our enemies and those we fear, not just ourselves or our friends.

Third, read it as a thrust in the intra-Christian argument about the concept of human rights.

We try to defuse the sometimes popular charge among academics that human rights is a modernist rather than Christian notion by exploring the rich but neglected Christian history of support for human rights. This is an important move that, so far, our critics have not challenged. This is good news, because Christian skepticism about the very validity of the concept of human rights can be quite damaging to our Christian moral witness in public life.

Notice that in our treatment of human rights we never say that combatants have the right not to be killed, or that it is immoral to kill on the battlefield. Some have derided the text's "pacifist leanings," but this is demagoguery, or at least a blatant misreading. Though some pacifists found themselves able to sign it, ours is not a pacifist statement. I personally take the (widely held) position that while killing an enemy combatant on the battlefield can be justified, torture of a detained and disarmed prisoner cannot be similarly justified.

Fourth, read it as an argument in favor of the validity of both international law and domestic laws that ban torture.

Having built our argument first on sanctity, and then on human rights, in section 5 we turn to a discussion of the various levels of moral responsibility that we have as individuals, churches, and governments to act to protect the human rights that we have been arguing are so important.

In section 6, we try to show that bans on torture are abundantly clear and unequivocal in both international law and U.S. law. The fact that we even cite international declarations, conventions, and treaties means that we are implicitly taking a stand in favor of honoring the significance and legitimacy of these instruments—which is noteworthy in its own right in light of conservative skepticism about international law. But we are always careful in the document to tie international obligations with U.S. law wherever that is possible.

Most of the drafters were theologians and ethicists rather than human-rights lawyers, and so this section turned out to need a bit of fine tuning once it saw the light of day in mid-March. We are grateful for the line-by-line refinements that various lawyers contributed to this section after its initial release. I learned from this process not just to appreciate international human rights and humanitarian lawyers but also that the United States had actually been edging away from its unequivocal support of international human-rights treaties and conventions for some time, not just since 9/11—and that it is actually a mistake to now describe our nation as a leader in protecting human rights. This is quite sad, really. Nothing I have heard has made me think that such an edging away from a strong stance on human rights by our government is anything other than a very bad idea, and one that ultimately weakens our international standing and role in the world.

Fifth, read it as praise of the Pentagon and not as a slam on the Bush administration!

One of the most important contributions of this particular section of the document (section 6) is the appeal to the revised U.S. Army Field Manual. After a considerable struggle within the Pentagon, the most recent revision of this manual contains an admirably detailed rejection of many of the particular interrogation techniques that at least arguably crossed the line into torture. Some would like to have seen the Pentagon go further and explicitly ban, for example, the use of stress positions and sleep deprivation, but it has at least banned some of the most notorious acts that were authorized, or permitted, or occurred despite not being permitted, after 9/11. Thus we are able to simplify our policy argument to ask flatly that all branches of the federal government should be playing by the rules instituted by the Pentagon, without exception.

"Do as the Pentagon does" is hardly a radical statement, and yet we have still been on the receiving end of predictable criticism from the right wing of the political-religious landscape for our "attack on the Bush administration."

When a Christian group such as our own drafting committee implicitly acknowledges that there has been a fissure within a particular administration, in which some have argued for respecting strict bans on torture and others have argued for loosening them, and we side with those who take the strict rather than loose stance, this is not an attack on a president, a party, or an administration. It is at least at one level an expression of support for those voices within that administration who have taken one view rather than another. We are glad that the more "strict constructivist" voices are gaining in strength in the latter days of the Bush administration. We reject the idea that our criticism of other voices is a "religious left" slam on that same administration. This is one reason why a mainstream evangelical group like the NAE, with strong ties, for example, to the military chaplaincy, could endorse this statement.

Sixth, read it as a broadening of concern from torture to overall detainee policies and finally to the rule of law.

The drafters came to the conviction that opposition to torture must not be the entirety of our policy agenda. Many features of the Military Commissions Act of 2006, for example, come in for criticism in this document. The use of the CIA for detentions, interrogations, and extraordinary renditions to other countries, all placed *in principle* beyond the reach of citizen oversight, creates concerns that are related to torture but also distinguishable from it. One might say that the agenda of the document in this sense evolved from "ban torture" through "protect detainees" to end up with "protect the rule of law in our land." These concerns are connected, of course. But many now join us in seeing that you cannot weaken constitutional protections anywhere without threatening them everywhere.

Seventh, read it as an expression of Christian discipleship.

One of the most distressing things about the sadly predictable criticism the document received was the immediate translation of the statement into a "culture wars" paradigm—and indeed, into the "evangelical culture wars" of latter days. To criticize the use of torture is seen as a thinly veiled partisan attack on the Republican president of the United States. To criticize the use of torture is seen as a victory for Rich Cizik and the NAE over against James Dobson and his cohorts on the Christian Right. (This latter identification occurred because of the timing of the NAE approval of the statement, just after a letter critical of Cizik was sent to the NAE board. Their "response" of approving our statement was seen as their approval of this declaration on human rights and torture. Therefore, score one for Cizik. Much news coverage of our declaration took this disappointing, "inside baseball," turn.)

All of this marks a sad degradation of evangelical moral discourse. Not to put ourselves in too lofty a crowd, but should we interpret Wilberforce as an anti-George III partisan? Was Bonhoeffer simply fronting for the Socialists? Was Solzhenitsyn just a CIA agent trying to bring down the Soviet regime? Should King be seen as one who used race as a wedge issue to elect a Democratic president in 1968? Is the evangelical movement against sex trafficking a hidden antiglobalization crusade secretly led by the Green Party?

What are Christians supposed to do who have actual *moral objections* to an action of their government? Could it be that they should gather together to test their views in community, analyze the issue as best they can, using the resources of the Christian tradition, and then offer a carefully and prayerfully crafted moral reflection that expresses dissent rooted in Christian conviction?

Or is there no room anymore for "speaking truth to power"—or even, perhaps, for following Jesus Christ as Lord?

Appendix 5

CLIMATE CHANGE: AN EVANGELICAL CALL TO ACTION

The Evangelical Climate Initiative (2006)

PREAMBLE

As American evangelical Christian leaders, we recognize both our opportunity and our responsibility to offer a biblically based moral witness that can help shape public policy in the most powerful nation on earth, and therefore contribute to the well-being of the entire world.[1] *Whether* we will enter the public square and offer our witness there is no longer an open question. We are in that square, and we will not withdraw.

We are proud of the evangelical community's long-standing commitment to the sanctity of human life. But we also offer moral witness in many venues and on many issues. Sometimes the issues that we have taken on, such as sex trafficking, genocide in the Sudan, and the AIDS epidemic in Africa, have surprised outside observers. While individuals and organizations can be called to concentrate on certain issues, we are not a single-issue movement. We seek to be true to our calling as Christian leaders, and above all faithful to Jesus Christ our Lord. Our attention, therefore, goes to whatever issues our faith requires us to address.

Over the last several years many of us have engaged in study, reflection, and prayer related to the issue of climate change (often called "global warming"). For most of us, until recently this has not been treated as a pressing issue or major priority. Indeed, many of us have required considerable convincing before becoming persuaded that climate change is a real problem and that it ought to matter to us as Christians. But now we have seen and heard enough to offer the following moral argument related to the matter of human-induced climate change. We commend the four simple but urgent claims offered in this document to all who will listen,

275

beginning with our brothers and sisters in the Christian community, and urge all to take the appropriate actions that follow from them.

CLAIM 1: HUMAN-INDUCED CLIMATE CHANGE IS REAL

Since 1995 there has been general agreement among those in the scientific community most seriously engaged with this issue that climate change is happening and is being caused mainly by human activities, especially the burning of fossil fuels. Evidence gathered since 1995 has only strengthened this conclusion.

Because all religious/moral claims about climate change are relevant only if climate change is real and is mainly human-induced, everything hinges on the scientific data. As evangelicals we have hesitated to speak on this issue until we could be more certain of the science of climate change, but the signatories now believe that the evidence demands action:

- The Intergovernmental Panel on Climate Change (IPCC), the world's most authoritative body of scientists and policy experts on the issue of global warming, has been studying this issue since the late 1980s. (From 1988–2002 the IPCC's assessment of the climate science was chaired by Sir John Houghton, a devout evangelical Christian.) It has documented the steady rise in global temperatures over the last fifty years, projects that the average global temperature will continue to rise in the coming decades, and attributes "most of the warming" to human activities.

- The U.S. National Academy of Sciences, as well as all other G8 country scientific Academies (Great Britain, France, Germany, Japan, Canada, Italy, and Russia), has concurred with these judgments.

- In a 2004 report, and at the 2005 G8 summit, the Bush administration has also acknowledged the reality of climate change and the likelihood that human activity is the cause of at least some of it.[2]

In the face of the breadth and depth of this scientific and governmental concern, only a small percentage of which is noted here, we are convinced that evangelicals must engage this issue without any further lingering over the basic reality of the problem or humanity's responsibility to address it.

CLAIM 2: THE CONSEQUENCES OF CLIMATE CHANGE WILL BE SIGNIFICANT AND WILL HIT THE POOR THE HARDEST

The earth's natural systems are resilient but not infinitely so, and human civilizations are remarkably dependent on ecological stability and well-being. It is easy to forget this until that stability and well-being are threatened.

Even small rises in global temperatures will have such likely impacts as: sea-level rise; more frequent heat waves, droughts, and extreme weather events such as torrential rains and floods; increased tropical diseases in now-temperate regions; and hurricanes that are more intense. It could lead to significant reduction in agricultural output, especially in poor countries. Low-lying regions, indeed entire islands, could find themselves under water. (This is not to mention the various negative impacts climate change could have on God's other creatures.)

Each of these impacts increases the likelihood of refugees from flooding or famine, violent conflicts, and international instability, which could lead to more security threats to our nation.

Poor nations and poor individuals have fewer resources available to cope with major challenges and threats. The consequences of global warming will therefore hit the poor the hardest, in part because those areas likely to be significantly affected first are in the poorest regions of the world. **Millions of people could die in this century because of climate change, most of them are our poorest global neighbors.**

CLAIM 3: CHRISTIAN MORAL CONVICTIONS DEMAND OUR RESPONSE TO THE CLIMATE-CHANGE PROBLEM

While we cannot here review the full range of relevant biblical convictions related to care of the creation, we emphasize the following points:

- Christians must care about climate change because we love God the Creator and Jesus our Lord, through whom and for whom the creation was made. This is God's world, and any damage that we do to God's world is an offense against God Himself (Gen. 1; Ps. 24; Col. 1:16).
- Christians must care about climate change because we are called to love our neighbors, to do unto others as we would have them do unto us, and to protect and care for the least of these as though each was Jesus Christ himself (Mt. 7:12; 22:34-40; 25:31-46).
- Christians, noting the fact that most of the climate-change problem is human induced, are reminded that when God made humanity, he commissioned us to exercise stewardship over the earth and its creatures. Climate change is the latest evidence of our failure to exercise proper stewardship and constitutes a critical opportunity for us to do better (Gen. 1:26-28).

Love of God, love of neighbor, and the demands of stewardship are more than enough reason for evangelical Christians to respond to the climate-change problem with moral passion and concrete action.

CLAIM 4: THE NEED TO ACT NOW IS URGENT. GOVERNMENTS, BUSINESSES, CHURCHES, AND INDIVIDUALS ALL HAVE A ROLE TO PLAY IN ADDRESSING CLIMATE CHANGE—STARTING NOW.

The basic task for all of the world's inhabitants is to find ways now to begin to reduce the carbon-dioxide emissions from the burning of fossil fuels that are the primary cause of human-induced climate change.

There are several reasons for urgency. First, deadly impacts are being experienced now. Second, the oceans only warm slowly, creating a lag in experiencing the consequences. Much of the climate change to which we are already committed will not be realized for several decades. The consequences of the pollution we create now will be visited upon our children and grandchildren. Third, as individuals and as a society, we are making long-term decisions today that will determine how much carbon dioxide we will emit in the future, such as whether to purchase energy-efficient vehicles and appliances that will last for 10-20 years, or whether to build more coal-burning power plants that last for 50 years rather than investing more in energy efficiency and renewable energy.

In the United States, the most important immediate step that can be taken at the federal level is to pass and implement national legislation requiring sufficient economy-wide reductions in carbon-dioxide emissions through cost-effective, market-based mechanisms such as a cap-and-trade program. On June 22, 2005, the Senate passed the Domenici-Bingaman resolution affirming this approach, and a number of major energy companies now acknowledge that this method is best both for the environment and for business.

We commend the Senators who have taken this stand and encourage them to fulfill their pledge. We also applaud the steps taken by such companies as BP, Shell, General Electric, Cinergy, Duke Energy, and DuPont, all of which have moved ahead of the pace of government action through innovative measures implemented within their companies in the United States and around the world. In so doing they have offered timely leadership.

Numerous positive actions to prevent and mitigate climate change are being implemented across our society by state and local governments, churches, smaller businesses, and individuals. These commendable efforts focus on such matters as energy efficiency, the use of renewable energy, low CO_2-emitting technologies, and the purchase of hybrid vehicles. These efforts can easily be shown to save money, save energy, and reduce global-warming pollution as well as air pollution that harm human health and eventually pay for themselves. There is much more to be done, but these pioneers are already helping to show the way forward.

Finally, while we must reduce our global-warming pollution to help mitigate the impacts of climate change, as a society and as individuals, we must also help the poor adapt to the significant harm that global warming will cause.

CONCLUSION

We the undersigned pledge to act on the basis of the claims made in this document. We will not only teach the truths communicated here but also seek ways to implement the actions that follow from them. In the name of Jesus Christ our Lord, we urge all who read this declaration to join us in this effort.

SIGNATORIES

Rev. Dr. Leith Anderson, President, National Association of Evangelicals (NAE); Senior Pastor, Wooddale Church, Eden Prairie, MN; **Robert Andringa**, Ph.D., President, Council for Christian Colleges & Universities (CCCU), Vienna, VA; **Rev. Jim Ball**, Ph.D., Executive Director, Evangelical Environmental Network, Wynnewood, PA; **Commissioner W. Todd Bassett**, National Commander, The Salvation Army, Alexandria, VA; **Dr. Jay A. Barber Jr.**, President, Warner Pacific College, Portland, OR; **Gary P. Bergel**, President, Intercessors for America; Purcellville, VA; **David Black**, Ph.D., President, Eastern University, St. Davids, PA; **Bishop Charles E. Blake Sr.**, West Angeles Church of God in Christ, Los Angeles; **Rev. Dr. Dan Boone**, President, Trevecca Nazarene University, Nashville; **Rev. Dr. Peter Borgdorff**, Executive Director, Christian Reformed Church, Grand Rapids, MI; **H. David Brandt**, Ph.D., President, George Fox University, Newberg, OR; **Rev. George K. Brushaber**, Ph.D., President, Bethel University; Senior Advisor, *Christianity Today*, St. Paul, MN; **Rev. Dwight Burchett**, President, Northern California Association of Evangelicals, Sacramento, CA; **Gaylen Byker**, Ph.D., President, Calvin College, Grand Rapids, MI; **Rev. Dr. Jerry B. Cain**, President, Judson College, Elgin, IL; **Rev. Dr. Clive Calver**, Senior Pastor, Walnut Hill Community Church; Former President, World Relief, Bethel, CT; **R. Judson Carlberg**, Ph.D., President, Gordon College, Wenham, MA; **Michael V. Carter**, Ph.D., President, Campbellsville University, Campbellsville, KY; **Rev. Dr. Paul Cedar**, Chair, Mission America Coalition, Palm Desert, CA; **Rev. John Chowning**, Vice President for Church and External Relations and Director of the Kentucky Hartland Institute on Public Policy, Campbellsville University, Campbellsville, KY; **David Clark**, Ph.D., President, Palm Beach Atlantic University; Former Chair/CEO, Nat. Rel. Broadcasters; Founding Dean, Regent University, West Palm Beach, FL; **Rev. Luis Cortes**, President and CEO, Esperanza USA and Host, National Hispanic Prayer Breakfast, Philadelphia, PA; **Andy Crouch**, Columnist, *Christianity Today*, Swarthmore, PA; **Rev. Paul de Vries**, Ph.D., President, New York Divinity School, New York; **Larry R. Donnithorne**, Ed. D., President, Colorado Christian University, Lakewood, CO; **Blair Dowden**, Ed.D., President, Huntington University, Huntington, IN; **Rev. Robert P. Dugan Jr.**, Former VP of Governmental Affairs, National Association of Evangelicals, Palm Desert, CA; **Craig Hilton Dyer**, President, Bright Hope International, Hoffman Estates, IL; **Philip Eaton**, Ph.D., President, Seattle Pacific University, Seattle, WA; **D. Merrill Ewert**, Ph.D., President, Fresno Pacific University, Fresno, CA; **Rev. Dr. LeBron Fairbanks**, President, Mount Vernon Nazarene University, Mount Vernon, OH; **Rev. Myles Fish**, President/CEO, International Aid, Spring Lake, MI; **Rev. Dr. Floyd Flake**, Senior Pastor, Greater Allen AME Cathedral; President, Wilberforce University, Jamaica, NY; **Rev. Scott Freeman**, Senior Pastor, Northside Church of Christ, Waco, TX; **Rev. Timothy George**, Ph.D., Founding Dean, Beeson Divinity School, Samford University; Executive

Editor, *Christianity Today*, Birmingham, AL; **Rev. Michael J. Glodo**, Stated Clerk, Evangelical Presbyterian Church, Livonia, MI; **Rev. James M. Grant**, Ph.D., President, Simpson University, Redding, CA; **Rev. Dr. Jeffrey E. Greenway**, President, Asbury Theological Seminary, Wilmore, KY; **Rev. Dr. David Gushee**, Professor of Moral Philosophy, Union University; Jackson, TN; **Gregory V. Hall**, President, Warner Southern College, Lake Wales, FL; **Brent Hample**, Executive Director, India Partners, Eugene OR; **Bishop Roger W. Haskins Jr.**, Free Methodist Church of North America, Glendora, CA; **Rev. Dr. Jack Hayford**, President, International Church of the Foursquare Gospel, Los Angeles; **Rev. Steve Hayner**, Ph.D., Former President, InterVarsity; Prof. of Evangelism, Columbia Theological Seminary, Decatur, GA; **E. Douglas Hodo**, Ph.D., President, Houston Baptist University, Houston, TX; **Ben Homan**, President, Food for the Hungry; President, Association of Evangelical Relief and Development Organizations (AERDO), Phoenix, AZ; **Rev. Dr. Joel Hunter**, Senior Pastor, Northland, A Church Distributed, Longwood, FL; **Rev. Bill Hybels,** Senior Pastor, Willow Creek Community Church, South Barrington, IL; **Bishop Joseph F. James**, Free Methodist Church of North America, Indianapolis, IN; **Bryce Jessup**, President, William Jessup University, Rocklin, CA; **Ronald G. Johnson**, Ph.D., President, Malone College, Canton, OH; **Rev. Dr. Phillip Charles Joubert Sr.**, Pastor, Community Baptist Church, Bayside, NY; **Jennifer Jukanovich**, Founder, The Vine, Seattle, WA; **Bishop David W. Kendall**, Free Methodist Church of North America, Greenville, IL; **Rev. Brian Kluth**, Senior Pastor, First Evangelical Free Church; Founder, MAXIMUM Generosity, Colorado Springs, CO; **Bishop James D. Leggett**, General Superintendent, International Pentecostal Holiness Church; Chair, Pentecostal World Fellowship, Oklahoma City; **Duane Litfin**, Ph.D., President, Wheaton College, Wheaton IL; **Rev. Dr. Larry Lloyd**, President, Crichton College, Memphis, TN; **Rev. Dr. Jo Anne Lyon**, Executive Director, World Hope, Alexandria, VA; **Rev. Dr. Gordon MacDonald**, Chair of the Board, World Relief; Editor-at-Large, *Leadership*; Canterbury, NH; **Jim Mannoia**, Ph.D., President, Greenville College, Greenville, IL; **Bishop George D. McKinney**, Ph.D., D.D., St. Stephens Church of God in Christ, San Diego; **Rev. Brian McLaren**, Senior Pastor, Cedar Ridge Community Church; Emergent Leader, Spencerville, MD; **Rev. Dr. Daniel Mercaldo**, Senior Pastor and Founder, Gateway Cathedral; Staten Island, NY; **Rev. Dr. Jesse Miranda**, President, AMEN, Costa Mesa, CA; **Royce Money**, Ph.D., President, Abilene Christian University, Abilene, TX; **Dr. Bruce Murphy**, President, Northwestern College, Orange City, IA; **Rev. George W. Murray**, D.Miss., President, Columbia International University, Columbia SC; **David Neff**, Editor, *Christianity Today*, Carol Stream, IL; **Larry Nikkel**, President, Tabor College, Hillsboro, KS; **Michael Nyenhuis**, President, MAP International, Brunswick, GA; **Brian O'Connell**, President, REACT Services; Founder and Former Executive Director, Religious Liberty Commission, World Evangelical Alliance, Mill Creek, WA; **Rev. Glenn R. Palmberg**, President, Evangelical Covenant Church, Chicago; **Roger Parrott**, Ph.D., President, Belhaven College, Jackson,

MS; **John E. Phelan Jr.**, President and Dean, North Park Theological Seminary, Chicago; **Kim S. Phipps**, Ph.D., President, Messiah College, Grantham, PA; **Charles W. Pollard**, Ph.D., J.D., President, John Brown University, Siloam Springs, AR; **Paul A. Rader**, D.Miss., President, Asbury College, Wilmore, KY; **Rev. Edwin H. Robinson**, Ph.D., President, MidAmerica Nazarene University, Olathe, KS; **William P. Robinson**, Ph.D., President, Whitworth College, Spokane, WA; **Rev. Scott Rodin**, Ph.D., President, Christian Stewardship Association; Former President, Eastern Baptist Theological Seminary; Author of *Stewards in the Kingdom*, Spokane, WA; **Lee Royce**, Ph.D., President, Mississippi College, Clinton, MS; **Andy Ryskamp**, Executive Director, Christian Reformed World Relief Committee, Grand Rapids, MI; **Scott C. Sabin**, Executive Director, Floresta USA, San Diego; **Rev. Ron Sider**, Ph.D., President, Evangelicals for Social Action, Philadelphia; **Matthew Sleeth**, M.D., Author of *Serve God, Save the Planet*, Wilmore, KY; **Bishop Richard D. Snyder**, Free Methodist Church of North America, Rock Hill, SC; **Richard Stearns**, President, World Vision, Federal Way, WA; **Rev. Jewelle Stewart**, Executive Director, Women's Ministries, International Pentecostal Holiness Church, Oklahoma City; **James Sundhome**, Director, Covenant World Relief, Evangelical Covenant Church, Chicago, IL; **Rev. Dr. Loren Swartzendruber**, President, Eastern Mennonite University, Harrisonburg, VA; **C. Pat Taylor**, Ph.D., President, Southwest Baptist University, Bolivar, MO; **Steven Timmermans**, Ph.D, President, Trinity Christian College, Palos Hights, IL; **Rev. Charles C. Tyler**, Pastor, New Covenant Presbyterian Church (PCA), Manning, SC; **Rev. Berten A. Waggoner**, National Director, Vineyard, USA, Sugar Land, TX; **Jon R. Wallace**, DBA, President, Azusa Pacific University, Azusa, CA; **Rev. Jim Wallis**, Founder and Editor of *Sojourners*, Washington, DC; **Rev. Dr. Rick Warren**, Senior Pastor, Saddleback Church; Author of *The Purpose Driven Life*, Lake Forest, CA; **John Warton**, President, Business Professional Network, Portland, OR; **Rev. Dr. Thomas Yung-Hsin Wang**, former International Director of Lausanne II, Sunnyvale, CA; **John D. Yordy**, Ph.D., Provost, Goshen College, Goshen, IN; **Adm. Tim Ziemer**, Director of Programs, World Relief, Baltimore, MD.

Appendix 6

"AN URGENT CALL TO ACTION"

Evangelicals and Scientists Unite to Protect Creation

January 17, 2007
National Press Club, Washington, D.C.

SUMMARY

Scientific and evangelical leaders recently met to search for common ground in the protection of the creation. We happily discovered far more concordance than any of us had expected, quickly moving beyond dialogue to a shared sense of moral purpose. Important initiatives were already underway on both sides, and when compared they were found to be broadly overlapping. We clearly share a moral passion and sense of vocation to save the imperiled living world before our damages to it remake it as another kind of planet. We agree not only that reckless human activity has imperiled the Earth—especially the unsustainable and short-sighted lifestyles and public policies of our own nation—but also that we share a profound moral obligation to work together to call our nation, and other nations, to the kind of dramatic change urgently required in our day. We pledge our joint commitment to this effort in the unique moment now upon us.

BACKGROUND

This meeting was convened by the Center for Health and the Global Environment at Harvard Medical School and the National Association of Evangelicals. It was envisioned as a first exploratory conference, based on a shared concern for the creation, to be held among people who were in some ways quite different in their

283

worldviews. It now seems to us to be the beginning point of a major shared effort among scientists and evangelicals to protect life on Earth and the fragile life-support systems that sustain it, drawing on the unique intellectual, spiritual, and moral contributions that each community can bring.

OUR SHARED CONCERN

We agree that our home, the Earth, which comes to us as that inexpressibly beautiful and mysterious gift that sustains our very lives, is seriously imperiled by human behavior. The harm is seen throughout the natural world, including a cascading set of problems such as climate change, habitat destruction, pollution, and species extinctions, as well as the spread of human infectious diseases, and other accelerating threats to the health of people and the well-being of societies. Each particular problem could be enumerated, but here it is enough to say that we are gradually destroying the sustaining community of life on which all living things on Earth depend. The costs of this destruction are already manifesting themselves around the world in profound and painful ways. The cost to humanity is already significant and may soon become incalculable. Being irreversible, many of these changes would affect all generations to come.

We believe that the protection of life on Earth is a profound moral imperative. It addresses without discrimination the interests of all humanity as well as the value of the nonhuman world. It requires a new moral awakening to a compelling demand, clearly articulated in Scripture and supported by science, that we must steward the natural world in order to preserve for ourselves and future generations a beautiful, rich, and healthful environment. For many of us, this is a religious obligation, rooted in our sense of gratitude for creation and reverence for its Creator.

One fundamental motivation that we share is concern for the poorest of the poor, well over a billion people, who have little chance to improve their lives in devastated and often war-ravaged environments. At the same time, the natural environments in which they live, and where so much of Earth's biodiversity barely hangs on, cannot survive the press of destitute people without other resources and with nowhere else to go.

We declare that every sector of our nation's leadership—religious, scientific, business, political, and educational—must act now to work toward the fundamental change in values, lifestyles, and public policies required to address these worsening problems before it is too late. There is no excuse for further delays. Business as usual cannot continue yet one more day. We pledge to work together at every level to lead our nation toward a responsible care for creation, and we call with one voice to our scientific and evangelical colleagues, and to all others, to join us in these efforts.

SIGNATORIES

Rev. Jim Ball Ph.D., Executive Director, Evangelical Environmental Network; **Steven Bouma-Prediger** Ph.D., John H. and Jeanne M. Jacobson Professor of

Religion, Hope College; **Eric Chivian** M.D., Director, Center for Health and the Global Environment, Harvard Medical School, Shared 1985 Nobel Peace Prize; **Rev. Richard Cizik** D.Min., M.Div, Vice President for Governmental Affairs, National Association of Evangelicals; **Rita R. Colwell** Ph.D., Distinguished University Professor, University of Maryland College Park and at the Johns Hopkins University Bloomberg School of Public Health; **Judith A. Curry** Ph.D., Professor and Chair of the School of Earth and Atmospheric Sciences, Georgia Institute of Technology; **Calvin B. DeWitt** Ph.D., Professor of Environmental Studies, University of Wisconsin–Madison; President, Academy of Evangelical Scientists and Ethicists; **Rev. Daryl Eldridge** Ph.D., President, Rockbridge Seminary; **Paul R. Epstein** M.D., M.P.H., Associate Director, Center for Health and the Global Environment, Harvard Medical School; **Howard Frumkin** M.D., Dr.P.H., Director, National Center for Environmental Health and Agency for Toxic Substances and Disease Registry, U.S. Centers for Disease Control and Prevention; **Rev. David P. Gushee** Ph.D., University Fellow and Graves Professor of Moral Philosophy, Union University; **James E. Hansen** Ph.D., Director, NASA Goddard Institute for Space Studies; Adjunct Professor, Columbia University Earth Institute; **Bernd Heinrich** Ph.D., Professor of Biology, University of Vermont; **Rev. Joel C. Hunter** D.Min., Senior Pastor, Northland—A Church Distributed; **Randall D. Isaac** Ph.D., Executive Director, American Scientific Affiliation; **Rev. Cheryl Bridges Johns** Ph.D., Professor of Christian Formation and Discipleship, Church of God Theological Seminary; **The Rt. Revd. James Jones** The Bishop of Liverpool; **Nancy Knowlton** Ph.D, Director, Center for Marine Biodiversity and Conservation; John Dove Isaacs Professor of Natural Philosophy, Scripps Institution of Oceanography; **James J. McCarthy** Ph.D., Agassiz Professor of Biological Oceanography, Harvard University; **Peter H. Raven** Ph.D., President, Missouri Botanical Garden, George Engelmann Professor of Botany, Washington University; **Carl Safina** Ph.D., President, Blue Ocean Institute; **Peter Seligmann** Ph.D., Chairman and CEO, Conservation International; **Joseph K. Sheldon** Ph.D., Distinguished Professor of Biology and Environmental Science, Messiah College; Professor of Environmental Studies, The Au Sable Institute of Environmental Studies; **James Gustave Speth** J.D., M.Litt., Dean, and Sara Shallenberger Brown Professor in the Practice of Environmental Policy, Yale School of Forestry and Environmental Studies; **Rev. Eric Steinkamp** Ph.D., Chair of the Department of Natural Sciences and Math; Professor of Environmental Sciences, Northwest University; Professor of Environmental Studies, The Au Sable Institute of Environmental Studies; **Loren Wilkinson** Ph.D., Professor of Philosophy and Interdisciplinary Studies, Regent College; **Edward O. Wilson** Ph.D., University Research Professor Emeritus, Harvard University; **Ken Wilson** Senior Pastor, Vineyard Church of Ann Arbor.

Institutional affiliation is given for identification purposes only. All signatories do so as individuals expressing their personal opinions and not as representatives of their organizations.

Appendix 7

RULES FOR EVANGELICAL POLITICS (2007)

It's election season again. Actually, it never ceases to be election season in our politics-obsessed culture—and in politics-obsessed evangelical America.

I have been thinking a lot about what happens at the intersection of evangelicals and politics. In a new book coming out this winter, I suggest that there are now three competing evangelical visions related to public life—I call them the evangelical right, left, and center. It is possible, I believe, to identify these visions with particular people, organizations, and policy priorities. In the book I also consider the enduring appeal of evangelical perspectives on politics and public engagement that primarily counsel distance or even withdrawal.

Here I want to propose some "rules for the game" for evangelical engagement with politics in the upcoming election season. These rules should apply to all evangelicals without regard to their political affiliation or their place on the evangelical spectrum.

The fundamental principles governing the political engagement of leaders representing Christian churches or "the Christian Church" must be the Lordship of Christ and the consequent political independence of the church in terms of earthly politics. The goal of those working as explicitly Christian leaders or representatives of Christian organizations is to bear faithful Christian public witness so that the Lord of the church might be pleased that we have represented him well. Therefore all who serve as Christian leaders must fiercely protect the mission of the church by refusing to compromise their political independence in both their words and their actions. The only way for us to do this is to remind ourselves constantly that we have an audience of One: Jesus Christ our Lord—and that we are accountable to Christ alone.

These key principles generate the following proposal for specific rules governing the public engagement of all who serve churches or parachurch organizations that are not explicitly organized as lobbying groups. For brevity, I will refer to leaders of all such groups as "Christian leaders." They include pastors, missionaries, evangelists, youth ministers, denominational officials, parachurch leaders, college presidents, and Christian ethics professors, among others.

1. Christian leaders must not officially or unofficially endorse political candidates or a political party.
2. Christian leaders must not distribute essentially partisan or single-issue voter guides that purport to be apolitical or nonpartisan.
3. Christian leaders must not publicly handicap or comment upon the political horse race.
4. Christian leaders must not provide private or public advice to particular politicians, parties, or campaigns concerning how they can strategize in order to win evangelical or Christian votes.
5. Christian leaders must not calibrate their public teachings or writings in order to affect the outcome of political elections or to gain and hold the support of politicians.
6. Christian leaders must not attend political rallies or campaign events of one candidate or party unless they are prepared to attend rallies and events of all candidates and parties.
7. Christian leaders must not invite political candidates to speak in church pulpits or on church grounds unless they are prepared to invite all political candidates of all parties to do so.
8. Christian leaders must not identify the potential or actual victory of any politician as a victory for God or God's kingdom.
9. Christian leaders must limit their direct contact with politicians or staff in order to avoid even the appearance of undue loyalty or involvement.
10. Christian leaders must not engage in voter registration campaigns or get out the vote efforts aimed at mobilizing the voters of one political party rather than another.
11. Christian leaders must not direct the funds of their churches or organizations toward direct or indirect support for a particular political candidate or party.
12. Christian leaders may not sidestep these rules by drawing a distinction between their activities as a "private individual" over against their service in their public role.
13. Christian leaders must offer Christian proclamation related to that large number of public issues that are clearly addressed by biblical principles or direct biblical teaching.
14. Christian leaders must encourage Christian people toward active citizenship, including studying the issues and the candidates and testing policy stances and candidates according to biblical criteria.

15. Christian leaders must model and encourage respectful and civil discourse related to significant public issues as well as political candidates.
16. Christian leaders must model and encourage prayer for God-ordained government, its leaders, and their policies.
17. Christian leaders must teach and model respect for the constitutional relationship between religion and the state as these are spelled out in the First Amendment.

There you have it—seventeen rules for Christians and politics. Who will come up with the other three to make it an even twenty? Who will join me in committing themselves to these rules for the 2008 election?

NOTES

CHAPTER 1

1 Kenneth J. Collins, *The Evangelical Moment* (Grand Rapids: Baker Academic, 2005).

2 Monique El-Faizy, *God and Country* (New York: Bloomsbury, 2006).

3 Chris Hedges, *American Fascists* (New York: Free Press, 2006); Kevin Phillips, *American Theocracy* (New York: Viking, 2006).

4 Karl Barth, *Church Dogmatics*, I/I, trans. G. W. Bromiley (Edinburgh: T & T Clark, 1975), xvi.

5 Richard J. Mouw, *Political Evangelism* (Grand Rapids: Eerdmans, 1973).

6 "For the Health of the Nation," accessed at www.nae.net/images/civic_responsibility.pdf, also in Ronald J. Sider and Diane Knippers, eds., *Toward an Evangelical Public Policy* (Grand Rapids: Baker, 2005), 363–75.

7 Dietrich Bonhoeffer, *Ethics* (Minneapolis: Fortress, 2005), 146–51.

8 Gregory A. Boyd. *The Myth of a Christian Nation* (Grand Rapids: Zondervan, 2005).

9 Glen H. Stassen and David P. Gushee, *Kingdom Ethics* (Downers Grove, IL: InterVarsity, 2003).

10 John Howard Yoder, *The Priestly Kingdom* (Notre Dame, IN: University of Notre Dame Press, 1984); Stanley Hauerwas, *A Community of Character* (Notre Dame, IN: University of Notre Dame Press, 1981); Stanley Hauerwas, *The Peaceable Kingdom* (Notre Dame, IN: University of Notre

Dame Press, 1983); Stanley Hauerwas and William H. Willimon, *Resident Aliens* (Nashville: Abingdon, 1989).

11 Craig A. Carter, *Rethinking Christ and Culture* (Grand Rapids: Brazon, 2006).

12 David Kuo, *Tempting Faith* (New York: Free Press, 2006).

13 Cal Thomas and Ed Dobson, *Blinded by Might* (Grand Rapids: Zondervan, 1999).

14 Timothy P. Weber, *On the Road to Armageddon* (Grand Rapids: Baker Academic, 2004).

15 John C. Green, "The American Religious Landscape and Political Attitudes: A Baseline for 2004," Ray C. Bliss Institute of Applied Politics, University of Akron, Akron, Ohio, 2004.

16 Peter Heltzel, *Lion on the Loose* (New Haven, CT: Yale University Press, 2008 forthcoming).

17 "Hispanic Voters," *Religion & Ethics NewsWeekly*, PBS, Episode no. 1006, October 6, 2006.

18 Michael O. Emerson and Christian Smith, *Divided by Faith* (Oxford: Oxford University Press, 2000), 3.

19 D. Eric Schansberg, *Turn Neither to the Right Nor to the Left* (Greenville, SC: Alertness Books, 2003).

20 George Lakoff, *Thinking Points: Communicating Our American Values and Vision* (New York: Farrar, Straus, & Giroux, 2006), ch. 2.

CHAPTER 2

1 Rose French, "As Southern Baptists gather in Nashville this week, Rev. Jerry Falwell applauds religion's role in politics." *Associated Press*, June 29, 2005.

2 Green, "The American Religious Landscape and Political Attitudes." For definitional purposes, I will employ the work of leading researcher John C. Green (Bliss Institute, University of Akron) in defining evangelicals as "individuals affiliated with historically white denominations and congregations in the Evangelical Protestant tradition." Green finds that 26 percent of the adult population fell within this definition of evangelicalism as of 2004. I am aware that evangelicalism is often defined in different ways, including by allowing those polled to define their own religious self-identity or by asking them a number of questions and letting the pollster determine "evangelical" status based on their answers. When either of these moves is made, some within historically "evangelical" denominations

define themselves out, whereas others outside those denominations define themselves in, on the basis of their religious convictions as they (or the pollsters) classify them.

3   Green, "The American Religious Landscape and Political Attitudes"; cf also David P. Gushee and Justin Phillips, "Moral Formation and the Evangelical Voter," in *Journal of the Society of Christian Ethics* 26, no. 2 (2006): 23–60.

4   The group has been mentioned in the press and is discussed by Weyrich himself at www.renewamerica.us/columns/weyrich/041203, accessed August 3, 2005.

5   All information and direct quotes gleaned from the Focus Web site: www. family.org.

6   All information gleaned from the FRC Web site: www.frc.org, accessed September 1, 2005.

7   Thomas B. Edsall, "Conservatives Rally for Justices," *Washington Post*, August 15, 2005.

8   All information gleaned from the ERLC Web site: www.erlc.com, accessed September 1, 2005.

9   All information gleaned from the AFA Web site: www.afa.net, accessed September 1, 2005.

10 All information gleaned from www.traditionalvalues.org, accessed September 5, 2005.

11 All information on CWA gleaned from their Web site: www.cwfa.org; for Eagle Forum, www.eagleforum.org, accessed September 5, 2005.

12 All information gleaned from www.faithandvalues.us/, accessed September 8, 2005.

13 All references gleaned from www.cc.org, accessed September 8, 2005.

14 All references are from www.himpactus.com, accessed April 1, 2007.

15 Steve Monsma and J. Christopher Soper, eds., *Equal Treatment of Religion in a Pluralistic Society* (Grand Rapids: Eerdmans, 1998).

16 Patrick Hynes, *In Defense of the Religious Right* (Nashville: Nelson Current, 2006), 157.

17 John Danforth, *Faith and Politics* (New York: Viking, 2006).

18 Ryan Sager, *The Elephant in the Room* (Hoboken, NJ: Wiley & Sons, 2006), 88–105; cf also Phillips, *American Theocracy*, 388–94.

19 Jimmy Carter, *Our Endangered Values* (New York: Simon & Schuster, 2005), 63–64; also worried over in many other books, such as Mel White, *Religion Gone Bad* (New York: Tarcher/ Penguin, 2006), Hedges, *American Fascists*, and Phillips, *American Theocracy*.

20 Randall Balmer, *Thy Kingdom Come* (New York: Basic Books, 2006).

21 March 1, 2007 letter to NAE board chair, www.citizenlink.org/pdfs/NAEletterfinal.pdf, accessed June 15, 2007.

22 James W. Skillen, *Recharging the American Experiment* (Grand Rapids: Center for Public Justice, 1994).

CHAPTER 3

1 A favorite line, Wallis often says this. See Michele Cottle, "Prayer Center," *New Republic*, May 23, 2005, 21.

2 Consider Jim Wallis, *The Call to Conversion* (San Francisco: Harper & Row, 1981).

3 Michael L. Cromartie, "The Evangelical Kaleidoscope: A Survey of Recent Evangelical Political Engagement," in David Gushee, ed., *Christians and Politics Beyond the Culture Wars* (GrandRapids: Baker, 2000), 15–28.

4 Cromartie, "The Evangelical Kaleidoscope," 15–28.

5 All information gleaned from www.tonycampolo.org, accessed on September 9, 2005.

6 www.tonycampolo.org.

7 Tony Campolo, *20 Hot Potatoes Christians Are Afraid to Touch* (Dallas: Word, 1988).

8 Tony Campolo, *Is Jesus a Republican or a Democrat?* (Dallas: Word, 1995); ibid, *Letter to a Young Evangelical* (New York: Basic Books, 2006); cf. also Tony Campolo, *Speaking My Mind* (Nashville: W Publishing Group, 2004).

9 All information gleaned from www.sojo.net, accessed on March 19, 2007.

10 Gustav Niebuhr, "Church Group Seeks Political Middle Ground," *The New York Times*, May 23, 1995.

11 All information gleaned from www.calltorenewal.org, accessed on September 9, 2005.

12 www.calltorenewal.org.

13 Jim Wallis, *God's Politics* (New York: HarperSanFrancisco, 2005); ibid, *The Soul of Politics* (New York: New Press/Maryknoll, NY: Orbis Books, 1994).

14 Wallis, *God's Politics*, 3–4.

15 Wallis, *God's Politics*, 4.

16 Heltzel, *Lion on the Loose*.

17 Wallis, *God's Politics*, 87–108.

18 Wallis, *God's Politics*, 121.

19 Robert Jewett, *Captain America and the Crusade against Evil* (Grand Rapids: Eerdmans, 2003).

20 Wallis, *God's Politics*, 173.

21 Wallis, *God's Politics*, part 4.

22 Wallis, *God's Politics*, 226, 228.

23 Wallis, *God's Politics*, part 5.

24 Eddie Gibbs and Ryan K. Bolger, *Emerging Churches: Creating Christian Community in Postmodern Culture* (Grand Rapids: Baker Books, 2005), 17–21.

25 www.emergentvillage.com/about/, accessed on May 1, 2007.

26 www.brianmclaren.net/archives/2004/10/im_not_ready_to_move_to_the_religious_left_either_111.html, accessed on May 1, 2007.

27 On War and Peace, Emergent Village Podcast, sponsored by Jossey-Bass, posted August 12, 2006; www.emergentvillage.com/podcast/brian-mclaren-discussing-peace-and-war, accessed on April 12, 2007.

28 www.precipicemagazine.com/brian-mclaren-interview.htm, accessed on April 19, 2007.

29 All quotations in this section are from this Web site: www.rainbowpush.org, accessed on May 1, 2007.

30 Obery M. Hendricks Jr., *The Politics of Jesus: Rediscovering the True Revolutionary Nature of Jesus' Teachings and How They Have Been Coopted* (Doubleday: New York, 2006), 250–53.

31 "Martin Luther King Jr., who in some ways might be seen as a founder," Martin Luther King Jr., *Where Do We Go from Here* (Boston: Beacon, 1967).

32 Wallis, *The Soul of Politics*, 166.

33 Monsma and Soper, *Equal Treatment of Religion*; Campolo, *Speaking My Mind*, 134.

34 Wallis, *God's Politics*, 299.

35 Stan Guthrie, "Jim Wallis: 'I see genuine soul-searching among Democrats.'" *Christianity Today*, February, 2005, 11.

36 Campolo, *Speaking My Mind*, 55–56.

37 Information gleaned from www.pbs.org/religionandethics/week734/interview.html, accessed on September 13, 2005.

38 Wallis, *God's Politics*, 333–34.

39 Campolo, *Speaking My Mind*, 155.

40 Wallis, *God's Politic*, 170.

41 Keith J. Pavlischek, "Can the Vital Center Hold? A Critique of the Evangelical Pacifist Left," *The Brandywine Review of Faith and International Affairs* (Spring 2005): 31–37.

42 Wallis, *God's Politics*, 299.

43 Stan Guthrie, "Soul-Searching Among Democrats: An Interview with Jim Wallis," *Christianity Today*, April 2005, 78–79. Here Wallis acknowledges

that he is consulting with Democratic leaders about how to reframe their message, reconnect with constituencies, and rethink their policy stances.

CHAPTER 4

1 Ronald J. Sider, *Rich Christians in an Age of Hunger*, 4th ed. (Dallas: Word, 1997).

2 For ESA's self-presentation of this event and of itself, see www.esa-online. org/about/#corevalues, accessed on September 13, 2005.

3 See www.creationcare.org, the EEN Web site, accessed on March 1, 2007.

4 Ron Sider's key book from this period, *Completely Pro-Life* (Downers Grove, IL: InterVarsity, 1987).

5 His view is widely shared among evangelicals of all types and not only evangelicals. One influential scholar who has helped crystallize this view among evangelicals is Calvin College political scientist Stephen Monsma. Among other works, see his *Positive Neutrality: Letting Religious Freedom Ring* (Grand Rapids: Baker, 1993).

6 Ronald J. Sider, *The Scandal of the Evangelical Conscience* (Grand Rapids: Baker, 2005).

7 Sider articulated key principles of such a vision, along with a call for a consensus statement, in "Toward an Evangelical Political Philosophy," in Gushee, *Christians and Politics Beyond the Culture Wars*.

8 Sider and Knippers, *Toward an Evangelical Public Policy*.

9 Information gleaned from the NAE Web site: www.nae.net/index.cfm? FUSEACTION=nae.history, accessed on September 13, 2005.

10 See Don Melvin, George Edmonson, "Influence of U.S. religious conservatives may remake world politics," Cox News Service, December 5, 2004. NAE agenda derived from quotes by Rich Cizik. Compare, "Interview: Richard Cizik, National Association of Evangelicals," *The Christian Post*, July 12, 2005; www.christianpost.com, accessed on July 14, 2005.

11 Susan Page, "Christian Right's alliances bend political spectrum," *USA Today*, June 15, 2005.

12 Information gleaned from chge.med.harvard.edu/media/releases/jan_ 17.html, accessed on January 27, 2007.

13 Information about the CCCU gleaned from its Web site: www.cccu.org, accessed on September 13, 2005.

14 See James A. Patterson, *Shining Lights: A History of the Council for Christian Colleges and Universities* (Grand Rapids: Baker, 2001), 81, 93.

15 "CCCU signs statement on affirmative action," CCCU news release, January 2003.

16 Robert Andringa, President's Self-Evaluation for CCCU Board, July 12, 2005. In that same report he mentioned government-relations priorities as follows: "IRA Charitable Rollover legislation, religious persecution, nonprofit reform legislation, support for HIV-AIDS, a solution in the Sudan, reasonable legislation on global warming, urging more attention to global poverty, etc."

17 Robert Andringa, CCCU Board Report, January 12, 2005.

18 "Worship as Higher Politics," *Christianity Today*, July 2005, 22.

19 Joseph Loconte and Michael Cromartie, "Let's Stop Stereotyping Evangelicals," *Washington Post*, November 8, 2006.

20 www.worldvision.org.

21 All quotationss gleaned from www.ijm.org, accessed on March 29, 2007.

22 Al quotations gleaned from www.ccda.org.

23 All information gleaned from www.tonyevans.org, accessed on April 11, 2007.

24 Tony Evans, *What a Way to Live!* (Nashville: Word, 1997), xiv, 404.

25 Evans, *What a Way to Live!*, 26.

26 Evans, *What a Way to Live!*, 429.

27 Evans, *What a Way to Live!*, 399–400.

28 Evans, *What a Way to Live!*, 418, 426.

29 All information gleaned from www.cpjustice.org, accessed on March 30, 2007.

30 Frances FitzGerald, "The Evangelical Surprise," *New York Review of Books*, April, 26, 2007.

31 Rick Warren, *The Purpose-Driven Church* (Grand Rapids: Zondervan, 2002); ibid, *Purpose-Driven Life* (Grand Rapids: Zondervan, 1995).

32 All information gleaned from www.vineyardusa.org, accessed on March 30, 2007.

33 Elysa Gardner, "Jones, Webb find faith their way," *USA Today*, April, 11 2007.

34 derekwebb.musiccitynetworks.com/index.htm?id=7013&inc=7&album_id=731#6052.

35 Michael Gerson, quoted in Collin Hansen, "How Then Shall We Politick?" *Christianity Today*, August 2006; accessed online at www.christianitytoday.com/CT/2006/august/9.38.html.

36 J. Christopher Latondresse, "The New Face of Politics," *Relevant*, November 2006, 74–77.

CHAPTER 5

1   Thomas E. Ricks, "Detainee Abuse by Marines Is Detailed," *Washington Post*, December 15, 2004, A1. The information in this article is from Defense Department documents.

2   Mark Danner, "Abu Ghraib: The Hidden Story, Part II," *New York Review of Books*, October 7, 2004, accessed online at www.ccmep.org/2004_articles/general/100704_abu_ghraib.htm. The information in the article is from the Fay-Jones Report for the Defense Department.

3   MG George R. Fay, "Investigation of the Abu Ghraib Detention Facility and 205th Military Intelligence Brigade," files.findlaw.com/news.findlaw.com/hdocs/docs/dod/fay82504rpt.pdf, 68.

4   Karen J. Greenberg and Joshua Dratel, *The Torture Papers: The Road to Abu Ghraib* (Cambridge: Cambridge University Press, 2005), 505.

5   Report of the International Committee of the Red Cross, February 2004, quoted in Mark Danner, "Torture and Truth," *New York Review of Books*, June 10, 2004, 259–60.

6   Dana Priest, "CIA Holds Terror Suspects in Secret Prisons," *Washington Post*, November 2, 2005, A1.

7   Evan Thomas and Michael Hirsh, "The Debate over Torture," *Newsweek*, November 21, 2005, 31.

8   Douglas Jehl and Tim Golden, "CIA Is Likely to Avoid Charges in Most Prisoner Deaths," *The New York Times*, October 23, 2005, 6.

9   Lisa Hajjar, "Torture and the Future," *Middle East Report Online*; www.merip.org/mero/interventions/hajjar_interv.html, 5.

10 Universal Declaration of Human Rights, www.un.org/overview/rights.html.

11 Geneva Conventions Relative to the Treatment of Prisoners of War, article 17, article 13; www.unhch.ch/html/menu3/b/91.htm.

12 UN Convention Against Torture, article 1, hrweb.org/legal/cat.html.

13 U.S. Army Field Manual, 34–52; www.globalsecurity.org/intell/library/policy/army/fm/fm34-52/chapter1.htm.

14 "Human Intelligence Collector Operations." *U.S. Army Field Manual* 2-22.3. September 6, 2006.

15 Mark Bowden, "The Dark Art of Interrogation," *Atlantic Monthly*, October 2003, 53.

16 Hajjar, "Torture and the Future," 3–4.

17 Michael Ignatieff, "Evil Under Interrogation," *Financial Times* (London), May 15, 2004, web.lexis-nexis.com/universe/printdoc, 2.

18 Hajjar, "Torture and the Future," 5.

19 UN Convention Against Torture, article 2.

20 Quoted in "The Roots of Torture," *Newsweek*, May 24, 2004; www.msnbc.msn.com/id/4989422/.

21 Mark Bowden, "The Dark Art of Interrogation," *Atlantic Monthly*, October 2003, 70.

22 This is a widely quoted remark from Rush Limbaugh's radio show. See www.smithersmpls.com/2004/05/more-rush-limbaugh-from-yesterday-it_13.html.

23 Robert G. Kennedy, "Can Interrogatory Torture Be Morally Legitimate?" a paper presented to the 2003 Joint Services Conference on Professional Ethics; www.usafa.ar.mil/jscope/JSCOPE03/Kennedy03.html, 3, 9.

24 Hajjar, "Torture and the Future," 6.

25 Richard John Neuhaus, "Speaking about the Unspeakable," *First Things*, March 2005, 61–62.

26 Gary A. Haugen, "Silence on Suffering," *Christianity Today Online*, October 17, 2005; www.christianitytoday.com/ct/2005/142/12.0.html, 2.

27 Dana Priest and Josh White, "Policies on Terrorism Suspects Come under Fire," *Washington Post*, November 3, 2005; www.washingtonpost.com, 2.

28 Bowden, "The Dark Art of Interrogation," 74.

29 Ignatieff, "Evil Under Interrogation," 3.

30 Alexander Solzhenitsyn, "What I Learned in the Gulag," quoted at www.freerepublic.com/forum/a3798e53e4620.htm.

31 John McCain, "McCain Statement on Detainee Amendments," October 5, 2005; mccain.senate.gov.

32 John McCain, "Torture's Terrible Toll," *Newsweek*, November 21, 2005, 35.

33 Jean Marie Arriga, "A Utilitarian Argument against Torture Interrogation of Terrorists," *Science and Engineering Ethics* 10, no. 3 (2004): 543–72.

34 Douglas Todd, "The Case against Torture," *Vancouver Sun*, June 4, 2005; www.lexis-nexis.com/universe/printdoc, 3.

35 Arriga, "A Utilitarian Argument," 551–60.

36 Among other sources, see Alan Dershowitz, "Let America Take Its Cues from Israel Regarding Torture," *Jewish World Review*, January 30, 2002; www.jewishworldreview.com/0102/torture.asp, 2.

37 Immanuel Kant, *Groundwork of the Metaphysics of Morals* (New York: Harper & Row, [1759], 1964), 73.

38 Adam Zagorin and Michael Duffy, "Inside the Interrogation of Detainee 063," *Time*, June 20, 2005, 33.

CHAPTER 6

1   For a discussion of the teaching dimension of marriage and divorce law, see Milton C. Regan Jr., "Postmodern Family Law: Toward a New Model of Status," ch. 7 in David Popenoe, Jean Bethke Elshtain, and David Blankenhorn, eds., *Promises to Keep* (Lanham, Md.: Rowman & Littlefield, 1996).

2   American Bar Association, *Guide to Family Law* (New York: Random House, 1996), 21.

3   Reported in archives.his.com/smartmarriages/0201/html.

4   *Kansas City Star*, March 12, 19983, in archives.his.com/smartmarriages/0113/html. To receive the money couples would also have to certify that they had never had a child, an abortion, or a sexually transmitted disease. These extra provisions are unhelpful.

5   Carl E. Schneider, "The Law and the Stability of Marriage: The Family as a Social Institution," in Popenoe et al., *Promises to Keep*, 196.

6   John Crouch, "Proposed language for pre-marital education provisions of divorce reform," www.divorcereform.org/mod.html.

7   B. J. Fowers and D. H. Olson, "Predicting Marital Success with PREPARE: A predictive validity study," *Journal of Marital and Family Therapy* 12, no. 4 (1986): 403–12.

8   Quoted in Pia Nordlinger, "The Anti-Divorce Revolution," *Weekly Standard*, March 2, 1998, 27.

9   www.divorcereform.org.

10 Crouch, "Proposed language."

11 See Michael J. McManus, *Marriage Savers*, 2nd ed. (Grand Rapids: Zondervan, 1998), ch. 7.

12 Milton C. Regan, "Postmodern Family Law," in Popenoe et al., *Promises to Keep*, 166.

13 Hewlett and West, *The War Against Parents*, 242.

14 Hewlett and West, *The War Against Parents*, ch. 9.

15 For the concept of marriage as a status relationship, see Regan, "Postmodern Family Law," 157–71.

16 Among the most common fault grounds that appear in state laws are adultery, physical and mental cruelty, attempted murder, desertion, habitual drunkenness, use of addictive drugs, insanity, impotence, infection of one's spouse with a venereal disease. American Bar Association, *Guide to Family Law*, 68–69.

17 For this analysis, see Mary Ann Glendon, *Abortion and Divorce in Western Law* (Cambridge, Mass.: Harvard University Press, 1987), 65.

18 Glendon, *Abortion and Divorce in Western Law*, 79–80, 66.

19 Christensen, "Taking Stock," 3.

20 Christensen, "Taking Stock," 4.

21 See Lenore J. Weitzman, *The Divorce Revolution: The Unexpected Social and Economic Consequences for Women and Children in America* (New York: Free Press, 1985). Weitzman's dramatic findings have been modified by later research, though the negative economic impact of divorce on women and children is a settled matter in current scholarship. For an authoritative recent analysis, see the *1998 Economic Report of the President*, chs. 3–4. Accessed at www.access.gpo.gov/eop.

22 See Barbara Dafoe Whitehead, "The Divorce Trap," *The New York Times*, January 13, 1997.

23 Daniel Sitarz, *Divorce Yourself: The National No-Fault Divorce Kit*, 3rd ed. (Carbondale, Ill.: Nova, 1994), 312.

24 Amy Black, "For the Sake of the Children: Reconstructing American Divorce Policy," *Crossroads Monograph Series on Faith and Public Policy* 1, no. 2 (1995): 40.

25 See www.divorcereform.org/wai.html.

26 Pia Nordlinger, "The Anti-Divorce Revolution," *Weekly Standard*, March 2, 1998, 26.

27 William A. Galston, "The Reinstitutionalization of Marriage: Political Theory and Public Policy," in Popenoe et. al., *Promises to Keep*, 285–86.

28 Glendon, *Abortion and Divorce in Western Law*, 77–78.

29 Carl E. Schneider, "The Law and the Stability of Marriage: The Family as a Social Institution," in Popenoe et al., *Promises to Keep*, 202.

30 Glendon, *Abortion and Divorce in Western Law*, 74.

31 My proposal resembles the "Classic Marriage" model proposed by John Crouch. See www.divorcereform.org/cla.html.

32 Elizabeth S. Scott, "Rational Decisionmaking About Marriage and Divorce," *Virginia Law Review* 76 (1990), qtd. in Schneider, "The Law and the Stability of Marriage," 200–201.

33 www.divorcereform.org/cov.html.

34 Etzioni, "How to Make Marriage Matter," *Time*, September 6, 1993, 6; for another early article, see Christopher Wolfe, "The Marriage of Your Choice," *First Things*, February 1995: 37–41.

35 DHH Office of Public Health Vital Records Registry, accessed at www. dhh.louisianagov/offices/publications/pubs-252/Marriage%20License%20 Packet.pdf.

36 Wolfe, "The Marriage of Your Choice," 37–41.

37 As reported by Religion News Service, November 11, 1997.

38 Galston, "The Reinstitutionalization of Marriage," 285–87.

39 See Judith S. Wallerstein and Sandra Blakeslee, *Second Chances: Men, Women, and Children a Decade After Divorce* (Boston: Houghton Mifflin, 1996). For a powerful glimpse at an all-too-typical young couple who both are children of divorce, see Tamara Jones, "The Commitment," *Washington Post Magazine*, May 10, 1998, 8–9.

40 Black, "For the Sake of the Children," 40.

41 Galston, "The Reinstitutionalization of Marriage," 286.

CHAPTER 7

1 Intergovernmental Panel on Climate Change (IPCC) 2001, Summary for Policymakers; www.grida.no/climate/ipcc_tar/wg1/007.htm. (See also the main IPCC Web site: www.ipcc.ch.) For the confirmation of the IPCC's findings from the U.S. National Academy of Sciences, see *Climate Change Science: An Analysis of Some Key Questions* (2001): books.nap.edu/html/climatechange/summary.html. For the statement by the G8 Academies (plus those of Brazil, India, and China) see Joint Science Academies Statement: *Global Response to Climate Change* (June 2005): nationalacademies.org/ onpi/06072005.pdf. Another major international report that confirms the IPCC's conclusions comes from the Arctic Climate Impact Assessment. See their *Impacts of a Warming Climate* (Cambridge: Cambridge University Press, 2004), 2; amap.no/acia/. Another important statement is from the American Geophysical Union, "Human Impacts on Climate," December 2003; www.agu.org/sci_soc/policy/climate_change_position.html. For the Bush administration's perspective, see *Our Changing Planet: The U.S. Climate Change Science Program for Fiscal Years 2004 and 2005*, 47: www.usgcrp.gov/ usgcrp/Library/ocp2004-5/default.htm. For the 2005 G8 statement, see www.number-10.gov.uk/output/Page7881.asp. In the winter and spring of 2007, the IPCC released its fourth assessment report on climate change. At the time of this book's publication, the full reports were forthcoming. To access the full report, go to www.ipcc.ch/.

2 John Houghton, *Global Warming*, 3rd ed. (Cambridge: Cambridge University Press, 2004).

3   IPCC 2001, Summary for Policymakers: www.grida.no/climate/ipcc_tar/wg1/007.htm.

4   Houghton, *Global Warming*, 297.

5   IPCC 2001, Summary for Policymakers; IPCC 2007, Summary for Policymakers.

6   IPCC 2007, Summary for Policymakers, 7.

7   Quoted in Deborah Zabarenko, "Global Warming Seen Pushing up Insurance Costs," *Reuters*, October 10, 2006.

8   "Investor Group Pushes Automakers for Action on Climate Change," www.greencarcongress.com/2006/05/investor_group_.html, accessed on May 20, 2006.

9   Nuhu Hatibu, "Rainwater Management: Strategies for Improving Water Availability and Productivity in Semi-arid and Arid Areas; www.iwmi.cgiar.org/home/rainwater.htm.

10 Arctic Climate Impact Assessment, *Impacts of a Warming Climate*, 499.

11 Ajay Mathur, Ian Burton, and Maarten van Aalst, eds., *An Adaptation Mosaic* (Washington, D.C.: World Bank, 2004).

12 Arctic Climate Impact Assessment, *Impacts of a Warming Climate*, 491.

13 IPCC 2007, Summary for Policymakers.

14 Arctic Climate Impact Assessment, *Impacts of a Warming Climate*, 502, 494.

15 The IPCC suggests that 80 to 90 million people worldwide could suffer hunger and malnutrition this century due to global warming. The *Africa–Up in Smoke?* report suggests that 70 to 80 percent of these victims will be in Africa. That is 56 to 72 million people. Also see IPCC, *Impacts*, Box 19-3, 938; www.grida.no/climate/ipcc_tar/wg2/674.htm, and; Andrew Simms, *Africa–Up in Smoke?*, New Economics Foundation, June 2005, 6; www.neweconomics.org/gen/z_sys_publicationdetail.aspx?pid=208.

16 Arctic Climate Impact Assessment, *Impacts of a Warming Climate*, 515, 507.

17 Andrew Simms, *Africa–Up In Smoke?*, 6; www.neweconomics.org/gen/z_sys_publicationdetail.aspx?pid=208, 25.

18 National Research Council and Ocean Studies Board, *Abrupt Climate Change: Inevitable Surprises* (Washington, D.C.: National Academy Press, 2002).

CHAPTER 8

1   Glen Stassen, *Just Peacemaking: Transforming Initiatives for Justice and Peace* (Louisville, Ky.: Westminster/John Knox, 1992).

2   "Just-War Divide," *Christian Century* 119, no. 17, August 24–27, 2002, 26–29.

3   James Turner Johnson, "The Broken Tradition—Just-War Doctrine," *The National Interest* (Fall 1996), accessed online at www.findarticles. com/p/articles/mi_m2751/is_n45/ai_18827110.

4   National Conference of Catholic Bishops, *Challenge of Peace: God's Promise and Our Response, a Pastoral Letter on War and Peace* (Edison, N.J.: Hunter, 1984).

5   National Conference of Catholic Bishops, *Challenge of Peace*, 29.

6   National Conference of Catholic Bishops, *Challenge of Peace*, 30.

7   National Conference of Catholic Bishops, *Challenge of Peace*, 37.

8   Keith Pavlischek, "Just War Theory and Terrorism: Applying the Ancient Doctrine to the Current Conundrum," a part of the Witherspoon Lectures, *Family Research Council*, November 21, 2001; www.frc.org/get. cfm?i=WT01K2.

9   Pavlischek, "Just War Theory and Terrorism," 15.

10 James W. Skillen and Keith J. Pavlischek, "Political Responsibility and the Use of Force," *Philosophia Christi*, 3, no. 2 (2001): 443.

11 National Conference of Catholic Bishops, *Challenge of Peace*, 37.

12 Pavlischek, "Just War Theory and Terrorism," 21.

13 Among other works, see J. Bryan Hehir, "What Can Be Done? What Should Be Done?" *America: The International Catholic Weekly*, October 8, 2001.

14 www.whitehouse.gov/news/releases/202/06/20020601-3/html, accessed September 20, 2002.

CONCLUSION

1   John Green and Steven Waldman, www.beliefnet.com/story_15355.html, accessed on September 1, 2005.

2   Mark Noll, *The Scandal of the Evangelical Mind* (Grand Rapids: Eerdmans, 1994).

APPENDIX 2

1   Sider and Knippers, *Toward an Evangelical Public Policy*.

2   Reinhold Niebuhr, *The Children of Light and Children of Darkness* (New York: Scribner's, 1944).

APPENDIX 3

1   Elie Wiesel, "Acceptance Speech for 1986 Nobel Peace Prize." Oslo, December 10, 1986; www.eliewieselfiundation.org/ElieWiesel/speech.html, accessed on September 28, 2006.

2   Robert A. Evans and Alice Frazer Evans, *Human Rights: A Dialogue Between the First and Third Worlds* (Maryknoll, N.Y.: Orbis Books, 1988), 3–4.

3   We use quotation marks for this term because we are not convinced of the precision or cogency of a war on "terror," which is at one level a tactic (terrorism) and at another level a feeling (terror). We do not use the term with quotation marks to downplay the significance of the terrorist acts that have been directed at other nations and our nation in the past two decades.

4   David P. Gushee, *The Sanctity of Life: A Christian Exploration* (Grand Rapids: Eerdmans, forthcoming).

5   David J. Atkinson, David Feld, Arthur F. Holmes, and Oliver O'Donovan, eds., *IVP New Dictionary of Christian Ethics and Pastoral Theology* (Downers Grove, IL: Intervarsity Press, 1995) 757–58.

6   Gushee, *The Sanctity of Life*, 3.

7   Pope John Paul II, *The Gospel of Life* (New York: Random House, 1995), 2–4.

8   Glen Stassen, "Foreword," in Christopher D. Marshall, *Crowned with Glory and Honor: Human Rights in the Biblical Tradition*, vol. 6, 11–14, *Studies in Peace and Scripture* (Telford, Penn.: Pandora Press, 2001), 11.

9   Per Sundman, "Human Rights, Justification, and Christian Ethics" (Ph.D. diss., Uppsala University, 1996), 41.

10 Sundman, "Human Rights," 45.

11 Stassen, "Foreword," 12.

12 Marshall, *Crowned with Glory and Honor*, 34.

13 An example from another context helps illustrate our point. In 2000, a young teenage girl in New Zealand was abducted by a neighbor. She was sexually violated and then buried alive. She died a horrible death. The murderer was tried, convicted, and imprisoned for life according to the laws of New Zealand, but this did not satisfy the girl's stepfather. He was subsequently convicted for repeatedly hurling murderous threats at her killer. Hailed as a hero, the stepfather had overwhelming public opinion in his favor. One supporter said of the girl's killer, "When you commit that kind of crime, you give up your rights. That kind of person is not even human." A columnist for the New Zealand Herald, however, wrote in support of the judge's decision. Criticizing the public's lust for vengeance, he

insisted that even the murderers of children "still have basic human rights and a decent society ensures those rights are upheld."

14 Sundman, "Human Rights," 38, 44.

15 Mary Ann Glendon, *Rights Talk* (New York: Free Press, 2004).

16 Stassen, *Just Peacemaking*, 138, 159.

17 Marshall, *Crowned with Glory and Honor*, 148.

18 Michael Westmoreland White, "Setting the Record Straight: Christian Faith, Human Rights, and the Enlightenment," *Annual of the Society of Christian Ethics* (1995): 75–96.

19 Marshall, *Crowned with Glory and Honor*, 29.

20 Marshall, *Crowned with Glory and Honor*, 29–30.

21 Stassen, "Foreword," 11–12.

22 Stassen, *Just Peacemaking*, 156.

23 Stassen, "Foreword," 13.

24 Pope John Paul II, *The Gospel of Life*, 129.

25 Vatican II: The Conciliar and Post Conciliar Documents, 64, Austin Flannery, O. P. ed., "Pastoral Constitution on the Church in the Modern World," *Gaudium et Spes*, December 7, 1965, 929.

26 Paul Marshall, "Human Rights," in Sider and Knippers, *Toward an Evangelical Public Policy*, 313.

27 Evans and Evans, *Human Rights*, 3.

28 "For the Health of the Nation," in Sider and Knippers, *Toward an Evangelical Public Policy*, 363–75, esp. 363.

29 Julie A. Mertus, *Bait and Switch: Human Rights and U.S. Foreign Policy* (New York: Routledge, 2004), 57.

30 Mertus, *Bait and Switch* , 58

31 As of March 18, 2007, parts of section 6 have been amended or revised in order to sharpen the treatment of issues related to international law.

32 United Nations Convention Against Torture, United Nations Department of Public Record (New York, February 4, 1985).

33 A dispute is still working its way through the judicial system regarding the scope of Common Article 3 of the Geneva Conventions. As President Bush has interpreted the treaty text, Common Article 3 applies only to civil wars completely internal to one signatory state. In *Hamdan v. Rumsfeld*, volume 126 Supreme Court Reporter page 2749 (2006), the Supreme Court disagreed. Although there are serious arguments on both sides of this issue, in the interest of the most expansive understanding and protection of human rights we support the broader interpretation of Article 3.

34 Geneva Convention (III): Relative to the Treatment of Prisoners of War (Geneva, 12 August 1949).

35 United Nations Convention Against Torture.

36 The United States took a reservation to this provision that says: "[T]he United states considers itself bound by article 7 to the extent that 'cruel, inhuman or degrading treatment or punishment' means the cruel and unusual treatment or punishment prohibited by the Fifth, Eighth, and/or Fourteenth Amendments to the Constitution of the United States." Our treaty obligation extends only to degrading treatment that is also "cruel and unusual" and that violates the Fifth, Eighth, and/or Fourteenth Amendment.

37 United Nations High Commission on Human Rights, Civil and Political Rights, Including the Questions of Torture and Detention, United Nations Department of Public Record (Geneva, Switzerland, December 23, 2005), 13.

38 International Covenant on Civil and Political Rights, United Nations General Assembly Resolution 2200A [XX1] (16 December 1966): www.cirp.org/library/ethics/UN-covenant (italics added), accessed on September 15, 2006.

39 United Nations Convention Against Torture.

40 Title 18 of the United States Code section 2340-2340a and Title 42 of the United States Code section 2000dd.

41 David Gushee and Cliff Kirkpatrick, "Rights of Detainees Must Not Be Violated," *Commercial Appeal*, September 27, 2006.

42 The Additional Protocols of 1977 were an opportunity for the United States to join the international community in updating the Geneva Conventions. Unfortunately, however, the Reagan administration chose not to do so.

43 Section 2 of the War Crimes Act of 1996, title 18 of the United States Code section 2401.

44 Ignatieff, "Evil Under Interrogation."

45 Katherine Shrader, "U.S. Has Detained 83,000 in War on Terror," Associated Press, November 16, 2005; www.sunherald.com, accessed on November 25, 2005.

46 "Intelligence Interrogation." U.S. Army Field Manual 34-52. September 28, 1992.

47 "Human Intelligence Collector Operations." *U.S. Army Field Manual* 2-22.3. September 6, 2006.

48 The United States has a moral obligation to train our military personnel in the best way to meet combat contingencies. That necessitates tough training in survival, escape, evasion, and rescue techniques. Also, history

demonstrates that our enemies often do not observe standards of international law or the Geneva Convention. Therefore, part of military training involves sleep deprivation, exhaustive marches, food deprivation, and even some pain or discomfort. While this training is closely monitored to guard against abuses, it also must be sufficiently rigorous to arm the individual with physical, psychological, and mental coping skills to endure the unimaginable if taken as a prisoner of war. The signatories understand that this is part of military training and do not intend to condemn it.

49 Military Commissions Act of 2006, 120 Statutes at Large 2600, Public Law 109-366 (October 17, 2006). Many of the act's sections are codified at title 10 United States Code section 948a and following.

50 President George W. Bush, in a speech made at the signing of the Military Commissions Act of 2006, Washington, D.C., October 17, 2006.

51 Section 7 of the Military Commissions Act, title 28 United States Code section 2241:

> (e)(1) No court, justice, or judge shall have jurisdiction to hear or consider an application for a writ of habeas corpus filed by or on behalf of an alien detained by the United States who has been determined by the United States to have been properly detained as an enemy combatant or is awaiting such determination.

52 Section 3 of the Military Commissions Act, title 10 of the United States Code section 948r and section 949a:

> 948r(c) STATEMENTS OBTAINED BEFORE ENACTMENT OF DETAINEE TREATMENT ACT OF 2005.—A statement obtained before December 30, 2005 (the date of the enactment of the Defense Treatment Act of 2005) in which the degree of coercion is disputed may be admitted only if the military judge finds that—
> "(1) the totality of the circumstances renders the statement reliable and possessing sufficient probative value; and "(2) the interests of justice would best be served by admission of the statement into evidence."
>
> 949a(E)(i) Except as provided in clause (ii), hearsay evidence not otherwise admissible under the rules of evidence applicable in trial by general courts-martial may be admitted in a trial by military commission if the proponent of the evidence makes known to the adverse party, sufficiently in advance to provide the adverse party with a fair opportunity to meet the evidence, the intention of the proponent to offer the evidence, and the particulars of the evidence

(including information on the general circumstances under which the evidence was obtained). The disclosure of evidence under the preceding sentence is subject to the requirements and limitations applicable to the disclosure of classified information in section 949j(c) of this title.

(ii) Hearsay evidence not otherwise admissible under the rules of evidence applicable in trial by general courts-martial shall not be admitted in a trial by military commission if the party opposing the admission of the evidence demonstrates that the evidence is unreliable or lacking in probative value.

53 Section 3 of the Military Commissions Act, title 10 United States Code section 948b:

(d) INAPPLICABILITY OF CERTAIN PROVISIONS.—(1) The following provisions of this title shall not apply to trial by military commission under this chapter: "(A) Section 810 (article 10 of the Uniform Code of Military Justice), relating to speedy trial, including any rule of courtsmartial relating to speedy trial."

54 Section 3 of the Military Commissions Act, title 10 of the United States Code section 948a:

(1) UNLAWFUL ENEMY COMBATANT.—(A) The term 'unlawful enemy combatant' means—"(i) a person who has engaged in hostilities or who has purposefully and materially supported hostilities against the United States or its co-belligerents who is not a lawful enemy combatant (including a person who is part of the Taliban, al Qaeda, or associated forces); or "(ii) a person who, before, on, or after the date of the enactment of the Military Commissions Act of 2006, has been determined to be an unlawful enemy combatant by a Combatant Status Review Tribunal or another competent tribunal established under the authority of the President or the Secretary of Defense."

55 Section 3 of the Military Commissions Act, title 10 of the United States Code section 948a:

56 The majority of the signatories of this document stand in the just-war tradition. Those who are pacifists believe government should carry out its important responsibilities using non-lethal methods.

57 Ignatieff, "Evil under Interogation."

58 Vatican II, The Concilar and Post Concilar Documents, 928.
59 "For the Health of the Nation," 363, 370.
60 "For the Health of the Nation," 373.
61 Haugen, "Silence on Suffering."
62 Ignatieff, "Evil under Interrogation."

APPENDIX 5

1 Cf. "For the Health of the Nation: An Evangelical Call to Civic Responsibility," approved by National Association of Evangelicals, October 8, 2004.

2 IPCC 2001, Summary for Policymakers. (See also the main IPCC Web site: www.ipcc.ch.) For the confirmation of the IPCC's findings from the U.S. National Academy of Sciences, see, Climate Change Science; http://books.nap.edu/html/climatechange/summary.html. For the statement by the G8 Academies (plus those of Brazil, India, and China) see Joint Science Academies Statement: Global Response to Climate Change. Another major international report that confirms the IPCC's conclusions comes from the Arctic Climate Impact Assessment, Impacts of a Warming Climate, 2/. Another important statement is from the American Geophysical Union, "Human Impacts on Climate," December 2003; www.agu.org/sci_soc/policy/climate_change_position.html. For the Bush administration's perspective, see Our Changing Planet, 47; www.usgcrp.gov/usgcrp/Library/ocp2004-5/default.htm. For the 2005 G8 statement, see www.number-10.gov.uk/output/Page7881.asp.

FURTHER READING

Adams, Lawrence E. *Going Public*. Grand Rapids: Brazos, 2002.

Albright, Madeleine. *The Mighty and the Almighty*. New York: HarperCollins, 2006.

Audi, Robert, and Nicholas Wolterstorff. *Religion in the Public Square*, Lanham, Md.: Rowman & Littlefield, 1997.

Balmer, Randall. *Mine Eyes Have Seen the Glory*. Oxford: Oxford University Press, 1993.

———. *Thy Kingdom Come*. New York: Basic Books, 2006.

Bane, Mary Jo, Brent Coffin, and Richard Higgins, eds. *Taking Faith Seriously*. Cambridge, Mass.: Harvard University Press, 2005.

Bauman, Michael, and David Hall, eds. *God and Caesar*. Camp Hill, Penn.: Christian Publications, 1994.

Benne, Robert. *The Paradoxical Vision*. Minneapolis: Fortress, 1995.

Bessenecker, Scott A. *The New Friars*. Downers Grove, Ill.: InterVarsity Press, 2006.

Blumenthal, Sidney. *The Rise of the Counter-Establishment*. Times Books, New York, 1986.

Boice, James Montgomery. *Two Cities, Two Loves*. Downers Grove, Ill.: Intervarsity Press, 1996.

Boxx, T. William, and Gary M. Quinlivan, eds. *Toward the Renewal of Civilization*, Grand Rapids: Eerdmans, 1998.

Boyd, Gregory A. *The Myth of a Christian Nation*, Grand Rapids: Zondervan, 2005.

Budziszewski, J. *Evangelicals in the Public Square* Grand Rapids: Baker Academic, 2006.

Campolo, Anthony. *Ideas for Social Action*, Grand Rapids: Zondervan, 1983.

———. *Is Jesus a Republican or a Democrat?*, Dallas, Tex.: Word, 1995.

———. *The Kingdom of God Is a Party*, Dallas, Tex.: Word, 1990.

———. *Letters to a Young Evangelical*. New York: Basic Books, 2006.

———. *Speaking My Mind*. Nashville: W Publishing Group, 2004.

———. *20 Hot Potatoes Christians Are Afraid to Touch*. Dallas, Tex.: Word, 1988.

Campolo, Tony, and Gordon Aeschliman. *101 Ways Your Church Can Change the World*, Ventura, Calif.: Regal Books, 1993.

Carter, Craig A. *Rethinking Christ and Culture* Grand Rapids: Brazos, 2006.

Carter, Jimmy. *Our Endangered Values*. New York: Simon & Schuster, 2005.

Carter, Stephen L. *The Culture of Disbelief*. New York: Basic Books, 1993.

Cerillo Jr., Augustus, and Murray W. Dempster. *Salt and Light*. Grand Rapids: Baker, 1989.

Charles, J. Daryl. *Between Pacifism and Jihad*. Downers Grove, Ill.: InterVarsity, 2005.

Christian Coalition. *Contract with the American Family*. Nashville: Moorings, 1995.

Clouse, Robert G., Richard V. Pierard, and Edwin M. Yamauchi. *Two Kingdoms*. Chicago: Moody, 1993.

Collins, Kenneth J. *The Evangelical Moment*. Grand Rapids: Baker Academic, 2005.

Cooey, Paula M. *Family, Freedom, and Faith*. Louisville, Ky.: Westminster/ John Knox, 1996.

Coulter, Ann. *Godless: The Church of Liberalism*. New York: Crown Forum, 2006.

Cromartie, Michael, ed. *Caesar's Coin Revisited*. Grand Rapids: Eerdmans, 1996.

———. *Religion and Politics in America*. Lanham, Md.: Rowman & Littlefield, 2005.

Danforth, John. *Faith and Politics*. New York: Viking, 2006.

Dionne Jr., E. J., Jean Bethke Elshtain, and Kayla M. Drogosz, eds. *One Electorate Under God?* Washington, D.C.: Brookings Institution Press, 2004.

Dorrien, Gary. *Soul in Society*. Minneapolis: Fortress, 1995.

Drinan, Robert F. *The Fractured Dream*. New York: Crossroad, 1991.

Dyson, Michael Eric. *The Michael Eric Dyson Reader*. New York: Basic Civitas Books, 2004.

Eberly, Don, ed. *Building a Healthy Culture*. Grand Rapids: Eerdmans, 2001.

El-Faizy, Monique. *God and Country*. New York: Bloomsbury, 2006.

Elshtain, Jean Bethke. *Democracy On Trial*. New York: Basic Books, 1995.

Emerson, Michael O., and Christian Smith. *Divided by Faith*. Oxrford: Oxford University Press, 2000.

Fackre, Gabriel, ed. *Judgment Day at the White House*. Grand Rapids: Eerdmans, 1999.

Feldman, Noah. *Divided by God*. New York: Farrar, Straus, & Giroux, 2005.

"For the Health of the Nation." National Association of Evangelicals, Washington, D.C., 2004.

Forrester, Duncan B. *Christian Justice and Public Policy*. New York: Cambridge University Press, 1997.

Fowler, Robert Booth. *A New Engagement*. Grand Rapids: Eerdmans, 1982.

———. *Unconventional Partners*, Grand Rapids: Eerdmans, 1989.

Frank, Thomas. *What's the Matter with Kansas?* New York: Henry Holt, 2004.

Gallagher, Michael. *Laws of Heaven*. New York: Ticknor & Fields, 1992.

Galston, William A. *Liberal Pluralism*. New York: Cambridge University Press, 2002.

Gamwell, Franklin I. *The Meaning of Religious Freedom.* Albany: State University of New York Press, 1995.

———. *Politics as a Christian Vocation.* New York: Cambridge University Press, 2005.

Garrison, Becky. *Red and Blue God, Black and Blue Church.* San Francisco: Jossey-Bass, 2006.

Gates Jr., Henry Louis, and Cornel West. *The Future of the Race.* New York: Knopf, 1996.

Gay, Craig M. *With Liberty and Justice for Whom?* Grand Rapids: Eerdmans, 1991.

Genovese, Eugene D. *The Southern Front.* Columbia: University of Missouri Press, 1995.

Gentile, Emilio. *Politics as Religion.* Princeton: Princeton University Press, Princeton, 2001.

George, Robert P. *The Clash of Orthodoxies* Wilmington, Del.: ISI Books, 2001.

Geyer, Alan. *Ideology in America.* Louisville, Ky.: Westminster/John Knox, 1997.

Gibbs, Eddie, and Ryan K. Bolger. *Emerging Churches: Creating Christian Community in Postmodern Culture.* Grand Rapids: Baker Books, 2005.

Gilbreath, Edward. *Reconciliation Blues.* Downers Grove, Ill.: InterVarsity Press, 2006.

Glendon, Mary Ann. *Abortion and Divorce in Western Law.* Cambridge, Mass.: Harvard University Press, 1987.

Goldberg, Michelle. *Kingdom Coming.* New York: Norton, 2006.

Green, John C., Mark J. Rozell, and Clyde Wilcox, eds. *The Values Campaign?* Washington, D.C.: Georgetown University Press, 2006.

Greenawalt, Kent. *Religious Convictions and Political Choice.* Oxford: Oxford University Press, 1998.

Gushee, David P., ed. *Christians and Politics Beyond the Culture Wars.* Grand Rapids: Baker Books, 2000.

———. *Toward a Just and Caring Society.* Grand Rapids: Baker Books, 1999.

Hall, Douglas John, and Rosemary Radford Ruether. *God and the Nations.* Minneapolis: Fortress, 1995.

Hankins, Barry. *Uneasy in Babylon*. Tuscaloosa: Univesity of Alabama Press, 2002.

Hauerwas, Stanley. *A Community of Character*. Notre Dame, Ind.: University of Notre Dame Press, 1981.

———. *The Peaceable Kingdom*. Notre Dame, Ind.: University of Notre Dame Press, 1983.

Hauerwas, Stanley, and William H. Willimon. *Resident Aliens*. Nashville: Abingdon, 1989.

Hedges, Chris. *American Fascists*. New York: Free Press, 2006.

Hellwig, Monika K. *Public Dimensions of a Believer's Life*. Lanham, Md.: Rowman & Littlefield, 2005.

Heltzel, Peter. *Lion on the Loose*. New Haven: Yale University Press, 2008 forthcoming.

Henderson, James W., and John Pisciotta, eds. *Faithful Economics*. Waco, Tex.: Baylor University Press, 2005.

Hendricks Jr., Obery M. *The Politics of Jesus*. New York: Doubleday, 2006.

Herron, Roy. *How Can a Christian Be in Politics?* Wheaton, Ill.: Tyndale, 2005.

Hertzke, Allen D. *Freeing God's Children*. Lanham, Md.: Rowman & Littlefield, 2004.

Hewlett, Sylvia Ann, and Cornel West. *The War Against Parents*. Boston: Houghton Mifflin, 1998.

Heyer, Kristin E. *Prophetic and Public*. Washington, D.C.: Georgetown University Press, 2006.

Horton, Michael S. *Beyond Culture Wars*. Chicago: Moody, 1994.

Hunter III, George G. *Christian, Evangelical, and . . . Democrat?* Nashville: Abingdon, 2006.

Hunter, James Davison. *Before the Shooting Begins*. New York: Free Press, 1994.

———. *Culture Wars*. New York: Basic Books, 1991.

Hynes, Patrick. *In Defense of the Religious Right*. Nashville: Nelson Current, 2006.

James, Kay Cole, with David Kuo. *Transforming America: From the Inside Out*. Grand Rapids: Zondervan, 1995.

Johnston, Douglas, and Cynthia Sampson, eds. *Religion, the Missing Dimension of Statecraft.* Oxford: Oxford University Press, 1994.

King Jr., Martin Luther. *A Testament of Hope.* Edited by James M. Washington. San Francisco: Harper & Row, 1986.

Kramnick, Isaac, and R. Laurence Moore. *The Godless Constitution.* New York: Norton, 1996.

Kuo, David. *Tempting Faith.* New York: Free Press, 2006.

Lakoff, George. *Thinking Points: Communicating Our American Values and Vision.* New York: Farrar, Straus, & Giroux, 2006.

Land, Richard. *The Divided States of America?* Nashville: Nelson, 2007.

Land, Richard, and Louis A. Moore, eds. *Citizen Christians.* Nashville: Broadman and Holman, 1994.

Lerner, Michael. *The Left Hand of God.* San Francisco: HarperCollins, 2006.

Linker, Damon. *The Theocons.* New York: Doubleday, 2006.

Lynn, Barry W. *Piety and Politics.* New York: Harmony, 2006.

Marsh, Charles. *Beloved Community.* New York: Basic Books, 2005.

Martin, William. *With God on Our Side.* New York: Broadway Books, 1996.

McCollough, Thomas E. *The Moral Imagination and Public Life.* Chatham, NJ: Chatham, 1991.

McDaniel, Charles. *God and Money.* Lanham, Md.: Rowman & Littlefield, 2007.

McLaren, Brian D. *A Generous Orthodoxy.* El Cajon, Calif.: Youth Specialties, 2004.

———. *A New Kind of Christian.* San Francisco: Jossey-Bass, 2001.

Meyers, Robin. *Why the Christian Right Is Wrong.* San Francisco: Jossey-Bass, 2006.

Miller, Keith Graber. *Wise as Serpents, Innocent as Doves.* Knoxville: University of Tennessee Press, 1996.

Minear, Paul S. *I Pledge Allegiance.* Philadelphia: Geneva Press, 1975.

Monsma, Stephen V. *Positive Neutrality.* Grand Rapids: Baker, 1993.

Monsma, Stephen V., and J. Christopher Soper, eds. *Equal Treatment of Religion in a Pluralistic Society,* Grand Rapids: Eerdmans, 1998.

Mouw, Richard J. *Political Evangelism.* Grand Rapids: Eerdmans, 1973.

Müller-Fahrenholz, Geiko. *America's Battle for God.* Grand Rapids: Eerdmans, 2007.

Neuhaus, Richard John. *America Against Itself.* Notre Dame, Ind.: University of Notre Dame Press, 1992.

———, ed. *Law and the Ordering of Our Life Together.* Grand Rapids: Eerdmans, 1989.

Noll, Mark A., and Carolyn Nystrom. *Is the Reformation Over?* Grand Rapids: Baker Academic, 2005.

O'Donovan, Oliver. *The Desire of the Nations.* Cambridge: Cambridge University Press, 1996.

———. *The Ways of Judgment.* Grand Rapids: Eerdmans, 2005.

O'Donovan, Oliver, and Joan Lockwood O'Donovan. *Bonds of Imperfection.* Grand Rapids: Eerdmans, 1999.

———, eds. *From Irenaeus to Grotius.* Grand Rapids: Eerdmans, 2004.

Penning, James M., and Corwin E. Smidt. *Evangelicalism: The Next Generation.* Grand Rapids: Baker Academic, 2002.

Perry, Michael J. *Love and Power.* Oxford: Oxford University Press, 1991.

———. *Under God?* Cambridge: Cambridge University Press, 2003.

Phillips, Kevin. *American Theocracy.* New York: Viking, 2006.

Ponnuru, Ramesh. *The Party of Death.* Washington, D.C.: Regnery, 2006.

Porpora, Douglas V. *Landscapes of the Soul.* Oxford: Oxford University Press, 2001.

Ramsay, William M. *The Wall of Separation.* Louisville, Ky: Westminster/John Knox, 1989.

Reed, Ralph. *Active Faith.* New York: Free Press, 1996.

Reichley, A. James. *The Values Connection.* Lanham, Md.: Rowman & Littlefield, 2001.

Roberts, Paul Craig, and Lawrence M. Stratton. *The Tyranny of Good Intentions.* Roseville, Calif.: Forum, 2000.

Sager, Ryan. *The Elephant in the Room.* Hoboken, N.J.: Wiley, 2006.

Sandel, Michael J. *Democracy's Discontent.* Cambridge, Mass.: Harvard University Press, 1996.

Schansberg, D. Eric. *Turn Neither to the Right Nor to the Left.* Greenville, S.C.: Alertness Books, 2003.

Schwarz, Sidney. *Judaism and Justice.* Woodstock, Vt.: Jewish Lights, 2006.

Sheldon, Garrett Ward, ed. *Religion and Politics.* New York: Peter Lang, 1990.

Sheler, Jeffery L. *Believers.* New York: Viking, 2006.

Shriver Jr., Donald W. *Honest Patriots.* Oxford: Oxford University Press, 2005.

Sider, Ronald J. *Just Generosity.* Grand Rapids: Baker, 1999.

———. *Rich Christians in an Age of Hunger.* Dallas, Tex.: Word, 1990.

———. *The Scandal of the Evangelical Conscience.* Grand Rapids: Baker, 2005.

Sider, Ronald J., and Diane Knippers, eds. *Toward an Evangelical Public Policy.* Grand Rapids: Baker, 2005.

Simon, Arthur. *Christian Faith and Public Policy.* Grand Rapids: Eerdmans, 1987.

Skillen, James W. *In Pursuit of Justice.* Lanham, Md.: Rowman & Littlefield, 2004.

———. *Recharging the American Experiment.* Grand Rapids: Baker, 1994.

———. *With or Against the World?* Lanham, Md.: Rowman & Littlefield, 2005.

Smidt, Corwin E., ed. *Pulpit and Politics.* Waco, Tex.: Baylor University Press, 2004.

Smiley, Tavis. *The Covenant.* Chicago: Third World Press, 2006.

Smith, Christian. *Christian America?* Berkeley: University of California Press, 2000.

Stetson, Brad, and Joseph G. Conti. *The Truth about Tolerance.* Downers Grove, Ill.: InterVarsity Press, 2005.

Storkey, Alan. *Jesus and Politics.* Grand Rapids: Baker Academic, 2005.

Strong, Douglas M. *They Walked in the Spirit.* Louisville, Ky.: Westminster/ John Knox, 1997.

Suarez, Ray. *The Holy Vote.* New York: HarperCollins, 2006.

Sweetman, Brendan. *Why Politics Needs Religion.* Downers Grove, Ill.: InterVarsity Press, 2006.

Taylor, Mark Lewis. *Religion, Politics, and the Christian Right.* Minneapolis: Fortress, 2005.

Thiemann, Ronald F. *Constructing a Public Theology.* Louisville, Ky.: Westminster/John Knox, 1991.

———. *Religion in Public Life.* Washington, D.C.: Georgetown University Press, 1996.

Thomas, Cal, and Ed Dobson. *Blinded by Might.* Grand Rapids: Zondervan, 1999.

Tinder, Glenn. *The Political Meaning of Christianity.* New York: HarperCollins, 1991.

Toulouse, Mark G. *God in Public.* Louisville, Ky.: Westminster/John Knox, 2006.

Villafañe, Eldin. *Beyond Cheap Grace.* Grand Rapids: Eerdmans, 2006.

Wallis, Jim. *The Call to Conversion.* San Francisco: Harper & Row, 1981.

———. *God's Politics.* San Francisco: HarperCollins, 2005.

———. *The Soul of Politics.* New York: New Press, 1994.

Walt, Stephen M. *Taming American Power.* New York: Norton, 2005.

Walzer, Michael. *Arguing about War.* New Haven: Yale University Press, 2004.

Watt, David Harrington. *Bible-Carrying Christians.* Oxford: Oxford University Press, 2002.

Weber, Timothy P. *On the Road to Armageddon.* Grand Rapids: Baker Academic, 2004.

West, Cornel. *Race Matters.* Boston: Beacon, 1993.

White, Mel. *Religion Gone Bad.* New York: Tarcher/Penguin, 2006.

Wills, Garry. *Under God.* New York: Simon & Schuster, 1990.

Witte Jr., John. *God's Joust, God's Justice.* Grand Rapids: Eerdmans, 2006.

Wogaman, J. Philip. *Christian Perspectives on Politics.* Louisville, Ky.: Westminster/John Knox, 2000.

Wolfe, Alan. *Moral Freedom.* New York: Norton, 2001.

———. *One Nation, After All.* New York: Penguin, 1998.

Wolterstorff, Nicholas. *Until Justice and Peace Embrace.* Grand Rapids: Eerdmans, 1983.

Wood Jr., James E., and Derek Davis, eds. *The Role of Government in Monitoring and Regulating Religion in Public Life.* Waco, Tex.: Dawson Institute of Church-State Studies, 1993.

INDEX OF NAMES AND TERMS

SUBJECT INDEX